9-70

The Chassidic Dimension

Interpretations of the Weekly Torah Readings
and the Festivals

Based on the Talks of
The Lubavitcher Rebbe
Rabbi Menachem M. Schneerson שליט״א

Vol. I

Published and Copyrighted by
"KEHOT" Publication Society
770 Eastern Parkway, Brooklyn, N. Y. 11213
5750 • 1990
הי׳ תהא שנת נסים

The Chassidic Dimension

Interpretations of the Weekly Torah Readings
and the Festivals

Based on the Talks of
The Lubavitcher Rebbe
Rabbi Menachem M. Schneerson שליט״א

Vol. I

Compiled by Rabbi Sholom B. Wineberg
Edited by Uri Kaploun

THE CHASSIDIC DIMENSION
VOL. I

Published and Copyrighted by
"KEHOT" PUBLICATION SOCIETY
770 Eastern Parkway, Brooklyn, N.Y. 11213
Tel. (718) 493-9250, 778-0226

5750 • 1990

Second Printing
Elul 5755 • September 1995

Printed in the U.S.A.

Library of Congress Cataloging-in-Publication Data
Schneersohn, Menahem Mendel, 1902
    [Likute Sihot, English Selections]
    The Chassidic dimension vol. 1:
    interpretations of the weekly Torah readings based on the talks of the
    Lubavitcher Rebbe, Rabbi Menachem Mendel Schneerson/compiled by
    Sholom B. Wineberg: edited by Uri Kaploun.
        p. 304   15 X 22 1/2 cm.
        Translation of: Likute sihot.
        Includes bibliographical references.
        ISBN 0-8266-0484-6
    1. Bible. O.T. Pentateuch—Commentaries. 2. Hasidim. 3. Habad. I. Wineberg,
Sholom B. (Sholom Ber) II. Kaploun, Uri. III. Title.
BS1225.3.S362513   1990
222'.107—dc20   90-4076
                                              CIP

Table of Contents

Publisher's Preface xiii
Compiler's Foreword xv

Sefer Bereishis

Bereishis
The Alef & Beis of Torah 3
Perfecting a Perfect World 5
Noach
Opening the Floodgates of Wisdom 7
Disembarking the Ark 9
Lech Lecha
The Birth of a Nation 12
In Sarah's Merit 14
Vayeira
Seasonable vs. Reasonable 17
The Akedah: The Ultimate Test 18
Chayei Sarah
One Moment, One Day, One Instant 21
Changing the Guard 23
Toldos
Avraham & Yitzchak: A Study in Contrasts 26
The Patriarchs as Models 28
Vayeitzei
Giving Names 31
An Honor Guard of Angels 33
Vayishlach
Gifts, Prayers & Battles 36
Healthy, Wealthy & Wise 38
Vayeishev
The Selling of Yosef 41
Vayeishev & Yud-Tes Kislev
Three Types of Liberation: Three Forms of Service 44
Mikeitz & Chanukkah
A Matter of Perspective 47
Chanukkah
Salvations, Miracles & Wonders 49
Vayigash
It Depends on How You Say It 52
The Flock of Yosef 54
Vayechi
To Take an Oath 56
To Reveal or Not to Reveal 58

Table of Contents

Sefer Shmos

Shmos
Descending into Egypt 63
Defying Pharaoh 65

Va'eira
Egyptian Exile: A Prelude to the Torah 68
Misplaced Criticism 70

Bo
Determining the New Month 73
The First Paschal Offering 75

Beshalach
Heavenly Bread & Earthly Bread 78

Tu biShvat
For Man is Like a Tree of the Field 81

Yisro
A United People: A United World 84
Seeing Voices, Hearing Visions 86

Mishpatim
Faith & Reason 89
Torah & Secular Wisdom 91

Terumah
Minutiae: An Entree to Holiness 94
A Matter of Give & Take 96

Tetzaveh
Moshe & His People: A Unique Relationship 99
A Tumult & a Still Small Voice 101

Ki Sisa
Two Sides of a Coin 104
Tying the Knot 106

Vayakhel
To Light a Fire 109

Pekudei
The Significance of a Name 111
Counting & Accounting 113

Table of Contents

Sefer Vayikra

Vayikra
A Small Alef 119
Let the Pure Engage in Purity 121

Tzav
A Jew's Relationship with G-d 124
Transforming Quantity into Quality 126

Shabbos HaGadol
A Truly Great Shabbos 128

Pesach
Matzos, Freedom & Passover 130
Celebrating the First & Final Redemptions 132

Shemini
Eighth: More than Just Another Number 135
Offerings & the Divine Presence 137

Tazria
Circumcision: A Family Affair 140

Metzora
The Effect of a Candle 142

Acharei
To Come before G-d 145
Mastery of Self 147

Kedoshim
Fruits of the Fifth Year 150

Lag baOmer
Rabbi Akiva's Disciples 152

Emor
What's in a Name? 155
The Four Kinds 157

Behar
The Loftiness of Humility 160

Bechukosai
Nullification of Self 163

Table of Contents

Sefer Bamidbar

Bamidbar
Counting the Jews: A Countdown to Shavuos 169

Shavuos
A Time to Eat & Rejoice 172
Eternal Torah in a Changeable World 174

Naso
A Modern-Day Levitical Tally 177
Princely Offerings 179

Behaalos'cha
Why Lose the Privilege? 182
Sounding the Trumpets 184

Shlach
Faithful Understanding 187
Challah: A Negation of Idolatry 189

Korach
Unity vs. Uniformity 192
The Desire to be a High Priest 194

Chukas
The Red Heifer: A Foundation of Torah 197
The Bond between Body & Soul 199

Balak & Yud-Beis Tammuz
The Ultimate Miracle 202

Pinchas
Pinchas' Reward: Peace & Priesthood 204
Personal & General Refinement 206

Matos & Masei
Of Staffs & Journeys 209

Masei
A Tale of Two Journeys 212

Table of Contents

Sefer Devarim

Devarim
Oil for a Silent Flame 217
Chazon: A Heavenly Vision 219
Vaes'chanan
Tearing Open Heaven & Earth 221
The Best of Both Temples 223
Eikev
Special Consideration 226
Mezuzah: A Unique Commandment 228
Re'eh
Beis HaBechirah & Beis HaMikdash 231
The Power of Repentance 233
Shoftim
The Purpose of a Monarch 235
Two Forms of Fear: Two Forms of Repentance 237
Seitzei
Even One Hundred Times 240
Building a Guard-rail 242
Savo
Gratitude to G-d & Brotherly Love 245
G-d's Concealed Treasure 247
Nitzavim
Blessing & Reigning: A Partnership 250
Rosh HaShanah
A Day of Shabbos: A Year of Shabbos 253
Vayeilech
Shemitah & Hakhel 256
Haazinu & Shabbos Teshuvah
Close to Heaven: Close to Earth 259
A Song of Repentance 261
Yom Kippur
The Very Day Brings Atonement 264
Sukkos
Uniting Jews through Union with G-d 267
Wine & Water: Two Forms of Joy 269
Berachah
Moshe & Aharon: Two Peacemakers 272

Key to Proper Names 275

Glossary 277

Subject Index 283

Publisher's Preface

The present volume, the pioneer of a series, is hereby offered to the English-speaking public in honor of *Yud* Shvat, 5750, a date which marks the fortieth anniversary of the passing of the Previous Lubavitcher Rebbe, Rabbi Yosef Yitzchak Schneersohn נ"ע, and forty years' leadership לאיוש"ט of the Lubavitcher Rebbe, Rabbi Menachem M. Schneerson שליט"א.

Side by side with the comprehensive and fully annotated editions of the public talks of the Rebbe *Shlita* on the weekly Torah readings and festivals, condensed versions have always been welcome. For the sheer diversity and approaches and levels in all the available translations, expositions, abridgments and adaptations of the Rebbe's voluminous teachings, allows each reader to drink from the life-giving wellsprings of *Chassidus* according to his thirst and according to his capacity.

Within each of the present essays, therefore, Rabbi Sholom Ber Wineberg has either compressed one of the focal points of one of the Rebbe's talks, or has combined and adapted the related ideas presented in a number of talks. For some years these essays were published in monthly collections entitled *From the Wellsprings of Chassidus*. Now, for the first time, the essays of the first two years appear in book form, complete with source references, a glossary and a subject index. This volume was edited by Uri Kaploun and prepared for publication by Rabbi Yonah Avtzon, Director of Sichos In English. Kehot Publication Society is confident that it will prove to be a versatile vessel that will enable many a reader to quench his thirst.

*   *   *

In the fortieth year of his leadership, Moshe Rabbeinu

tells his people: "G-d did not give you a heart to understand nor eyes to see nor ears to hear — until this day."[1] The Sages comment: "From this we learn that no man understands his Rebbe's teachings in all their depth until the passage of forty years."[2]

After forty years such as these, it is our earnest prayer that the ever-broadening publication of the past and future teachings of the *Rebbe* Shlita will help grant us — and our readers — a heart to understand and eyes to see and ears to hear.

Vaad L'Hafotzas Sichos

Motzaei Shabbos, Rosh Chodesh Shvat, 5750
Brooklyn, NY

---

1. *Devarim* 29:3.
2. *Avodah Zarah* 5b; and see *Rashi* on the above verse.

ב"ה

Compiler's Foreword

Perhaps the most eagerly sought Jewish commodity in today's hurried world is — *a pithy teaching that will flex the mind, warm the heart and ignite the soul.* Who seeks it? Often it is the man in the street who hankers after relevance as he reviews the weekly Torah reading; it may be a rabbi in his pulpit; it may be a writer, an educator or youth leader; it may be a participant in a family *simchah;* it may be a host who realizes that he has to serve up something more substantial than chicken soup if he is to enable his Friday evening guest to savor the sweet spice of the *Shabbos* experience; or it may be that very same Friday evening guest, whom experience has taught to arrive at his host's table fully equipped — with a quotable (but different!) *dvar Torah* up his sleeve.

These and many others, seeking original and multidimensional interpretations of the weekly Torah readings and of the festivals,[1] have learned to turn to the published talks of the Lubavitcher Rebbe, Rabbi Menachem M. Schneerson, שליט"א. Their original Yiddish and Hebrew version, in 27 volumes to date, is entitled *Likkutei Sichos* ("Collected Talks").[2]

The present work (and likewise its forthcoming second volume) is a condensation in English of over a hundred of these talks, supplemented by source references, a glossary and a subject index. Each essay herein provides the reader with the main thrust of the parent discourse, usually in the

---

1. Certain of the talks below refer to the connection between a festival and the weekly Torah reading with which it coincided in a particular year. Needless to say, from year to year the calendar allows for a certain degree of variance.
2. Three volumes have so far appeared in an English translation by Rabbi Jacob Immanuel Schochet *(Likkutei Sichot;* Kehot, N.Y.).

XV

form of a systematic abridgment, and sometimes as a more free-flowing exposition of its message. Those who desire to drink more deeply, and who are able to relish the full vintage flavor of the original undiluted talks, will be rewarded by a unique blend — intelligible erudition and usable inspiration.

*   *   *

In this volume, too, as in a number of previous titles, my endeavors have had the good fortune to have been edited by Uri Kaploun and prepared for publication by Rabbi Yonah Avtzon, Director of Sichos In English — for "a threefold cord is not quickly broken" (Koheles 4:12).

Sholom B. Wineberg
Kansas City

Rosh Chodesh Kislev, 5750 (1989)
The fortieth year of the leadership
of the Lubavitcher Rebbe שליט״א

ספר בראשית

Bereishis

The Alef & Beis of Torah

The first letter of *Bereishis*, the first portion of the Torah, is *beis*, which is the second letter of the Hebrew alphabet. Why doesn't the Torah begin with the first letter of the alphabet, which is *alef?*

On the verse, "Why was the land destroyed?... For they have forsaken My Torah,"[1] our Sages comment: "They failed [before studying] to first recite the blessing for the Torah."[2]

The Rabbis[3] explain this to mean that although the Jews of the time studied Torah extensively, they were not fired by the proper inner intention — of "cleaving to the holiness and spirituality of the Torah and becoming one with it, and of drawing down the Divine Presence through their Torah study."

Torah study comprises two aspects:[4] (a) studying and understanding its logic; (b) cleaving and uniting with G-d, the Giver of the Torah.[5] This latter aspect symbolizes the inherent sanctity and essence of Torah that transcends logic. Before a Jew embarks on the study of Torah, he should cleave to its essence, which eclipses intellect. In the words of our Sages: *"First* he should recite the blessing for Torah," and only afterwards should he study it with his own intellect.

Being the first letter of the alphabet, *alef* signifies that which comes first, while *beis*, the second letter, alludes to that

---

1. *Yirmeyahu* 9:11-12.
2. *Nedarim* 81a; *Bava Metzia* 85b.
3. *Bach, Orach Chayim,* ch. 47; cf. *Ran* on *Nedarim, loc. cit.; Shulchan Aruch Admur HaZaken, Orach Chayim,* beginning of ch. 47.
4. Cf. introduction to *Tiferes Yisrael (Maharal).*
5. As stated in the blessing over the Torah: "...and has given us *His* Torah. Blessed are You, L-rd, Who gives the Torah."

which occupies second place. The Torah begins with a *beis* and not with an *alef* because our study and reading is only its second aspect, the *beis* of Torah. The first aspect, the *alef* of Torah, is its bond with G-d, the Giver of Torah. At this superior level the Torah transcends not only intellect, but also the very letters into which it is distilled.

Approaching Torah in such a fashion has a positive impact on: (a) the Torah itself; (b) the individual who studies the Torah; and (c) the manner in which Torah will affect the world as a whole. When instead one studies Torah and lacks devotion to G-d, the Giver of Torah, then the Torah one studies becomes — heaven forbid — separated from G-dliness.[6] The person does not sanctify the Torah, and something entirely opposite to holiness may result.[7] When, however, Torah study is prefaced by the individual's attachment to G-d, then the Torah being studied is completely united with Him.

With regard to a person studying Torah our Sages state: "If one merits it [; i.e., spiritually purifies himself, from the root], it becomes for him a healing medicine; if not it becomes a deadly poison."[8] For the student who is aware of the *alef* of Torah, its sanctity, the Torah becomes "a healing medicine." Should he begin with the *beis* of Torah and ignore the *alef*, it may very well have an opposite effect.

Furthermore, should a person begin Torah from the perspective of logic, from the letter *beis*, and forget about the *alef*, the sanctity of Torah, he will not sanctify and elevate the world to holiness. In order for Torah to properly affect the world so that G-d's dominion be felt throughout, it is necessary that within the Torah that one studies — the *beis* of Torah — there be felt the Giver of Torah. For this is the *alef* of Torah.

Based on Likkutei Sichos, Vol. XV, pp. 1-5.

---

6. Cf. *Or HaTorah, Bereishis* 11a.
7. See *Hilchos Talmud Torah* (in *Shulchan Aruch Admur HaZaken*) 4:3; see also fn. to *Likkutei Sichos*, Vol. IV, p. 1351.
8. *Yoma* 72b.

Perfecting a Perfect World

With regard to the first *Shabbos*, the *Shabbos* that followed the Six Days of Creation, Scripture states: "G-d blessed the Seventh Day and made it holy, for on it He rested from all His work which G-d created to function."[1] The *Midrash*[2] adduces from this verse that "all that was created during the Six Days of Creation must be rectified and made [by man] to function," for the verse does not state "...which G-d created and made functional," but "...which G-d created to function," thereby indicating that it is incumbent upon *man* to make all of creation functional.

This statement seems to flatly contradict the saying of our Sages[3] that "the world was created in a *completed* state." How are we to reconcile these two teachings?

During the Six Days of Creation the world was indeed created "in a completed state [and lacking nothing]." As a result, however, of the ensuing day of *Shabbos*, "all that was created during the Six Days of Creation must be made [by man] to function." This means that within the "same" world there existed a difference between its state of being during the Six Days of Creation and its state of being on the day of *Shabbos*. According to the conditions of the first six days it was indeed "complete"; according to the elevated status it enjoyed on *Shabbos* the world was seen to be lacking; it was in need of rectification in order for it to be made functional.

This recalls the Alter Rebbe's explanation in *Tanya*[4] with regard to repentance. He states there that "repentance resides mainly within the heart, which comprises a multitude of levels." For this reason, "even if one has already repented properly," his subsequent advance to a higher spiritual level necessitates a higher form and level of repentance.

---

1. *Bereishis* 2:3.
2. *Bereishis Rabbah* 11:6.
3. *Ibid.*, 14:7; see also *ibid.*, 12:6, 13:3.
4. Ch. 29.

A similar explanation is offered[5] as to why our request to "pardon us, our Father, for we have sinned..." is expressed during the *Amidah*, rather than at the beginning of the daily prayers. Once the individual has elevated himself to a loftier level through prayer, he realizes that he must now achieve a loftier manner of repentance. Though his previous manner of spiritual service was considered "complete" during his previous state, it is now wanting.

The *mitzvah* of distributing charity — according to one's means — serves as a simple but effective example. Understandably, when a person becomes wealthier his obligation increases commensurately; what formerly constituted a perfect fulfillment of the *mitzvah*, is now insufficient.

*   *   *

The effect of the Divine union a Jew achieves through Torah study and the performance of *mitzvos* is everlasting.[6] Therefore, when a Jew is elevated to a higher spiritual level he takes along with him (so to speak) the Torah that he had studied and the *mitzvos* that he had fulfilled while on the lower level. In order to elevate his *previous* Torah and *mitzvos* (which on his new spiritual level are found wanting), it is necessary for him to repent.

The same is true here. During the Six Days of Creation the world was as complete as it could be during the six creative work days. However, once the seventh day of *Shabbos* arrived and the world was elevated to a higher level, then the previously "complete" and "perfect" world was suddenly found to be wanting; rectification was now called for, so that the world could be uplifted to the new and loftier state of *Shabbos*.

Based on *Likkutei Sichos*, Vol. XXV, pp. 14-17.

---

5. See *Torah Or, Va'eira* 55d, *Megillas Esther* 95c.
6. *Tanya*, ch. 25.

Noach   נח

Opening the Floodgates of Wisdom

In the Torah portion of *Noach* it is written: "It was in the 600th year of Noach's life...all the wellsprings of the great deep burst forth and the floodgates of the heavens were opened."[1]

The *Zohar* comments on this verse: "In the six-hundredth year of the sixth millenium the gates of supernal wisdom will be opened as will be the wellsprings of lower wisdom. The world will then be rectified, enabling it to enter the seventh millenium."[2]

The "gates of supernal wisdom" and the "wellsprings of lower wisdom" mentioned in the *Zohar* allude to the "floodgates of heaven" and the "wellsprings of the great deep" mentioned in the verse. One refers to Torah wisdom and the other to secular wisdom, respectively.[3]

Indeed, we find that during this period there was a great flurry of revelation of the esoteric depths of Torah. The blossoming of secular scientific knowledge began during this period as well.

That the revelation of the esoteric and inner dimension of Torah serves as a preparation to the "seventh millenium" is readily understandable.[4] For during the Messianic era "the earth will be filled with the knowledge of G-d."[5] It is only fitting that as a prelude[6] to that era the esoteric portion of

---

1. *Breishis 7:11.*
2. *Zohar* I, 117a. The year 5600 after Creation corresponds to 1840 C.E.
3. Commentary of *Ashmores HaBoker* (R. Moshe ben Avraham Kastro).
4. See *Toras Shalom*, p. 237.
5. *Yeshayahu* 11:9.
6. See *Tanya*, beginning of ch. 37.

Torah should be revealed, since it is similar to the Torah that will be taught by *Mashiach*.

However, what possible connection can there be between the revelation and development of secular disciplines, and preparing the world for the "seventh millenium"?

Our Sages say that the world and all that it contains were created "for the sake of Torah and the Jewish people,"[7] and "*All* that G-d created in His world *was created only* for His glory."[8] Thus, the ultimate purpose and intent of every created being and thing is realized when it is utilized by Jews in their service of G-d.

Likewise, the burgeoning of secular knowledge ultimately takes place for the purpose of its being utilized "as a means for serving G-d and gaining a better understanding of His Torah."[9] Secular wisdom, when used toward this end, enables one to visualize how G-dliness will be perceived in the seventh millenium." Moreover, it also serves as a powerful lesson in our service of G-d, here and now.

Some examples: Man has recently discovered and developed the science of telecommunications, whereby a sound or image may be instantaneously transmitted to all corners of the globe.

This serves as a tangible and perceptible paradigm of G-d's ability to see and hear all. For if man can instantaneously hear and see all that takes place in the farthest reaches of the earth, then surely, "Shall He Who implants the ear not hear? Shall He Who forms the eye not see?"[10]

This concrete example of *instantaneous* communication helps one immeasurably in his contemplation of the statement, "'And behold G-d stands over him...' and He looks upon him and 'searches his reins and heart' [to see] if he is serving Him as is fitting."[11] This example enhances a man's

---

7. *Osiyos deRabbi Akiva* 2; commentary of *Rashi*, beginning of *Bereishis*.
8. *Avos*, end of ch. 6.
9. *Tanya*, end of ch. 8.
10. *Tehillim* 94:9.
11. *Tanya*, beginning of ch. 41.

imagery, so that G-d's omnipotence becomes more palpable to him. It therefore affects him to a greater degree — emotionally, as well as in his thought, speech and action.

In the "seventh millenium" G-d's absolute unity will be revealed. We will then be able to *physically*[12] perceive how the multiplicity of creation directly results from His unity. Since the world exists because of G-d's absolute unity this unity should, in some way, be found in the physical world itself.

Science used to believe that the key factors in the world's composition were the different and divergent elements and forces. The further science advances, the more it realizes that this diversity is secondary in importance to the essential unity of matter and energy. The analogue of G-d's absolute unity creating a multitude of created beings and forces is readily apparent.

Based on *Likkutei Sichos,* Vol.XV, pp. 42-48.

---

12. *Shaar HaEmunah,* ch. 25ff.; cf. *Tanya,* ch. 36.

Disembarking the Ark

The Torah reading of *Noach* relates[1] that "by the second month... the land was completely dry. G-d spoke to Noach, saying, 'Leave the ark.... Take out with you every living creature.... They shall be fruitful and multiply upon the earth.'"

Since the land was already "completely dry" and there was no further reason for Noach to remain in the ark, why was it necessary for him to be commanded by G-d to disembark; why did he not leave of his own volition? Furthermore, the command to Noach to leave the ark should have sufficed not only for himself and his family, but also for the animals; why

---

1. *Bereishis* 8:14-17.

did G-d issue a separate command, "Take out with you every living creature..."?

Our Sages explain[2] that within Noach's ark a state of peace and tranquillity existed among the animals and wild beasts, similar to the state that will exist during the Messianic era, at which time "the wolf will dwell with the lamb.... They shall do no evil, nor shall they destroy...."[3]

The simple meaning of the text supports this view as well: It is extremely difficult to suppose that according to the common laws of nature one can confine a multitude of beasts of prey in a very small space for *over a year's time*. We must therefore say that while in the ark the very nature of the beasts of prey underwent a radical change, similar to the change that will be effected during the Messianic era.

Since in the ark Noach found himself in a state that mirrored the Messianic era, he was understandably reluctant to leave; his departure entailed embarking into a lower level of spiritual life. A Divine command was therefore necessary. And if this was so with regard to Noach's own departure, it surely applied to the release of the animals, for Noach was obviously reluctant to set them free and allow them to resume their former destructive natures. G-d therefore had to specifically command him that not only were he and his family to leave the ark, but all the animals were to leave as well.

On the other hand, since G-d did so command, evidently a greater purpose could be served by the ark's inhabitants outside the ark than within it. How could this be, when their life in the ark was on so lofty a level?

Because of the ark's confined space it was impossible for the ark's inhabitants to breed. Indeed, the first command and blessing given to Noach upon leaving the ark was, "Be fruitful and multiply upon the earth." Since the flood had "obliterated

2. See *Sefer HaMaamarim Es'halech — Liozna*, discourse titled *Ki Padah; Or HaTorah, Noach* (Vol. III), p. 669a ff.

3. *Yeshayahu* 11:6-9.

every organism"[4] it was Noach's task to replenish the world's population, thereby enabling the Creator to fulfill His desire of having the *corporeal* world transformed into a "dwelling place for G-d,"[5] the loftiest possible form of spiritual service — superior by far to the spiritual state that existed within the ark.

Our generation has experienced its own deluge, with a major portion of the Jewish people obliterated by the storm-waters of the Holocaust. We must know that first and foremost there lies an obligation on those who by G-d's grace were spared, as well as on their children, to replenish our people physically. There will then be Jews with whom spiritual achievements too can be accomplished.

Based on *Likkutei Sichos*, Vol. XXV, pp. 28-33.

---

4. *Bereishis* 7:23.
5. *Tanya*, ch. 36.

Lech Lecha   לך לך

The Birth of a Nation

The Torah portion of *Lech Lecha* opens with G-d saying to Avraham: "Go away from your land and birthplace....I will make you into a great nation...."[1]

Why does the Torah not preface this statement by mentioning at least briefly that Avraham was a G-d-fearing individual, similar to the way Noach is introduced with the statement, "Noach was a righteous man"?[2] Surely such a statement would be appropriate with regard to Avraham, for the Midrashic literature is replete with incidents that testify to his piety, righteousness and self-sacrificing devotion to G-d while still living in Ur Casdim and Charan.

The Jewish nation begins with Avraham, the first Jew. Yet his sterling qualities notwithstanding, his selection by G-d from among all the people on earth only came about when G-d said to him, "Go away from Your land...." The Torah begins its narrative with this command in order to indicate the essential qualities of Avraham in particular, as well as of the Jewish people as a whole.

The relationship of all the other nations with the Creator results from their knowledge and understanding of Him. This causes them to bind themselves to Him and obey His laws. By contrast, the Jewish people's relationship with G-d and their own existence as a nation is primarily based on the fact that it was *G-d* who chose them, not that they uplifted *themselves* to come to know Him and to bind themselves to Him.

Since this relationship emanates from G-d and not from

---

1. *Bereishis* 12:1ff.
2. *Bereishis* 6:9.

man, it is readily understandable that Jews are not only a more elevated category of created beings, but are in fact qualitatively different. All created beings are and remain created entities; Jews, however, are essentially a G-dly entity that is found within the context of creation.

The same is true with regard to the contrast between the commandments given to the Jewish people and those commanded to other nations. There is not merely a quantitative difference (between seven and 613), but a qualitative difference as well.[3]

The main function of the commandments given to non-Jews is to ensure an orderly world[4] and to refine the world and man, so that both the world as a whole and man in particular conduct themselves properly. This is also why all the commandments of the various nations can be performed solely out of logical imperative.[5] The *mitzvos* given by G-d to the Jewish people, however, are quite different. Not only are they given for the sake of purifying man and the world, but most importantly in order to effect "unification and attachment"[6] with G-d.

Since Creator and created are separated by an infinite gulf, it is self-evident that just as created beings are as nothing in G-d's eyes, the same is true of their service. The only way that "unification and attachment" can be achieved between Creator and created is for G-d to choose this unification as a result of the fulfillment of His commands.

This concept is stressed in the Torah at the very beginning of the first Jewish relationship with G-d. It was not Avraham's own unique qualities and his personal divine service that singled him out; rather, *G-d* chose him. His "union and attachment" to G-d resulted from his being chosen and commanded by G-d, and from his fulfillment of His commands.

Based on *Likkutei Sichos*, Vol. XXV, pp. 47-50.

---

3. See *Likkutei Sichos*, Vol. V, p. 159ff.; Vol. XV, p. 150.
4. See *Yeshayahu* 45:18.
5. See *Rambam, Hilchos Melachim*, end of ch. 8.
6. *Likkutei Torah, Bechukosai* 45b.

In Sarah's Merit

The Torah portion of *Lech Lecha* relates how Avraham and his wife Sarah went to Egypt to escape the famine in the land of Canaan. Before they arrived in Egypt Avraham said to Sarah: "I realize that you are a good-looking woman. When the Egyptians see you, they will say, 'This is his wife,' and kill me, allowing you to live. Please say that you are my sister. They will then be good to me for your sake, and my life will be spared because of you."[1]

The classical commentaries ask:[2] How could Avraham have placed Sarah in a position of potential danger, allowing her to be taken to Pharaoh's palace, in order for his own life to be saved? Even more puzzling is Avraham's ability to think about the benefits he would receive by placing his wife in such jeopardy. Even if Avraham were forced to let Sarah be taken in order to spare his life, how could he possibly say, "They will then be good to me..."?

Earlier on, G-d had promised Avraham that by leaving his birthplace and going to Canaan he would — among other things — be blessed with wealth.[3] Avraham was sure that this forced departure from Canaan to go to Egypt was in some way related to this blessing. Seeing his journey to Egypt as a possible vehicle for G-d's blessing of wealth — "They will then be good to me...," Avraham asked Sarah to "Please say that you are my sister."

Spiritually as well, Avraham's departure from his birthplace was intended to enable him to attain spiritual elevation by sifting and refining the sparks of holiness found within the physical world. This, too, was the spiritual intent of his jour-

---

1. *Bereishis* 12:11-13.
2. See commentaries of *Abarbanel* and *Alshech* on *Lech Lecha*; cf. commentaries on *Rashi* 12:13.
3. *Ibid.* 12:1-2.
4. Discussed at length in *Likkutei Sichos*, Vol. V, p. 61ff.; cf. sources noted there.

ney to Egypt — to elevate the "lost" sparks of holiness found there.[4]

The performance of *mitzvos*, whose overall purpose is the spiritual refinement of the physical world, is to be done, as a rule, through natural means.[5] Avraham therefore said to Sarah, "Please say that you are my sister," for by doing so, "They will then be good to me...." By being granted material gifts Avraham's mission of elevating the materiality that came into his possession would be fulfilled in as natural a manner as possible.

The question, however, remains: How could Avraham allow Sarah be drawn into a situation where she might possibly become dishonored, for the sake of his personal benefit? "G-d has many agents through which He provides [physical as well as spiritual] sustenance to those who fear Him;"[6] should Avraham not have relied on G-d to help him in a manner which would not cause Sarah to face such great anguish?

The *Zohar* answers this question by stating that Avraham "did not rely on his own merit but rather on the merit of his wife — that he would acquire wealth in her merit, for one acquires wealth in the merit of one's wife."[7]

Spiritually as well, Avraham's descent into Egypt for the sake of "spiritual wealth" could only be accomplished in the merit of Sarah. Toward that end she had to descend to Pharaoh's house.

Since the ultimate intent of the descent into Egypt could only be accomplished in this manner, the *Zohar* concludes that Avraham was correct in "relying on Sarah's merit; in her merit he would not be harmed, nor would any harm befall her."

In spiritual terms, Avraham and Sarah are symbolic of soul and body, respectively.[8] That both of them had to des-

---

5. See *ibid.*, p. 80ff.; cf. sources noted there.
6. *Bamidbar Rabbah* 18:18.
7. Zohar III, 52a.
8. *Ibid.*, I, 78b.

cend to Egypt in order for them to accomplish their spiritual missions in life, teaches us a lesson as well. Only through partnership with the body can the soul reach its supreme elevation.

Based on *Likkutei Sichos*, Vol. XX, pp. 38-41.

Vayeira   וירא

Seasonable vs. Reasonable

In the weekly reading of *Vayeira* we learn of the circumcision of Yitzchak that took place when he was eight days old.[1] The *Midrash* relates that "Yitzchak and Yishmael argued. One said: 'I am cherished more than you, for I was circumcised at thirteen years of age.' The other said: 'I am more cherished than you, for I was circumcised when I was but eight days old.'"[2]

One can easily understand why Yishmael felt more cherished because his circumcision took place at the age of thirteen: at that age he was old enough to protest. That he did not do so was surely reason enough for him to feel himself to be superior. But why did Yitzchak reason that he was the more cherished of the two?

The overall theme of circumcision is, as the verse says: "This shall be My covenant in your flesh, an eternal covenant."[3] Circumcision effects an *eternal* bond between the individual and G-d, like a covenant formed between two dear friends who desire to ensure thereby that their friendship will remain eternally unmarred. There is no ironclad guarantee that an interpersonal covenant will truly be everlasting, for mortals are subject to change. When, however, it is G-d who makes the covenant — in this case, His covenant with the Jewish people through circumcision — then it is immutable and truly eternal.

The reason that circumcision is performed at the tender age of eight days — at a time the infant has absolutely no say in the matter — may be understood accordingly.

Whatever a person does on his own initiative requires

---

1. *Bereishis* 21:4.
2. *Bereishis Rabbah* 55:4.
3. *Bereishis* 17:13.

preparation; adequate time must therefore be allowed. However, the covenant that is set in motion through circumcision is effected entirely by G-d. In other words, circumcision is not an act through which a person binds himself to G-d. Quite the contrary: when a Jew is circumcised *G-d binds Himself* to the person with an "eternal covenant." Thus, there is no reason to tarry until the time the infant will come of age and consciously affirm and participate in this act, for in any event he does nothing at all — the entire covenant comes from G-d. He is therefore circumcised at the earliest age possible.

Accordingly, we now understand that the merit of Yitzchak's circumcision at eight days surpassed not only that of Yishmael, but also the circumcision of his father Avraham. For Avraham was given the commandment of circumcision after he had already prepared himself through his previous spiritual service. His service was such that he attained the highest degree of perfection possible for a created being to achieve on his own. Thus, Avraham's circumcision lacked the indisputable indication that the covenant, which came about as a result of the circumcision, came *entirely* from G-d.

The same was true of Yishmael's circumcision. Since it was performed when he was already intellectually mature, he entered into it with the decision that *he* desired to bind himself to G-d.

Only with the circumcision of Yitzchak, at the age of eight days, was it clear for all to see that this was a covenant that had nothing whatever to do with this created being, but was entirely dependent on G-d.

Based on *Likkutei Sichos*, Vol. XXV, pp. 86-90.

The Akedah: The Ultimate Test

Our Sages tell us that G-d tested Avraham ten times.[1] The final and most difficult test was the *Akedah*, the binding of Yitzchak upon the altar. This is related at length in the Torah

---

1. *Avos* 5:3.

portion of *Vayeira*, which recounts how G-d said to Avraham, *"Please* take your son, your only son, whom you love, Yitzchak...and offer him as a burnt-offering...."[2]

The *Gemara* explains why G-d pleaded with Avraham to offer his son and did not simply command him to do so. G-d was, in effect, saying to Avraham: "I have tested you on numerous occasions and you have successfully passed all the trials. Please withstand this test as well, so that it not be said: 'The earlier tests were meaningless.'"[3]

The *Gemara's* explanation needs to be understood. Even if Avraham's self- sacrifice would not have been strong enough to withstand the final test, in no way would this have negated his ability in withstanding the previous ones, since the last test was by far the most difficult of all. Why, then, would it be said that "the earlier tests were meaningless"?

The passage describing the *Akedah* is deemed so important that it takes a prominent place in our daily prayers.[4] Why do we constantly recall this event, which ended with Avraham and Yitzchak receiving a last-minute reprieve, when the whole course of Jewish history is one long, unbroken chain of Jewish martyrs who actually gave their lives for the sanctification of G-d's Name?[5] Moreover, they willingly faced martyrdom without having first received a direct communication from G-d![16]

Chassidus explains[7] that Avraham was unique in that he was the *first* individual to withstand the test of *mesirus nefesh,* total sacrifice of self for the sake of G-d. He did so notwithstanding the fact that "All beginnings are difficult."[8] Once he broke this barrier, it became easier for those who came after

---

2. *Bereishis* 22:2.
3. *Sanhedrin* 89b.
4. Commentary of *Abarbanel* on *Lech Lecha.*
5. *Ikkarim, Maamar* 3:36.
6. *Iggeres HaKodesh,* Epistle 21.
7. *Sefer HaMaamarim 5678,* p. 283; *Sefer HaMaamarim 5688,* p. 102; *Likkutei Sichos,* Vol. X, p. 46.
8. *Mechilta* and *Rashi* on *Shmos* 19:5.

him to follow in his footsteps and reveal within themselves too the power of *mesirus nefesh*.

Attaining true *mesirus nefesh* is exceedingly difficult. It involves total renunciation of self; sacrificing to G-d one's very soul and being. It is a level of dedication to G-d that transcends all bounds of logic and emotion.

Even offering one's life for G-d is not conclusive proof of true *mesirus nefesh*, inasmuch as a person may be doing so because of a logical imperative — logic might dictate that it is proper to sacrifice one's life for the sake of a greater good. Only when the act transcends all human bounds of logic, emotion, possible rewards, etc., is it deemed true *mesirus nefesh*.

This level of *mesirus nefesh* was first palpably revealed by Avraham at the time of the *Akedah*. There was absolutely no rhyme nor reason for Avraham to offer his son other than the fact that G-d asked him to do so; no possible personal benefit could accrue to him from this act.

The *Gemara's* answer — "...so that it not be said that 'the earlier tests were meaningless'" — will be understood accordingly.

Had Avraham not withstood the tenth and final test of the *Akedah* it could well be said that his previous successes were a result of the fact that they made spiritual sense to him. We would still not know how he would respond to a test that required absolute and total *mesirus nefesh*.

By rising to the challenge of the *Akedah*, Avraham not only proved that he was now capable of absolute *mesirus nefesh*, but also proved that this spirit of total self-abnegation had permeated him when he withstood the earlier tests as well.

The ability to serve G-d with true *mesirus nefesh* was bequeathed by Avraham to every Jew. Even when a Jew's self-sacrifice may seem to stem from external factors, it contains the same degree of self-nullification to G-d which Avraham displayed at the *Akedah*.

Based on *Likkutei Sichos*, Vol. XX, pp. 73-78.

Chayei Sarah   חיי שרה

One Moment, One Day, One Instant

The *Zohar*[1] on the Torah portion of *Chayei Sarah* speaks of a merit possessed by penitents that even the truly righteous lack. The truly righteous make daily spiritual progress in an orderly fashion, ultimately attaining an extremely exalted state of union with G-d. Their spiritual progress is similar to Avraham's, of whom the verse says: "Avraham grew old, advancing in days...."[2] Our Sages comment: "Every day saw Avraham advance spiritually."[3]

Penitents, however, says the *Zohar*, surpass even the truly righteous in that "in one moment, in one day, in one instant, they draw close to G-d."

Likkutei Levi Yitzchak asks the following question: "This does not seem to follow in proper sequence. The *Zohar* should surely have stated *day, moment* and *instant*. In this order each time segment would be briefer than the one preceding it. It would then be telling us that repentance may be accomplished not only in a *day*, but even in a *moment*, and indeed, even in an *instant*. Furthermore, if one *instant* suffices [for repentance], why the need to mention a *moment* or a *day*?"[4]

The author answers these questions by explaining that there are three levels of repentance. The lowest level is "turning away from evil";[5] the next level is "doing good";[6] and the third and highest level of repentance is that of "seeking peace

---

1. I, 129a ff.
2. *Bereishis* 24:1.
3. See *Zohar* I, 224a; *Torah Or* 16a, 79b.
4. Commentary on *Zohar* I, p. 81.
5. *Tehillim* 34:15.
6. *Ibid.*

and pursuing it."[7] The third level refers to the study of Torah, for "all of its paths are peace."[8]

The lowest level of repentance may be accomplished in a *moment*, the next takes a *day* to achieve, while the third and highest level can be effected in an *instant*.

This, however, must be understood: A penitent can *"immediately* be elevated and cleave to G-d,"[9] because repentance inherently transcends orderly progression. It is therefore possible for one who just a while ago was in a spiritual abyss to rise to the uppermost heights. All this results from the fact that repentance emanates from the level of a person's soul that transcends boundaries. This makes it possible for the spiritual feat of repentance to be accomplished within a framework of time that transcends boundaries — in a *moment* or an *instant*.

This being so, why is it that the intermediary level of "doing good" takes a *day* to accomplish, and cannot be achieved — as can the lowest level of repentance — in a *moment?*

Brevity and length apply not only to time, but also to intellect. "One should always teach one's pupil in a succinct style," state our Sages.[10] On the other hand, we find that in order for a student to fully understand his master's teachings, it is necessary for the master to elaborate and explain a given concept at length. The difference between the two situations is obvious: The initial concept should be transmitted in a pithy manner; elucidation of the concept calls for further elaboration.

There is yet another instance of conceptual brevity: a concept as it exists within its source will invariably be brief, since the *essence* of the concept is revealed there.

Within the realm of repentance, too, there exist varying

---

7. *Ibid.*
8. *Mishlei* 3:17.
9. *Zohar* I, 129b.
10. *Pesachim* 3b; *Chullin* 63b.

degrees of length and brevity. The repentance of "seeking peace and pursuing it" because of its intrinsic loftiness (like a lofty concept within its source) is necessarily brief — "one *instant*." The repentance of "turning away from evil" is of but "one *moment's*" duration because of its very simplicity. However, the repentance of "doing good," like an intricate concept transmitted to a student, cannot be mastered immediately, therefore a full *day* is required.

Based on *Likkutei Sichos*, Vol. XX, pp. 86-89.

Changing the Guard

According to Jewish law the *Haftorah* reading from the Prophets is to be "in the spirit of the Torah portion";[1] moreover, it is to be "similar" to the conclusion of the Torah portion.[2]

The relationship between the Torah reading of *Chayei Sarah* and its *Haftorah* is readily discernible. The *Haftorah* chronicles the activities of King David when he was "old, well advanced in years."[3] This closely parallels the portion of *Chayei Sarah* which speaks for the most part about the time when "Avraham was old, well advanced in years."[4]

Indeed, the *Haftorah* parallels not only the time frame, but also the events that then took place. The *Haftorah* tells of the rivalry between David's two sons, Adoniyah and Shlomo, and of how Adoniyah boasted, "I shall be the [next] king."[5] It then goes on to recount the events that eventually resulted in

---

1. *Tur* and *Shulchan Aruch* (so too *Shulchan Aruch Admur HaZaken*) *Orach Chayim*, beginning of Section 284; *Tur* and *Rama, ibid.*, end of Section 428.
2. See *Beis Yosef* on *Tur Orach Chayim* (and similarly in *Shulchan Aruch Admur HaZaken*), end of Section 283.
3. Beginning of I *Melachim*.
4. *Bereishis* 24:1.
5. I *Melachim* 1:5.

David's declaration to Bas-Sheva that his oath, "For Shlomo, my son, will reign after me...," would be fulfilled on "this very day."[6]

This closely parallels the rivalry between Avraham's two sons, with Yishmael telling Yitzchak, "I am greater and more cherished than you,"[7] and thus claiming to be Avraham's true heir. However, Avraham made his younger son Yitzchak his rightful heir, transferring to him all his possessions.[8] Thus, just as David chose his younger son, Shlomo, to reign after him and carry on his dynasty, so did Avraham choose his younger son, Yitzchak, to continue *his* dynasty, thereby rejecting Yishmael and the other children.

However, there still remains a noteworthy detail found in the Torah portion but lacking in the *Haftorah*. The former passage also speaks of the time after Avraham's demise, when "G-d blessed his son, Yitzchak...."[9] Why does not the *Haftorah* as well go on to cite the later verses which relate how "Shlomo sat on the throne"?[10]

After King David swore that he would see to it "on this day" that Shlomo would become king, Bas-Sheva said, "May my master, *King David, live forever.*" As explained by Maimonides,[11] this means to say that "sovereignty will *forever* not be severed from David's progeny." Maimonides goes on to say that even when David's descendants do not conduct themselves fittingly, G-d forbid, they still retain the reins of kingdom. The reason for this is that "G-d had so promised him (David)."[12] Since David's reign resulted from his being chosen by G-d, there can be no change.

This resembles the selection of the Jewish people in that they are the descendants of Avraham, Yitzchak and Yaakov.

---

6. *Ibid.*, v. 30.
7. *Sanhedrin* 89b.
8. See *Bereishis* 24:36, 25:5 and *Rashi's* commentary.
9. *Ibid.* 25:11.
10. *I Melachim* 1:46.
11. *Rambam, Hilchos Melachim* 1:7.
12. *Ibid.*

That which the Patriarchs transmitted to all the Jewish people endures eternally, for G-d's choice of Avraham is not subject to change.

Herein lies the striking parallel between the Torah reading and the *Haftorah*. David's kingship was actually perpetuated when his son, Shlomo, reigned after him. In the Torah portion, as well, G-d's choice in Avraham found expression in Yitzchak's continuation of the dynasty and in Yaakov after him.

The reason the *Haftorah* does not go on to mention Shlomo's actual reign may be understood accordingly. For in the Torah portion as well we have yet to encounter Yaakov, whose life brought the divine service of the Patriarchs to its consummation. It was only with his birth that the self-sufficient entity of the three Patriarchs came into being — the three illustrious individuals who jointly became the foundation of the Jewish people, and its source of spiritual sustenance until this very day.

Based on *Likkutei Sichos*, Vol. XXV, pp. 106-114.

Toldos   תולדת

Avraham & Yitzchak: A Study in Contrasts

The Torah portion of *Toldos* begins by relating that "Avraham was the father of Yitzchak."[1] Our Sages note: "The cynics of that generation were saying that 'Avimelech fathered Yitzchak.' What did G-d do? He caused Yitzchak's countenance to resemble Avraham's. Everybody then testified that 'Avraham was the father of Yitzchak.'"[2]

Since our Sages inform us of the above through a process of *question and answer* — "What did G-d do? [I.e., "What could G-d possibly do to remedy the situation?"] He caused Yitzchak's countenance etc." — and do not simply state that G-d made Yitzchak look like Avraham, it is obvious that making Yitzchak resemble Avraham involved a singular accomplishment on G-d's part.

This is strange indeed: it is the most natural thing in the world for a father and son to look alike.[3] In fact, there would have to be a special reason for them not to look alike. Why, then, do our Sages indicate that making Yitzchak look like Avraham was a particular feat?

There are a number of things which the *Gemara* deems to be as "difficult" for G-d to do as the classical "difficulty" of splitting the sea for the Jewish people soon after their exodus from Egypt.[4] Why was splitting the sea considered to be difficult for G-d?

The Rabbis explain[5] that the difficulty was not so much in

---

1. *Bereishis* 25:19.
2. *Rashi, loc. cit.;* cf. *Tanchuma, Vayeira* 1; cf. *Bava Metzia* 87a.
3. See *Eduyos* 2:9, and commentary of the *Rambam* there.
4. *Pesachim* 118a; *Sotah* 2a.
5. See *Shaar HaEmunah*, ch. 32.

the actual splitting of the sea, but in a related matter. At that moment two opposites came to pass simultaneously — the Egyptians were smitten and the Jews were saved.[6] This was done notwithstanding the fact that the Attribute of Justice then complained: "What difference is there between the two [nations]? Both are idolatrous!"[7]

Treating the Jewish people preferentially and the Egyptians harshly, by completely ignoring the protestations of the Attribute of Justice — which generally is given credence — is considered to be "difficult" for G-d.[8]

The same is true with regard to Avraham and Yitzchak. Father and son were different in many critical areas. Avraham was totally dedicated to G-d out of love for Him, while Yitzchak was wholly devoted to G-d out of fear and awe of Him.[9]

Since intellect is the cause and root of the emotions, it follows that the reason Avraham and Yitzchak differed so radically in their spiritual emotions was that they differed intellectually as well.

Avraham and Yitzchak differed, too, in their manner of spiritual service. Avraham's service of G-d involved hospitality and making Him known to the populace — revealing G-dliness from *above downwards*. Yitzchak's spiritual service was symbolized by his digging of wells, involving as it did removing the obstructions that concealed the wellsprings and revealing the well-water that flowed from *below upwards*.

A son will truly resemble his father when both father and son share similar personalities, and are like intellectually, emotionally, and so forth. Avraham and Yitzchak, however, possessed completely different personalities. They should therefore have had totally different appearances — Avraham a kind countenance, Yitzchak a stern one.

---

6. See *Yeshayahu* 19:22; *Zohar* II, 36a.
7. See *Zohar* II, 170b; *Mechilta, Beshalach* 14:28.
8. As the *Zohar* states, *loc. cit.*: "It is difficult for Him to resist the Attribute of Justice."
9. *Torah Or* and *Toras Chayim*, beginning of the portion of *Lech Lecha*.

Herein lies the "difficulty": What could be done to these "opposites" — Avraham and Yitzchak — to forestall the scoffing of the cynics who said that "Avimelech fathered Yitzchak"?

In order to discredit their words, G-d did something "difficult": He changed the order of things and saw to it Himself that Yitzchak look like Avraham, so that all would testify that "Avraham was the father of Yitzchak."

Bearing in mind that Avraham is symbolic of kindness and Yitzchak of severity, we learn an important lesson from the fact that G-d made Yitzchak look like Avraham, rather than the reverse. Whenever a Jew is faced with a decision regarding his spiritual service, whether to serve his Maker with the attribute of benevolence or with the attribute of severity, he should choose to act kindly and benevolently.

Based on *Likkutei Sichos,* Vol. XX, pp. 100-105.

The Patriarchs as Models

In the Torah reading of *Toldos* we learn of the famine in the land of Canaan during the time of Yitzchak.[1] G-d appeared to him and said: "Do not go down to Egypt.... Remain in this land, and I will be with you and bless you...." Our Sages explain[2] that Yitzchak was a "complete, wholly-consumed offering," therefore "Diaspora is unfit for you."[3] G-d thus told him that he was not to follow in the footsteps of his father Avraham, who had gone down to Egypt when a similar famine had struck in his time.

There is a well-known saying of our Sages, "All that transpired with the Patriarchs serves as a sign to their progeny."[4] This means to say that these events not only serve as

---

1. *Bereishis* 26:1ff.
2. See *Bereishis Rabbah* 64:3; *Rashi* and *Ramban* on verses cited above.
3. *Rashi* and *Ramban, loc. cit.*
4. See *Tanchuma, Lech Lecha* 9; *Bereishis Rabbah* 40:6.

guideposts for the conduct of their children, but in addition pave the way and provide fortitude, so that the children will be able to conduct themselves in the selfsame manner.

The lesson here is unequivocal. A Jew's true place is not in exile but "at his Father's table";[5] i.e., G-d should redeem him from exile and lead him to *Eretz Yisrael*. For when a Jew finds himself in exile he can find neither peace nor true happiness, knowing as he does that this is not his true place and state of existence. He therefore prays and demands three times a day: "Speedily cause the scion of David Your servant to flourish...,"[6] and "May our eyes behold Your return to Zion in mercy."[7]

To remain exclusively in the Land of Israel was unique to Yitzchak, for both Avraham and Yaakov found themselves on a number of occasions outside the Land. It is self-understood that the lessons gleaned from the life of the Patriarchs, especially those events which characterized the unique personality of each, apply to all Jews, at all times, in all places — even as they find themselves in exile. What can we learn from the Patriarchs with regard to their places of residence, Avraham and Yaakov residing both in the Land of Israel and outside of it, and Yitzchak dwelling only in the Land?

Jews may generally be divided into two categories: those who wholly devote their lives to Torah study, and those who engage in worldly pursuits in order to make a living. Since the latter engage in mundane affairs with "all their deeds being done for the sake of heaven,"[8] they imbue the physical world as well with holiness.

The ability for all Jews to perform both these manners of service — for every Jew ought to engage both in Torah and in good deeds — is bequeathed to every Jew by the Patriarchs. Avraham descended into the straits and spiritual constric-

---

5. See *Berachos* 3a.
6. Liturgy, weekday *Amidah*.
7. Liturgy, *Amidah* of weekdays and *Shabbos*.
8. Cf. *Avos* 2:12.

tions of Egypt, yet there too, as he had done previously in other places, he influenced people to come to know G-d and serve Him. Yitzchak, by contrast, did not leave the Land of Israel. Furthermore, even while there we do not find him oft venturing from his own territory and devoting himself to others. His service was directed more inwardly.

Avraham's approach to divine service teaches and enables all Jews to work with others. Even those Jews who are immersed in Torah study are obliged from time to time to leave their environs and imbue the "outside" world with holiness, bringing their fellow Jews closer to G-d and His Torah.

Yitzchak's approach instructs and inspires all Jews in the more inwardly-directed manner of service. Even those who are mainly involved in permeating the world at large with holiness and bringing their fellow Jews closer to G-d and His Torah, must from time to time serve Him in the way that Yitzchak did; i.e., they should separate themselves at times from the rest of the world and wholly immerse themselves in the study of Torah.

Based on *Likkutei Sichos*, Vol. XXV, pp. 123-125.

Vayeitzei   ויצא

Giving Names

In the Torah portion of *Vayeitzei* we learn of the birth of eleven of Yaakov's twelve sons and the names given them by the Matriarchs. The reasons for the names of these children — who later went on to establish the twelve tribes of Israel — are stated explicitly in the Torah. This is in marked contrast to the names of the Patriarchs, Avraham, Yitzchak and Yaakov, where the Torah does not explicitly spell out the reasons for the names given them at birth. Why the difference?

The Jewish name[1] possessed by an individual is not mere happenstance;[2] there is a direct connection between the name of a person and the very essence of his soul.[3] While it is indeed true that the soul itself, prior to its descent within a body, has no name at all,[4] still it is the person's name that connects the soul and the body, acting as it does as the conduit for the soul's life-force to animate the body.[5]

More specifically, in this process of soul-body animation, the name serves two distinct purposes:[6] (a) essentially, it effects a general connection between soul and body, the effect of which is the same in all individuals; (b) in its revealed form — as a specific name of a particular person — it serves as a personal expression of the particular qualities and personality of the individual so named.

---

1. *Or Torah* 4b; *Likkutei Torah, Behar* 41c; *Or HaTorah, Shmos* 103ff.; the *maamar* entitled *Atah Echad,* 5702.
2. *Likkutei Torah, loc. cit.*
3. *Ibid.*
4. *Ibid.,* and *Balak* 67c; *Or HaTorah, loc. cit.*
5. *Likkutei Torah, ibid.*
6. See sources cited in fn. 1.

The Alter Rebbe explains in *Torah Or*[7] that the spiritual
level of the Patriarchs is to be found "at all times within all
individuals, for 'only Avraham, Yitzchak and Yaakov are
entitled Patriarchs.'"[8]

He goes on to say: "This level of 'Patriarchs' was
bequeathed by them to all their progeny in each and every
generation.... However, the other degrees of saintliness,
such as those of the tribes of Reuven, Shimon, Levi..., may
not necessarily be found at all within some individuals. This is
not so with regard to the level of 'Patriarchs'; this level must
be found within each and every Jew, for they are the source
and root of all Jewish souls."

Thus, we understand that the level of "Patriarchs" is to be
found within all Jews because of something that relates to the
very essence of their being Jewish: they are part of the greater
Jewish whole, which consists of the entire Jewish people. It
therefore follows that all Jews possess this level equally.

This is not so regarding the individual tribes: their levels
are found in varying degrees and in different forms among
the Jewish people,[9] personifying the *particular* manner of
service of each and every Jew.

The differences between the names of the Patriarchs and
Yaakov's sons, the founders of the tribes, will be understood
accordingly. The names of the Patriarchs reflect the collective
quality of Judaism found within each and every Jew, while the
names of the tribes allude to the specific levels of different
Jews in accordance with their individual qualities.

Since the names of the tribes are indicative of specific
forms and levels, each name is accompanied by its revealed
and specific rationale, in keeping with the particular level and
manner of divine service that characterized the individual son
of Yaakov so named. No reason, however, is given for the
names of the Patriarchs, inasmuch as their names are of a

---

7. Beginning of section *Va'eira.*
8. *Berachos* 16b.
9. Cf. *Likkutei Sichos*, Vol. VI, p. 304.

general and collective nature, applying as they do to all the Jewish people at all times and in all places.

This also explains why the names of the tribes were provided by the Matriarchs, for the *revealed* and developed shape of a child is formed through the nine months of gestation.[10] Since the founders of the tribes embody *revealed* and particular spiritual levels, as opposed to the essential and general level of the Patriarchs, it follows that their names, too, should be determined by those who are themselves responsible for their particular development and revelation — the Matriarchs.

Based on *Likkutei Sichos*, Vol. X, pp. 96-98.

---

10. See *Pirush HaMillos*, ch. 111.

An Honor Guard of Angels

At the conclusion of the Torah portion of *Vayeitzei* we read how Yaakov, on his way back to the Land of Israel, encountered "angels of G-d."[1] *Rashi*,[2] quoting the Sages,[3] says: "Angels of *Eretz Yisrael* came toward him, in order to escort him into the Land."

Since Yaakov already had an escort of angels outside the Land of Israel whose function it was to protect him,[4] it is evident that the angels who left the Land in order to escort him as he re-entered it served more as members of an honor guard than as guardian angels. What spiritual purpose did these angels serve?

Yaakov's departure from Beersheba and journey to Charan, which is described at the outset of the Torah portion,[5]

---

1. *Bereishis* 32:2.
2. *Loc. cit.*
3. See *Tanchuma* (and *Tanchuma, Buber*) *Vayishlach* 3; *Tanchuma, Buber, Vayeishev* 2; see also *Midrash Lekach Tov* on this verse.
4. See *Rashi* on *Bereishis* 28:12.
5. *Ibid.* 28:10.

parallels the Jewish exile.[6] Indeed, being the journey of one of the three Patriarchs "whose deeds serve as a sign to their progeny,"[7] Yaakov's journey to Charan and his exile in the house of Lavan served as the forerunner of all subsequent Jewish exiles. Just as Yaakov departed from the Land of Israel not only to flee his brother's wrath, but also to "marry a woman...and become an assembly of nations,"[8] so, too, with regard to the exile of the Jewish people from *Eretz Yisrael*.

Although it is true that "because of our sins we were exiled from our land,"[9] nevertheless, the ultimate intent of exile is to purify the entire world and elevate it to holiness. This is accomplished by each and every Jew through transforming the Diaspora into a spiritual "Land of Israel." For by making the entire world a dwelling place for G-d,[10] it becomes a spiritual Land of Israel. (Indeed, there was once a follower of the *Tzemach Tzedek* who desired to move to *Eretz Yisrael*. As a devoted *chassid*, he consulted him as to the wisdom of such a move. The *Tzemach Tzedek* told him: "Transform *this* place into *Eretz Yisrael*."[11])

These, then, were the two types of angels. The angels who escorted Yaakov within the Land of Israel *before* he left and entered a state of exile, provided him with the strength to withstand the vicissitudes of exile and enabled him to perform his spiritual service there. Then, having accomplished his task of transforming the Diaspora into a spiritual Land of Israel through his divine service, Yaakov merited an encounter with the angels of the Land of Israel, who came to him while he was still outside it, to symbolize his transformation of the Diaspora into the Land of Israel.

*   *   *

---

6. *Bereishis Rabbah* 68:13; see also *Zohar, Vayeitzei* 149b.
7. See *Tanchuma, Lech* 9; *Bereishis Rabbah* 40:6.
8. *Bereishis* 28:2-3.
9. Liturgy, *Amidah* of *Musaf* for the Festivals.
10. See *Tanchuma, Naso* 16; *Tanya,* beginning of ch. 36.
11. See *Igros Kodesh* of Rabbi Yosef Yitzchak Schneersohn, Vol. I, p. 485; *Likkutei Sichos,* Vol. II, p. 621.

The purpose of the entire Torah is to teach us how to better serve G-d. What lesson is to be learned from Yaakov's angels?

When the Torah informs us that angels are sent to us while in exile in order to escort us to the Land of Israel, it does so in order to reveal to all Jews the critical importance of their divine service during the time of exile. This in turn provides the encouragement and strength needed to perform this service, notwithstanding the difficulties that are encountered. Even when in exile, each and every Jew is assured that not only does he have nothing to fear for there are protective angels who accompany him, but more importantly, G-d sends angels of the Land *of Israel* to escort him and provide him with an honor guard.

Not only should a Jew not be fazed by the alien spirit of exile, but he should act moreover as if he were already in a state of redemption. For he is being escorted by the angels of the Land of *Israel*; there is nothing to fear, and all his spiritual tasks will be accomplished in the most dignified fashion.

Such knowledge is especially desirable now, at the end of exile, for it helps Jews to steadfastly pursue their divine mission of purifying and elevating the last remnants of exile, and hastening their entrance into the Land of Israel through the speedy coming of our Righteous *Mashiach*.

Based on Likkutei Sichos, Vol. XXV, pp. 150-158.

Vayishlach   וישלח

Gifts, Prayers & Battles

In the Torah portion of *Vayishlach* we learn of the preparations Yaakov made to confront his brother Esav after learning that his brother was marching towards him with four
hundred men.

Regarding Yaakov's manner of preparation *Rashi* comments: "He *repaired himself* in three ways: to give gifts [to Esav
and thereby appease him]; to pray [to G-d to save him from
his brother's clutches]; and to do battle."[1]

Why does *Rashi* use the unusual expression *"repaired* himself" rather than the more common expression "prepared
himself"?

When a person "prepares himself" for what is about to
come, it may mean either that in preparation he acts in a
particular fashion, or he mentally readies himself for the
event through prayer and the like. *"Repairing* himself" —
implying rectification — indicates more than mere preparation: it is indicative of a person's "repairing" and "rectifying"
himself; he changes something *within himself* in order to prepare
to do that which must be done.

This was the case with Yaakov: he prepared himself for
"gifts, prayer and battle" by "repairing" something within
himself.

Our Sages note[2] that it angered Yaakov that he had to
appease his brother by giving him gifts. In order for the gifts
to be given — as gifts should be given — with a cheerful

---

1. *Bereishis* 32:9.
2. See *Rashi* on 32:22.

countenance, Yaakov had to effect and *repair* a change of attitude *within himself.*

Yaakov was also fearful that his merits may have been diminished as a result of all the kindness G-d had shown him.[3] For this reason he was not sure that G-d's promise — "I shall deal very kindly with you"[4] — would stand him in good stead in saving him from his brother's wrath. It was therefore necessary to effect a change *within himself,* and once again merit G-d's blessings, through the vehicle of prayer.

This was also the case with regard to Yaakov's preparations to do battle, for "he feared and it anguished him."[5] In order for him to mentally prepare himself to do battle, an emotional change had to transpire *within himself.*

These three changes that Yaakov effected within himself — "repaired himself" — were accomplished in such a manner that they all manifested themselves within him at one and the same time. Simultaneously, he was prepared for "gifts, prayer and battle."

Granting gifts presupposes an attitude of closeness and kindness, while doing battle requires a feeling of distance and severity. Both of these are interpersonal in nature, while prayer beseeches *Divine* mercy.

It is self-understood that a human being cannot harbor these three very different emotions simultaneously without effecting a radical change within himself. This, then, is an additional reason why it was necessary for Yaakov to "repair himself" — so that he could harbor these conflicting emotions within himself at the same moment.

As Yaakov is symbolic of holiness and Esav of evil, and their confrontation symbolizes the battle between them, it is understandable why these three different attributes must manifest themselves at one and the same time.

In a physical battle victory will be assured when, in a

---

3. *Rashi* on 32:11.
4. *Bereishis* 32:13.
5. *Ibid.* 32:8.

pincer movement, three divisions converge upon one of the enemy's divisions. In doing so, victory over the outnumbered and outgunned enemy division is assured. This strategy is then repeated — with the same successful results — with a second enemy division, and so on.

So, too, the three attributes of kindness, severity and mercy — when they stem from an unholy source — are successfully vanquished when their three holy counterparts join ranks, attacking and subduing each unholy attribute in turn. This is exactly what Yaakov did when at the same time he "repaired himself" to confront Esav with "gifts, prayer and battle" — kindness, mercy and severity.[6]

Based on *Likkutei Sichos*, Vol. XV, pp. 265-272.

---

6. See *HaTamim* III, 120a; cf. *Likkutei Torah, Vaes'chanan* 5a.

Healthy, Wealthy & Wise

In the Torah reading of *Vayishlach* we learn that Yaakov arrived in the city of Shechem in a "complete" state.[1] Comments *Rashi*: "Complete in body, complete in wealth, complete in his [knowledge of the] Torah."[2] *Rashi* goes on to explain: "'Complete in body' — having been healed of his limp [inflicted by Esav's angel]; 'complete in wealth' — although he had given such a large gift [to appease Esav] he lacked nothing because of it; 'complete in his [knowledge of the] Torah' — he did not forget his learning while in Lavan's house."

Yaakov's journey to Charan parallels the descent of the Jewish people into exile.[3] Yaakov's ascent out of exile thus parallels the Jewish people's redemption from exile. Just as Yaakov returned to Israel "complete", so, too, are the Jewish

---

1. *Bereishis* 33:18.
2. *Ibid.*
3. *Bereishis Rabbah* 68:13; see also *Zohar, Vayeitzei* 149b.

people assured that when they return from exile they will lack nothing because of the experience.

There are three aspects of exile concerning which the Jewish people must be assured that it will cause them no loss.

The *first* corresponds to Yaakov's being "'complete in body' — having been healed of his limp."

A focal element of the divine service of the times of exile is *actual self-sacrifice* for G-d. The afflictions of exile result from G-d's putting us to the test, so as to arouse within us this very power of self-sacrifice. One might mistakenly think that since these afflictions emanate from Above, they are therefore (G-d forbid) permanent. We are therefore assured that although Yaakov's limp resulted from Esav's *angel*, i.e., it came from Above, nevertheless it was completely healed.

So, too, once the Jewish people accomplish their divine service in exile, all their afflictions become *completely nullified*, for in truth they never were real: they were nothing but a test.

The *second* corresponds to Yaakov's being "'complete in wealth' — although he had given such a large gift [to appease Esav] he lacked nothing because of it."

The ultimate intent of exile is not only that the Jew emerge unscathed, but that he should transform the very exile into *his wealth*, i.e., transform it into holiness. This resembles Yaakov's experience: not only was he saved from the clutches of Esav and Lavan, but he also managed to acquire a tremendous amount of wealth which was claimed by Lavan "to be his." Later his bountiful gift to Esav transformed Esav's homicidal rage into feelings of love.

Similarly, during the time of exile, it is necessary for the Jew to descend from his intrinsic level and garb himself in mundane garments in order to elevate the world. Since this is not merely a test, but an actual descent into the world in order to transform it, the Jew may think that this descent too is (G-d forbid) permanent.

He is therefore assured that even this investment of his time and "money" within the world is only temporary; eventually he will be "complete in his wealth." When a Jew is redeemed his physical "wealth" is redeemed with him — all together they are elevated and encompassed within holiness.

The *third* corresponds to Yaakov's being "'complete in his [knowledge of the] Torah' — he did not forget his learning while in Lavan's house."

To study Torah properly requires separation from mundane affairs. A Jew's plaint is, therefore: Since he is required to descend into exile and engage in purifying and elevating the mundane world, how can he maintain his level of Torah knowledge?

He is therefore told that "Yaakov did *not forget* his Torah knowledge in *Lavan's house.*" Exile may indeed cost one's person and one's wealth an actual loss, albeit a temporary one. With regard to Torah, however, no loss can occur in the first place, for while the Jew's body is subject to exile, his soul — his Torah and his spiritual affairs — is not subject to exile at all.

Based on *Likkutei Sichos*, Vol. XXV, pp. 168-176.

Vayeishev   וישב

The Selling of Yosef

The Torah portion of *Vayeishev* chronicles the sale of Yosef by his brothers — a sale through which he eventually found himself in Egyptian bondage. The *Zohar* notes[1] that G-d brought this about in order to implement His decree that the Jews would be exiled in Egypt.

G-d's plan for Yosef to be in Egypt could have been realized in countless ways, almost all of them less objectionable than being sold by his own brothers. Why was it accomplished in *this* manner?

The *Zohar* answers[2] this by going on to explain that the brothers' treatment of Yosef before his descent into Egypt (to the extent that they sold him as "a master who sells his slave") made him the "servant of his brothers." This ensured that even when the Jews were ultimately enslaved by the Egyptians, their enslavement was not total. Since Yosef ruled the Egyptians and he, in turn, was ruled by his brothers, thus, "the Jews ruled over them all."[3]

The *Zohar's* commentary offers additional insight into that which Scripture already indicates regarding the sale of Yosef. Notwithstanding the less than honorable intentions of the brothers in selling him, in reality the entire episode ended up for the good. For, as Yosef later said to his brothers, "G-d has sent me ahead of you to insure your survival in the land and keep you alive through a great deliverance."[4]

According to the *Zohar's* explanation that selling Yosef

---

1. *Zohar* I, 184a.
2. See commentary of *Or HaChamah*, *loc. cit.*
3. See commentaries of *Or HaChamah* and *Mikdash Melech*, *loc. cit.*
4. *Bereishis* 45:5-7.

established the brother's dominance not only over Yosef but also over the Egyptians, his sale not only proved to be for the good when he later became viceroy of Egypt, but the actual sale itself also gave Jews the ability to "rule over them all" and assured their subsequent "great deliverance" from Egypt.

We thus observe that the sale of Yosef accomplished two opposites at one and the same time: The unworthy intent of the brothers to sell Yosef into slavery led to the enslavement of the Jewish people — the Egyptian *exile;* the fact that ultimately "G-d brought all this about" was the reason that this selfsame sale harbored the seeds of their *redemption.*

The realization that ultimately G-d brought all this about, for "it is not you who sent me here, but G-d,"[5] and "[while] you meant to do me harm, G-d made it come out good,"[6] not only enabled Yosef not to be angry with his brothers, but moreover enabled him to act towards them with "kindness and abundant love..., repaying the offenders with beneficence."[7]

* * *

The progeny of Yosef and his brothers, the Jewish people, are expected to act with a similar intensity of love of their fellows,[8] even when treated by them as Yosef was treated by his brothers.

This kind of love can come more readily when an individual contemplates what the Alter Rebbe explains in *Tanya*[9] — that everything is providential; although an individual's evil dealings with another are a result of the perpetrator's having freely chosen to act evilly, "nevertheless, as regards the person harmed, this was already decreed from heaven."[10]

Furthermore, since "all that G-d does is for the good,"[11]

---

5. *Ibid.,* v. 8.
6. *Ibid.,* 50:20.
7. *Tanya,* end of ch. 12.
8. *Ibid.*
9. *Iggeres HaKodesh,* Epistle 25 (p. 276).
10. *Ibid.*
11. *Berachos* 60b.

there is a measure of benefit involved even in the harmful act itself,[12] just as the sale of Yosef ultimately brought about the deliverance of the Jewish people from Egypt, as the *Zohar* explains. Additionally, acting with selfless love of a fellow Jew can have the effect of minimizing and sometimes totally negating the harm done by the other.

In this way, increasing one's love for fellow Jews to the degree of loving the undeserving without any basis or reason, will nullify the exile that resulted from baseless and senseless hatred,[13] for selfless and reasonless love negates the tragic effects of baseless and senseless hatred. And this in turn will lead to the immediate arrival of *Mashiach*, speedily in our days.

Based on *Likkutei Sichos*, Vol. XX, pp. 187-191.

---

12. See *Likkutei Sichos*, Vol. V, p. 247, fn. 48.
13. *Yoma* 9b.

Vayeishev   וישב
Yud-Tes Kislev   י"ט כסלו

Three Types of Liberation: Three Forms of Service

There is a famous statement of the *Shaloh*[1] that all Jewish festivals are related to the Torah reading of the week in which they occur. Included in this are those festivals that took place long after the relevant passages were written. We thus understand that the festival of *Yud-Tes* Kislev, the festival of the liberation of the Alter Rebbe and the day of liberation of the teachings of *Chassidus*, is also alluded to in the Torah portion of the week of *Vayeishev*, the portion in which the festival almost always occurs.

At first glance the very opposite seems to be the case. *Vayeishev* speaks of the events leading up to and including Yosef's sale as a slave in Egypt and his subsequent incarceration. How does this relate to the Alter Rebbe's *liberation* from prison?

This may be understood by first considering the *Midrash* on the verse, "And Yosef was taken down to Egypt."[2] The Hebrew word for "taken down" *(hurad)* is explained by the *Midrash* to be related to the similar roots that mean "conquest" and "dominion". Thus, according to the *Midrash*, Yosef's descent to Egypt not only *eventually* resulted in his becoming the viceroy of Egypt, without whom "no man will lift a hand or foot in all Egypt,"[3] but it also *immediately* involved "conquest" and "dominion".

*   *   *

There are three ways in which a person may be redeemed

---

1. *Cheilek Torah Shebichsav*, beginning of the portion of *Vayeishev*.
2. *Bereishis* 39:1.
3. *Ibid.*, 41:44.

from a state of exile. The first is liberation through battle — one fights off one's oppressor and vanquishes him. Yet although the enemy may be completely routed, such a victory is somewhat hollow, for in order to secure this liberation one had to lower oneself to the enemy's standards, up to and including the shedding of blood.

There is a superior form of victory and liberation — "peace through strength"; i.e., the individual is so powerful that his enemy is afraid to engage him in battle. However, here as well, although actual bloodshed is avoided the victory is only temporary; the enemy still exists and if he becomes more powerful he may well engage in battle.

The greatest form of peace and liberation from oppressors comes about when the oppressor himself is encountered and *transformed* into a steadfast friend. In this instance there is no need to worry about an eventual attack from the enemy, for the enemy has ceased to exist. He has become a friend.

These three forms of liberation parallel the spiritual service of (a) the brothers of Yosef who founded the tribes, (b) the Patriarchs, and (c) Yosef.

The founders of the tribes chose to be shepherds, cut off from the world, so that worldly matters would not interfere with their divine service of cleaving to G-d. Their spirituality was such that they feared that if they were to engage their spiritual enemy in battle — lowering themselves to do battle with the world in order to refine and elevate it — this would inevitably cause them to be tainted.

The Patriarchs by contrast were of so lofty a level that they knew that even while they were within the world they could transcend it, so that it did not affect them in the slightest. The world was (as it were) afraid to do battle with them. They did not, however, vanquish evil; they stood above it.

The highest level of all was that of Yosef. On the one hand he was "taken down" into Egypt and was wholly engaged in conducting the affairs of state, but on the other hand, he did not permit this involvement to affect his constant cleaving to G-d — even in the midst of conducting his affairs. Yosef thus engaged Egypt and transformed it.

The same was true with regard to the arrest and liberation of the Alter Rebbe. Although incarcerated by extremely coarse individuals who sought to destroy him, he was able — during this very same period — to engage them in conversation and debate, thereby transforming them so that they came to recognize him as a "wise and holy man,"[4] whom they ultimately released in a wondrous manner.

Based on *Likkutei Sichos*, Vol. XXV, pp. 193-199.

---

4. *Beis Rebbe* I, ch. 15.

Mikeitz
Chanukkah

מקץ
חנוכה

A Matter of Perspective

In the Torah portion of *Mikeitz* we read that after Yaakov reluctantly acceded to his sons' request to return to Egypt together with Binyamin, he said to them: "May G-d Almighty grant that the man have pity on you and release your other brother and Binyamin."[1]

Yaakov's fear and trepidation was greater than that of his children. Although they, too, were aware that this whole event had unfortunate undertones — as they themselves said, "We deserve to be punished because of what we did to our brother... that is why this great misfortune has come upon us" — they nevertheless looked upon it as a *personal* misfortune.[2] Yaakov, however, saw this event as a continuation of his previous trials and tribulations. More importantly, he viewed this affair in light of the *forthcoming* tragedy of the Jewish people in Egyptian exile.[3]

The reason Yaakov and his children viewed this event differently has to do with the basic difference between Yaakov and his children, the founders of the tribes.

As one of the three Patriarchs of the Jewish people, Yaakov viewed all events that involved him as a "sign" and forerunner of events that would occur with later generations of Jews. The founders of the tribes, however, not being at the spiritual level of the Patriarchs, were unable to see these events as being of a general nature; they were only able to view them in terms of personal misfortune. In other words, they viewed these events as they related to the course of nature; Yaakov, who was on a far superior spiritual plane,

---

1. *Bereishis* 43:14.
2. *Ibid.,* 42:21.
3. See *ibid.,* v. 2, and commentary of *Rashi.*

was able to see these selfsame events insofar as they transcended the bounds of nature.

*   *   *

This distinction also relates to the festival of Chanukkah. Although the events surrounding this festival actually came about through miraculous means, superficially one might think that these miracles were bounded by nature, because the deliverance of the Jewish people from the hands of the Syrian-Greeks involved actual physical warfare.

This shortsighted view misses the truth — that the victory involved nothing less than miracles that utterly burst the bounds of nature. For the victorious Jews overcame vastly superior odds, "the mighty [being delivered] into the hands of the weak, the many into the hands of the few...."[4]

From this we may learn that whatever a Jew engages in, even if it seems to be completely within the realm of nature, he should not think that he need only act according to natural means. His actions must always be accompanied by — indeed, preceded by — a prayer for success. While it is true that he ought to act according to the laws of nature — for the Torah exhorts, "G-d your L-rd will bless you in all you do"[5] — he must at the same time know that his connection with nature is but an external garb. Essentially, he is bound to G-d Who transcends nature. Thus, when a Jew desires (for example) wealth, what counts is that he "pray to Him to Whom all wealth belongs."[6] So, too, with regard to all one's needs, both material and spiritual.

When a Jew acts in this manner he is privileged to behold the miracles that are *clothed* in the garments of nature, and moreover the miracles that utterly *transcend* nature — and, ultimately, the miracles too that will be revealed with the coming of our Righteous *Mashiach*.

Based on Likkutei Sichos, Vol. XXV, pp. 227-234.

---

4. Chanukkah, *VeAl HaNissim* prayer.
5. *Devarim* 15:18; see also *Sifri, loc. cit.*
6. *Niddah* 70b; see also *Derech Mitzvosecha* 107ff.

Chanukkah   חנוכה

Salvations, Miracles & Wonders

During the eight days of Chanukkah the kindling of the festive lights is followed by the prayer of *HaNeiros Halalu*. The prayer begins with the words: "We kindle these lights [to commemorate] the salvations, miracles and wonders which You performed for our forefathers in those days...." It concludes: "...so that we may offer thanks and praise to Your great Name for Your miracles, for Your wonders, and for Your salvations."[1]

We observe that the order of the wording "salvations, miracles and wonders" used at the beginning of the prayer, changes at the conclusion of the prayer to "miracles, wonders and salvations." Why the change?

The prayer of *HaNeiros Halalu* comprises two parts. The first part speaks of the three forms of miracles, wonders, etc., which were "performed for our *forefathers* in *those* days," while the conclusion of the prayer emphasizes *our* emotional response of "offering thanks and praise to Your great Name" for having made those miraculous and wondrous events come to pass.

Chronologically, the "miracles" of the festival of Chanukkah were preceded by "salvations" and were follows by "wonders". Concerning our emotional response, "miracles" elicit the most obvious response of "thanks and praise," followed by "wonders" and finally "salvations".

The reason this is so will be understood by first considering the difference between the three above-mentioned terms.

---

1. The prayer as quoted here follows the text of Tractate *Sofrim* 20:6; *Tur, Orach Chayim* 676; *Siddur Admur HaZaken*. In many other *Siddurim*, etc., there are textual variations.

In order for a person to be *assured* of victory when fighting his equal, he must be blessed with G-d's help and *salvation*, for in the natural course of events sometimes one person wins and sometimes the other. Yet G-d's assistance and salvation notwithstanding, winning such a victory may seem to have occurred entirely by natural means.

A miracle, however, is surely involved when a totally outnumbered and much weaker force emerges victorious over its enemy; in the natural course of events a puny force cannot vanquish its much more formidable foe — a miracle must occur.

Wonders refer to those occurrences which, while not being clear-cut miracles, nevertheless, arouse astonishment and wonder in the eyes of the beholder; while these events may not be miracles, still, they are beyond the pale of the ordinary.

The beginning of the Chanukkah saga, the Hasmonean victory over the Greek soldiers in Modi'in, involved one small force opposing another — Mattisyahu and his sons overwhelmed the small local Greek garrison.[2] While G-d's help and *salvation* was surely involved, in no way was this an obvious miracle.

Later on, when the greatly outnumbered and much weaker Jewish army vanquished the mighty army of Antiochus,[3] it was evident to all that a miracle had occurred and that "G-d stood by them in their time of distress and waged their battle."[4]

When the Hasmoneans finally routed the Greeks, they entered the Holy Temple and found only one cruse of untainted olive oil with which to kindle the *Menorah*.[5] This phenomenon, that one cruse should remain pure while all the others were defiled, was "wondrous" indeed. Although an argument could be made that a miracle was involved, it was

2. *Yosifun*, ch. 20.
3. See *Megillas Antiochus, Midrash Chanukkah*.
4. Text of *Al HaNissim* recited on Chanukkah.
5. *Shabbos* 21b.

also possible that the Greeks just happened to overlook that cruse of oil. Therefore, this event was not a "miracle" but a "wonder". Hence the order — "salvations, miracles and wonders."

When it comes to our emotional reactions to these events — the conclusion of the *HaNeiros Halalu* prayer — the order of the wording changes in line with our emotional response: We are initially moved by clearly evident miracles, and for these we "thank and praise Him." Only after further contemplation are we able to realize that G-d's hand is also involved in "wonders" and even in "salvations".

Based on *Likkutei Sichos,* Vol. XV, pp. 366-369.

Vayigash　　　　　　　　　　ויגש

It Depends on How You Say It

The Torah portion of *Vayigash* begins by relating how Yehudah requested permission of the Egyptian viceroy to speak personally to him,[1] not realizing that in reality he was addressing his own brother, Yosef. Yehudah did this in his desire to obtain the release of his youngest brother, Binyamin, who was seemingly enslaved by Yosef after Yosef's silver chalice was found in Binyamin's pack.

Yehudah prefaced his remarks by saying, "Do not be angry with me." *Rashi* notes that this indicates that Yehudah "spoke to him harshly,"[2] in effect saying to him: "Do not be angered by the harsh words you are about to hear from me."

Why did Yehudah attempt to free his brother from bondage by speaking harshly to the second most powerful person in all of Egypt? Would it not have made more sense for him to begin by speaking mildly? Quite possibly he would have been able to accomplish more that way than by speaking harshly. If the mid-mannered approach failed, Yehudah could then change tactics.

By way of explanation: Were the matter under discussion to have been of secondary importance, Yehudah would have conducted himself in a wholly rational manner; before he spoke he would have given careful consideration as to whether a gentle or harsh approach would be more effective. However, he was faced with a situation that impacted on the very life of Binyamin as well as of his father Yaakov, "whose soul was bound up with his [Binyamin's] soul."[3] In this

---

1. *Bereishis* 44:18ff.
2. *Ibid.* v. 18.
3. *Ibid.* v. 30.

instance logic could not possibly serve as the final arbiter; the situation was so grave that Yehudah's emotions came to the fore. He therefore began to speak with great feeling, in line with the folk-saying: "When something hurts — you scream."

Furthermore, Yehudah sensed that a greater impression would be made upon the viceroy when he realized how critical the issue was to him. He would become aware of this, Yehudah felt, when he noticed that diplomatic niceties were not being observed and that his words were not couched in the honeyed tones of tactful politesse.

When a speaker conveys the message that the matter at hand is so vital that it penetrates to the very core of his being, this motivates the hearer to grant his request.

Herein lies an important lesson for Jews at all times and in all places.

When the issue at hand is saving a Jewish child from the clutches of Egyptian slavery, i.e., saving him from being enslaved to cultures and ideologies alien to Judaism, then tough speech and immediate action are required.

Then is not the time to appoint committees of so-called "experts" who will ponder the issue with due deliberation, and who will, after a slow and careful process, finally propose a solution predicated on the availability of ample funds, and whose conclusions will then be subject to the vote of a general committee which has the final say in determining whether or not to spend money to save Jewish children from Egyptian slavery.

A situation such as this is perilous and life-threatening. Immediate action of the most vociferous kind is required to save Jewish children from Egyptian education and culture, to save them from a lifestyle that leads to assimilation and intermarriage.

This firm type of approach will assure their liberation from Egyptian bondage. It will guarantee that they will be trained — to their eternal benefit and happiness — in the hallowed traditions of Judaism.

Based on Likkutei Sichos, Vol. XX, pp. 212-217.

The Flock of Yosef

Scripture states: "Shepherd of Israel, listen closely [to our prayers]; You Who lead the flock of Yosef....appear [to us]."[1] Our Sages comment: "All of Israel are known by the name Yosef, for it was he who sustained them during the time of the famine."[2]

Now why should Jews be *forever* known by the name of Yosef, when his good deed took place thousands of years ago, and only for a short time at that? Moreover, the above verse consists of a supplication on the part of the Jewish people for G-d to "listen closely" and "appear" to them. Thus, when Jews are described in the verse by the appellation "Yosef", obviously the intention is that the quality represented by that name should stand them in good stead. How can Yosef's personal support of the Jewish people be considered a *collective* merit?

Everything in this physical world possesses a spiritual counterpart from which it derives. Here, too, the fact that Yosef sustained the Jewish people *physically* during the famine, resulted from the support he provided them during times of *spiritual* famine, during times when G-dliness was not manifest.

We can now perceive the inner meaning of the above quotation, "it was he who sustained them during the time of the famine." Yosef drew down into the Jewish people *his* lofty qualities, qualities that enabled them to surmount the obstacles of spiritual famine.

It is for this reason that Jews are known by the name "Yosef" for eternity, for Yosef provided them with eternal qualities previously possessed by him alone. These qualities became, through Yosef's beneficence, the heritage of every single Jew.

* * *

This may be explained as follows. Yosef differed from his

---

1. *Tehillim* 80:2.
2. See *Rashi, Radak* and *Metzudas David, loc. cit.*

brothers in that he alone was exiled among strangers; only Yosef was "a captive of the nations."[3] This applied not only when he was a slave in the residence of Potiphar and then a jailed prisoner, but later on as well. Even after he was freed and was proclaimed viceroy of Egypt, he was still subject to the whims of a capricious Pharaoh.

The difference between Yosef and his brothers was a natural outgrowth of their different lifestyles and approaches to divine service. His brothers, the founders of the tribes, chose to be shepherds. Such a lifestyle guaranteed them freedom from worldly distractions and excessive toil, and enabled them to serve G-d without hindrance.

Yosef, however, led an extremely involved and active life, and was immersed in worldly affairs. This was his lifestyle in the house of Potiphar,[4] and continued to be so while he was in prison.[5] It goes without saying that Yosef was even busier when he was conducting all the affairs of Egypt,[6] a task that required a prodigious expenditure of time and energy. Nevertheless, all this did not hinder him in the least in his divine service; at the very same time that he was engaged in these mundane tasks he was also in a state of ultimate attachment to G-d.

His brothers, on the other hand, were able to cleave to G-d only when they separated themselves from worldly affairs. Understandably, such a manner of service cannot exist in a state of exile, when a Jew is under the thumb of those who seek to sever his bonds with G-d.

Only Yosef's approach to divine service — being immersed in worldly affairs yet not being fazed by them in the least — is capable of sustaining Jews during the long and dark exile, and leading them to the luminous redemption through our Righteous *Mashiach.*

Based on *Likkutei Sichos,* Vol. XXV, pp. 252-254.

---

3. *Rashi* on *Bereishis* 47:31.
4. See *Bereishis* 39:4-6.
5. *Ibid.,* verses 22-23.
6. *Ibid.,* 41:40.

Vayechi   ויחי

To Take an Oath

The beginning of the Torah reading of *Vayechi* relates[1] that
when Yaakov sensed that he would soon die he called for his
son, Yosef, and besought him, "Do not bury me in Egypt...."
After Yosef replied, "I will do as you say," Yaakov said to him,
"Swear to me," and Yosef did so.

The commentators ask: Why was Yaakov not satisfied
with Yosef's promise? Did he fear, G-d forbid, that his son
would not fulfill his promise?[2]

The difference between a promise and an oath lies in the
following. When one undertakes to do something under oath
he binds himself in such a manner that the thing *must* be done
under any and all circumstances. Even if numerous difficulties should arise, that individual will still be bound to fulfill his
oath. Furthermore, when someone promises to do something
in the future, the promise will not necessarily remain uppermost in his mind; rather, when the time comes to fulfill it he
will *then* do whatever he can to do so. When one takes an oath,
however, he thinks about it constantly, for he knows that he
must fulfill it, come what may.

While residing in Egypt, Yaakov and Yosef were in a
foreign country where it was impossible to know what the
future held in store; difficulties might later arise that could
deter Yosef from then fulfilling his promise. Yaakov therefore sought means at the very outset to forestall any difficulties that would later arise, by making Yosef take an oath.

This answer, however, still leaves something to be
desired, for Yosef knew as well what difficulties might later

---

1. *Bereishis* 47:29-31.
2. See *Ramban, Sforno, Kli Yakar* and *Or HaChayim* on v. 31.

be encountered. His promise, "I will do as you say," thus indicating that he was ready to overcome any future difficulties, should therefore have sufficed. Why did Yaakov insist on an oath?

We find a difference between Yaakov and Yosef regarding their desire not to be buried in Egypt. Yaakov said, "Do not bury me in Egypt," i.e., he refused to remain there after his demise even on a temporary basis. Yosef, however, only told the Jewish people that when they left Egypt "you must bring up my remains out of this place."[3]

The reason for this difference lies in the fact that Yaakov was *loftier* than the Egyptian exile. For this reason, even when he descended to Egypt his place of residence was Goshen, which was separated from the rest of the country.[4] Yosef, however, descended into Egypt amongst the Egyptians.

It was therefore impossible for Yaakov's body to find rest in Egypt even on a temporary basis. Yosef, by contrast, whose spiritual task it was to function *within* Egypt, remained there throughout the Egyptian exile, so that he (and his merit) would remain with the Jewish people for as long as they were subject to it. Yosef, however, made his brethren swear that "you must *bring up* my remains out of this place," for the whole intent of the descent into Egypt was the subsequent ascent. When the Jews left Egypt and "brought up" Yosef with them, they thereby elevated the sparks of holiness that were hidden there.

From Yosef's perspective Yaakov should have remained temporarily in Egypt "so that his merit would protect his children"[5] as they found themselves within the Egyptian exile. This would have enabled them to better refine and elevate the coarseness of Egypt. Yaakov therefore made Yosef take an oath — an oath being something that commits one to perform even if it totally transcends his intellect — so

---

3. *Bereishis* 50:25.
4. See *ibid.*, 45:18, and *Rashi*.
5. *Zohar* I, p. 222a.

that he would be assured that his remains would not stay in Egypt even temporarily. For from Yaakov's perspective he had absolutely no connection with the exile of Egypt.

Based on *Likkutei Sichos*, Vol. XXV, pp. 270-273.

To Reveal or Not to Reveal

The Torah portion of *Vayechi* relates that Yaakov assembled his children before his death. Among the things he said to them was this: "I shall tell you that which will transpire at the End of Days."[1]

Say our Sages: "Yaakov desired to reveal to his children the End of Days (i.e., the time that the exile would end and *Mashiach* would come), but the Divine Presence (i.e., prophecy) departed from him."[2]

If his intention was to ease from them and future generations the terrible pain of exile, what could he have possibly hoped to accomplish by revealing to them that a few thousand years were still to pass before the exile ran its course and *Mashiach* would finally come? If anything, this knowledge could only serve to dishearten them.

The *Zohar* comments[3] that had the Jewish people been meritorious and had their spiritual service been of the highest calibre, then the exodus from Egyptian exile would have also served as the true and complete redemption through *Mashiach* — a redemption after which there is no further exile. Thus, at the time Yaakov desired to reveal the End of Days to his children, his intention was to reveal to them that if they would shine in their spiritual service, they would merit the speedy coming of *Mashiach* at the end of the Egyptian exile.

His good intentions notwithstanding, G-d caused His presence (the prophetic spirit) to depart from him, so that he would be unable to make his children privy to this knowledge.

---

1. *Bereishis* 49:1.
2. *Pesachim* 56b.
3. III, 221b.

What was G-d's reasoning in keeping Yaakov from revealing to his children that their exemplary spiritual behavior would have the effect of speedily bringing *Mashiach?*

The ultimate manner of spiritual service that enables a person to be deemed "meritorious" is when — to the greatest extent possible — he serves G-d with his own sweat and toil, rather than relying on the spiritual help granted to him by G-d.

It was for this reason that the Divine Presence departed from Yaakov. Were he to have revealed to his children that their excelling in spiritual service would lead to the speedy arrival of *Mashiach,* that service would have become much easier as they would have known that it would soon be richly rewarded. G-d therefore saw to it that the spiritual tasks of the Jewish people should be accomplished in the most meritorious way possible — without their knowing of the ample reward involved.

Yaakov was also aware of the fact that spiritual service is at its best when it is most difficult, and that revealing to his children the benefit of their service would slightly diminish its quality. He was nevertheless ready to forego this additional measure of quality, so long as this would enable his children to more speedily be rid of the pain and indignity of exile, and be ushered in to the era of the true and complete Redemption.

G-d, however, desired that the redemption be as complete as possible. In order for it to be so, it was necessary that the spiritual labor of the Jewish people — the labor that brings about this redemption — should also be as spiritual as possible. This could only be achieved when the Jewish people were not fully aware of the great rewards they would reap. He therefore caused His Divine Presence to depart from Yaakov,[4] who was thus unable to reveal to his children the time of the End of Days.

Based on *Likkutei Sichos,* Vol. XX, pp. 228-232

---

4. See also *Likkutei Sichos,* Vol. XV, p. 430ff.

ספר שמות
Shmos

Shmos   שמות

Descending into Egypt

The Torah reading of *Shmos* opens with the words: "These
are the names of Israel's sons who came to Egypt...."[1] However, the verse does not actually use the past tense, "who
came"; rather, it uses the present tense, "who are coming."

This leads the *Midrash*[2] to ask the following question: "Had
they not already arrived in Egypt a long time earlier?" Why,
then, is the present tense used, as if they had just arrived?

The *Midrash* answers: "As long as Yosef was still alive the
Jews did not have the oppressive Egyptian yoke thrust upon
them. When Yosef died the yoke was placed upon them. The
verse therefore states 'who are coming': it was as if they had
arrived in Egypt that very day."

There is an explanation of the Alter Rebbe[3] along similar
lines. The portion of *Shmos*, says the Alter Rebbe, recounts for
the second time the story of the Jews' descent to Egypt as it
was already related earlier on in *Vayigash*.

The Torah does so because the "coming into Egypt"
related in *Shmos* involved a far greater spiritual descent than
did the move to Egypt related in *Vayigash*. So much so, that it is
considered as if the Jewish people entered Egypt anew.

Just as the Egyptian *exile* involved two stages of descent,
so, too, the *liberation* from Egypt consists of two distinct stages
of "elevation" — that of the Exodus, and that which will take
place at the time of the ultimate redemption.

That the "oppressive Egyptian yoke," which began immediately after the demise of Yosef, is considered a second

1. *Shmos* 1:1.
2. *Shmos Rabbah, ibid.,* 4; *Midrash Tanchuma, ibid.,* 3.
3. *Torah Or,* beginning of *Shmos.*

descent, teaches us that this descent was of far greater magnitude than was its predecessor. This explains why it cannot simply be considered yet another aspect of the original descent, but must be considered as a descent in its own right.

What, exactly, was it that caused the second descent — brought on by Yosef's death — to be so severe?

The underlying concept of "Egypt" (which in Hebrew is etymologically related to the word meaning "straits" and "limitations"[4]) is that of stifling any revelation of G-dliness that transcends nature.[5] It was for this reason that when Moshe told Pharaoh that *Havayah* — the Divine Name that transcends nature[6] — had said, "Send out My people," Pharaoh responded by saying, "Who is *Havayah*...? I do not know *Havayah*."[7] Pharaoh neither knew, nor cared to know, of G-dliness insofar as it transcends nature.

Before the Jews descended into Egypt they lived in *Eretz Yisrael*, a land where Divine Providence is clearly *revealed* — "a land under the scrutiny of *Havayah* your L-rd; the eyes of *Havayah* your L-rd are on it at all times."[8] Descending from such a land to Egypt, which "knows not *Havayah*" surely involved a mighty fall.

Nevertheless, this first descent pales in comparison to the second, which began with Yosef's demise, for the following reason.

Our Rabbis tell us[9] that the Patriarch Yaakov represented a level that transcended this corporeal world by far. In order for his spiritual level to permeate this world the intermediary of Yosef was required; only Yosef could stand "before Pharaoh" and reveal within Egypt that which essentially tran-

---

4. *Ibid.*, 71c ff.
5. *Ibid.*, and 50b.
6. *Shaar HaYichud VehaEmunah*, ch. 7; *Likkutei Sichos*, Vol. IX, p. 55, fn. 32.
7. *Shmos* 5:1-2.
8. *Devarim* 11:12, and *Bachya ad loc.*
9. See *Biurei HaZohar* (of the Mitteler Rebbe) 30a ff.; see also *Or HaTorah* II, *Vayechi* 386a, b; see also the above essay on *Vayechi* entitled "To Take an Oath."

scended Egypt — that it is G-d who rules the world and all that it contains.

Thus, it is understandable that with Yosef's passing this feeling which had until then permeated Egypt, ceased as well. Egypt then reverted to its original heathen self.

As long as Yosef was still alive, this characteristic of Egypt was not yet felt by the Jews to be the "oppressive yoke" it truly was; with Yosef's passing and the consequent cessation of G-dly revelation within Egypt, the Jewish people felt "as if they had arrived in Egypt that very day."

Based on *Likkutei Sichos*, Vol. VI, pp. 28-32.

Defying Pharaoh

When Moshe and Aharon relayed G-d's message to Pharaoh, "Let My people go,"[1] the Egyptian king said to them: "...Why are you distracting the people from their work? Get back to your own business!"[2]

Our Sages tell us[3] that "your *own* business" indicates that Moshe, Aharon and indeed, the whole tribe of Levi, were not subject to slave labor. As *Ramban*[4] explains, Pharaoh permitted the Jews — as was customary in every nation — to have their wise men and teachers. Teaching was the task of the Levite tribe,[5] and it was to this task that Pharaoh commanded them to return.

In effect, Pharaoh said to them: "It should suffice that you are free from slave labor and are permitted to study and teach the Jews Torah. Why do you also desire to mix into other

---

1. *Shmos* 5:1.
2. *Ibid.*, v. 4.
3. *Shmos Rabbah* 5:16; commentary of *Rashi* on *Shmos* 5:4; see also *Tanchuma, Va'eira* 6.
4. In his commentary on this verse; see also commentary of *Rabbeinu Bachye, loc. cit.*
5. See also commentary of *Chizkuni, loc. cit.*

aspects of their lives, telling them that they should not conduct themselves according to the laws of Egypt?"

Pharaoh's remarks were quite logical. Egyptian bondage was so absolute that "not even one slave could flee from Egypt,"[6] let alone the entire Jewish nation. Any thoughts of liberation were obviously futile. Furthermore, their enslavement was in line with the divine decree that the Jews' servitude in Egypt would last "four hundred years."[7] What, then, did Moshe and Aharon think they could accomplish?

As logical as the argument was, it was, however, *Pharaoh's* logic, and if the Jews had succumbed to his argument, any future hope of redemption would have been lost. For as our Sages tell us,[8] if the Jews had remained in Egypt any longer than they did, they would have become so mired in Egyptian profanity that they would never have been liberated. Only by disregarding Pharaoh's words were they released from bondage.

While Pharaoh's argument followed a certain logic, Jews transcend the bounds of nature and logic; although the Jews of that time could never hope to escape by natural means, they could manage to escape through miraculous means. Notwithstanding the decree of "four hundred years of exile," G-d could circumvent this time frame[9] and release them much earlier.

* * *

As to us: A Jew should not be misled into thinking that it suffices that he studies Torah regularly on his own and only occasionally takes time to teach others as well, not really caring further about his fellow Jew's spiritual welfare.

It is vital for Jews to know that "mind your own business" was first uttered by *Pharaoh*. It is not at all a Jewish attitude.

---

6. *Mechilta, Yisro* 18:11; *Rashi, ibid.,* v. 9.
7. *Bereishis* 15:13.
8. *Siddur HaAriZal; Haggadah shel Pesach,* commentary on: *"Matzah Zu";* *Tzror HaMor,* and others.
9. See *Pesikta deRabbi Kahana* and *Pesikta Rabasi, Parshas HaChodesh; Shir HaShirim Rabbah* 2:8(1).

When there is a fire raging in another's house, one does not stop to ponder whether he should do something about saving his neighbor from the conflagration, or whether he should perhaps simply "mind his own business." Any right-thinking individual will surely do his utmost to save his friend.

Surely this applies, to an even greater degree, to saving a fellow Jew from a spiritual conflagration, rescuing him from a holocaust of the spirit.

The Baal Shem Tov declared[10] that the obligation to love a fellow Jew extends even to those Jews whom one has never met. Furthermore, says the Baal Shem Tov,[11] the love felt towards him should be boundless, for we are exhorted to love our fellow Jews "as we love ourselves." Just as our love of self is boundless, so should be our love of fellow Jews.

And just as our boundless self-love leads us to constant self-improvement, so too should our boundless love for our fellow Jews lead us to constantly seek the betterment of their physical and spiritual lot.

Based on *Likkutei Sichos*, Vol. XVI, pp. 29-31.

---

10. See *Sefer HaArachim-Chabad*, s.v. *Ahavas Yisrael*, p. 623ff., and sources cited there; *Kuntreis Ahavas Yisrael*, Section 9 and onward.
11. See *Sefer HaArachim*, *ibid.*, Section 5, and sources cited there.

Va'eira   וארא

___

Egyptian Exile: A Prelude to the Torah

The Torah portion of *Va'eira* begins by continuing the subject discussed at the end of the preceding portion of *Shmos*. There the Torah[1] tells us of the Jews' complaint to Moshe and Aharon — that since the two brothers had gone to Pharaoh demanding their release from slavery, conditions had worsened for them. Moshe, in turn, relates their complaint to G-d.

G-d's answer to their complaint comes at the opening of *Va'eira*, when He tells Moshe: "I have also heard the groaning of the Jews...and I have remembered My covenant. ...I will take you away... I will free you... I will liberate you.... I will take you to Myself.... I will bring you to the land....."[2] The Torah then relates how G-d began to smite the Egyptians with the ten plagues.

How does all this answer the complaint that Moshe and Aharon's intercession with Pharaoh had only made things worse for the Jews? G-d could just as easily have hearkened to the moans of the Jewish people much earlier, and could then have "remembered His covenant." In this way the additional labor Pharaoh foisted upon the Jews would have been avoided altogether.

All this indicates that G-d's remembering His covenant and taking them out of Egypt could only take place after their having first undergone further, more intense, suffering. But why did this have to be?

The Egyptian exile served as a preparation for the most cataclysmic phenomenon in our history: receiving the Torah

___

1. *Shmos* 5:21ff.
2. *Ibid.*, 6:5ff.

at Mount Sinai.[3] At that time it first became possible for Jews to perform G-d's commandments — thereby attaching themselves to Him[4] —- solely because these commands emanated from G-d, without any ulterior motive whatsoever.

This was so not only with regard to the suprarational statutes, but with regard to rational commands as well. For a person to perform a nonrational command without the intervention of his own intellect or emotions is not a difficult task. To perform *logical* precepts only because G-d so commanded, and not because of their inherent logic, was a feat that Jews could accomplish only after G-d gave the Torah on Sinai.

The same is true of Torah study. Notwithstanding the fact that Torah is understood, encompassed and grasped by a person's intellect,[5] nevertheless, this is not the logic of mortals, but G-d's Torah. As such, it remains transcendent of human logic even as it descends into the realm of rationality.[6]

Self-effacement — a true lack of egocentricity — is a prerequisite to the study of the Torah at this level. Undergoing the hardships of the exile enabled the Jews to reach this state. For we observe that when a person (heaven forbid) undergoes suffering, he ceases to be wrapped up in himself.

Thus, the self-nullification that came about as a result of the Jews' suffering at the hands of the Egyptians, enabled them to absorb the spirituality required for the proper study of Torah and the performance of G-d's commands.[7]

Additionally, this nullification which enabled the Torah to be received, had to pervade not only the Jewish people but also the world at large. This was achieved by G-d's smiting the Egyptians and causing Pharaoh's downfall,[8] for Pharaoh ruled not only Egypt, but also the whole world.[9]

3. *Torah Or* 49a, 74a ff.
4. *Likkutei Torah, Bechukosai* 45c; also cited elsewhere.
5. See *Tanya*, beginning of ch. 5.
6. *Ibid.,* ch. 4.
7. See also *Likkutei Sichos,* Vol. XV, p. 81.
8. See *Torah Or* 57a,b; *Or HaTorah, Shmos,* p. 260ff.
9. *Mechilta, Beshalach* 14:5.

When the selfsame Pharaoh who previously stated, "Who is G-d that I should obey Him,"[10] changes his tune because of the plagues and admits, "G-d is just; I and my people are wicked,"[11] then the world has been purified enough. It can now receive the Torah.

Based on *Likkutei Sichos*, Vol. XXI, pp. 46-48.

---

10. *Shmos* 5:2.
11. *Ibid.*, 9:27.

Misplaced Criticism

The Torah reading of *Va'eira* begins with G-d's response to Moshe's question, "Why did You mistreat Your people?"[1] G-d answered: "I revealed Myself to Avraham, Yitzchak and Yaakov...."[2]

Rashi comments[3] that G-d said to Moshe: "Woe to those who have passed on, and whose likes are not to be found. I lament the passing of the Patriarchs.... They were not critical of My behavior, and *you* said, 'Why did You mistreat....'"

One of the fundamentals of Jewish faith is that Moshe was the "most superlative individual of all mankind."[4] This refers both to all those individuals who followed him, as well as those individuals who preceded him — including the Patriarchs. How is it then possible to say that Moshe was "critical of G-d's behavior," emphasizing, moreover, that this was in contrast to the conduct of the Patriarchs who did *not* act in such a manner?

The *Tzemach Tzedek* explains[5] that Moshe was at the level of

---

1. *Shmos* 5:22.
2. *Ibid.*, 6:3.
3. On 6:9, based on *Sanhedrin* 111a.
4. *Pirush HaMishnayos LehaRambam, Sanhedrin*, ch. *Cheilek*, 7th Fundament; see also *Turei Zahav, Yoreh Deah* 242:36.
5. *Or HaTorah, Shmos*, p. 133.

d'etre of Torah and *mitzvos* in relation to the world as a whole, so, too, does it reveal the effect of Torah and its commandments upon the Jewish people.

The Jewish people are likened by our Sages to the orb of the moon.[15] Their development and growth demonstrates their *chiddush* and ascent as accomplished by their performance of Torah and *mitzvos*. This is done in two ways: (a) elevating their innermost levels through rational spiritual service; (b) elevating their essential soul levels through their nullification to the Divine will insofar as it transcends rationality.

These two manners of divine service are both to be found in the spiritual context of the manner in which the new month is determined. The internal and rational level of service is alluded to by declaring the new month according to astronomical calculation — a completely rational decision. The sighting of the new moon by witnesses alludes to that level of service that transcends rationality. For a person believes what he witnesses with his own eyes even when it defies all the rules of logic.

Based on *Likkutei Sichos*, Vol. XXI, pp. 64-67.

_____

15. See *Bereishis Rabbah* 6:3; *Sukkah* 29a.

The First Paschal Offering

One of the differences between the first Paschal sacrifice, the one that was offered in Egypt, and all subsequent offerings, was the obligation to "take the Paschal lamb" on the tenth day of the month of Nissan.[1]

Rashi,[2] citing the *Mechilta*,[3] explains why this was so. "The

_____

1. *Shmos* 12:3.
2. On v. 6.
3. *Ibid.*

verse states, 'And I passed over you....'[4] [G-d said: 'The time] has arrived for Me to fulfill My oath to Avraham redeem his children.' However, they were lacking *mitzvos* with which to occupy themselves, and by virtue of which they would be liberated,' as it is written 'and you were naked [i.e., 'you were lacking good deeds']....' G-d therefore gave them two *mitzvos*: the blood of the Paschal offering and the blood of circumcision...."

Rashi goes on to say: "Moreover, they were immersed in idolatry. G-d therefore said to them, 'Draw and get for yourselves':[6] Draw yourselves away from idolatry, and get for yourselves sheep with which to perform a *mitzvah*."[7]

Now why did G-d desire that the Jewish people perform *two* commandments? If He merely desired to remove the stigma of their lacking good deeds, then one command would have sufficed; if He wanted to provide them with a multitude of merits, why were two sufficient?

We must therefore assume that each of the two commandments succeeded in removing a specific aspect of their spiritual nakedness.

At that time the Jewish people were deficient in two respects — in their positive performance of commandments, and in their separation from the evil that pervaded Egypt.

Their lack of performance hindered their ability to go out of Egypt and receive the Torah, for upon leaving Egypt they were to serve G-d "upon this mountain."[8] I.e., it was in the merit of their ultimate ability to receive the Torah that they left Egypt in the first place.

The people were then also lacking in their separation from the evil of Egypt, the "abomination of the earth," which had fastened itself on them. Thus, even if they were to have "*mitzvos* with which to occupy themselves," they would still

4. *Yechezkel* 16:8.
5. *Ibid.* v. 7.
6. *Shmos, ibid.,* v. 21.
7. *Mechilta* there.
8. *Shmos* 3:12, and *Rashi* there.

not be able to rid themselves of the evil that had invaded them to the core. Had they departed in such a state they would have taken the Egyptian evil along with them.

They were therefore given two commandments. The commandment of the "blood of circumcision" brought them into a divine covenant; the other commandment, involving the "blood of the Paschal offering," purged them from Egyptian evil.

But how is the the commandment of the "blood of the Paschal offering" related to the negation of evil?

This is explained by *Rashi* in the continuation of his commentary, when he says, "Moreover, they were immersed in idolatry. G-d therefore said to them, 'Draw and get for yourselves': Draw yourselves away from idolatry, and get for yourselves sheep with which to perform a *mitzvah*." The commandment of the Paschal lamb nullified the Jews' prior preoccupation with idolatry. For earlier on the Torah informed us[9] that sheep were deified and worshiped by the Egyptians. Taking a lamb, the Egyptian idol, in order to bring it as a sacrifice for G-d, thus had the effect of negating idolatry and Egyptian evil from the midst of the Jewish people.

This also explains why the Jews were commanded to take their sheep four days before its offering. Merely taking it and immediately slaughtering it would not have the effect of undoing their immersion in idolatry. Only by holding it for a period as long as four days, in order to eventually slaughter it, were they able to rid themselves totally of Egyptian evil and idolatry.

Based on Likkutei Sichos, Vol. XVI, pp. 114-119.

---

9. *Ibid.,* 8:22, and *Rashi* there.

Beshalach   בשלח

Heavenly Bread & Earthly Bread

In the Torah portion of *Beshalach* we read that G-d said to Moshe: "I will make bread rain down to you from the sky."[1] This refers to the heavenly bread, the manna, that the Jews ate during their forty-year sojourn in the desert.

There is a curious anomaly regarding this miraculous bread. On the one hand its production required no human labor at all, there was no need for Jews to plough, sow, or reap; it simply descended from the sky. On the other hand, some effort was necessary in its preparation, as indicated by the statements of our Sages concerning the manna: "For the righteous it descended fully baked, for the intermediate it descended as dough, while the wicked had to grind and pound it [into flour]." Moreover: "The righteous had it descend at the entrance to their tents, the intermediate went out to gather it, while the wicked had to wander farther out to gather it."[2]

Thus, even the righteous had to exert some measure of effort in gathering the manna, since it descended in front of their tents rather than appearing within their tents or upon their table, in which instance no work at all would be necessary.

Why, indeed, was labor involved in obtaining this miraculous, heavenly bread; why not have the manna appear in a manner that completely obviated the need for human toil; since its appearance was miraculous anyway, why not have a totally miraculous event?

The difference between earthly and heavenly bread is the

---

1. *Shmos* 16:1.
2. *Yoma* 75a.

following. Man-made bread is inextricably dependent upon human toil: a man must labor to provide a natural vessel, a vehicle for G-d's bountiful blessings. Heavenly bread, however, requires no man-made vehicle; toil is thus not a prerequisite.

Understandably, one's emotional response to these two forms of bread varies accordingly. One knows full well that his exertions to produce man-made bread are but an instrument for the fulfillment of the verse that promises that "G-d will bless you in all that you do."[3] Nevertheless, since the bread ultimately was produced by his own efforts, it is quite possible for one to be over-impressed by his own input, and to attribute to his part in this joint venture more than its due.

This not at all so with the manna. In this instance the Jews clearly perceived that their labor was superfluous. This in turn, aroused within them a feeling of complete reliance on G-d.

Although the manna was wholly miraculous and consequently man's labor was not at all necessary, G-d nevertheless, desired that man's efforts be involved, for the following reason. The gift of the manna prepared the Jews for their entry into the Promised Land, where they would have to toil for their earthly bread, by revealing to them that their needs were provided by G-d Himself. This enabled them to recall this fact even when their daily bread became dependent upon their own efforts; even upon entering *Eretz Yisrael* and producing their own bread they would know that it was "He Who gives you the power to become prosperous."[4]

Were heavenly bread to be provided in a manner wherein the individual's labor was entirely irrelevant, it would then have no connection whatsoever with earthly bread. This might then lead to the erroneous conclusion that complete faith and trust in G-d as Provider is necessary only when He is entirely responsible for seeing to the person's needs; in the

---

3. *Devarim* 15:18.
4. *Ibid.*, 8:18.

instance of earthly bread, however, this faith and trust is not a prerequisite.

Providing the manna in a manner whereby the Jews' labor was also necessary demonstrated that even then, complete trust in G-d is vital, for even earthly bread is heavenly bread: man's labors are wholly secondary to G-d's in providing him with his daily bread.

Based on *Likkutei Sichos*, Vol. XVI, pp. 174-178.

Tu biShevat   ט״ו בשבט

For Man is Like a Tree of the Field

The fifteenth day of the Hebrew month of Shevat, or *Tu biShevat*, is known as the "New Year for Trees."[1] Since man is likened by the Torah to "a tree of the field,"[2] this day is — by extension — celebrated by man as well.

A tiny seedling's germination and development into a full-fledged fruit-producing tree is one of the most inspiring transformations in all of G-d's creation. First and foremost comes the development of the tree's root system. Thereafter the trunk and body of the tree as well as the branches and leaves come into being. Finally there comes the time when the tree bears fruit.

The roots are for the most part concealed from the eyes of the beholder. Nevertheless, it is from them that the tree derives its main life-force. While it is true that the leaves also nurture it by absorbing sunlight, and so on, the roots are its mainstay; sever them, and the tree will soon wither and die.

Furthermore, the roots enable the tree to be firmly embedded in the earth and to withstand strong gusts of wind or other elements that seek to uproot it.

The trunk and body of the tree, including the leaves, constitute the overwhelming majority of the actual mass of the tree. This part of the tree is generally in a constant state of growth — with thicker trunk and boughs, additional leaves, and so on. Furthermore, the age of the tree may be ascertained from its trunk and body, especially from its annual rings.

The physical predominance of the trunk and body of the

---

1. *Rosh HaShanah* 1:1.
2. *Devarim* 20:19 and commentary of *Rashi*.

tree notwithstanding, the tree attains a state of completion only when it bears fruit. This is so to an even greater degree when the kernel contained within the fruit serves as the forebear and seed for future trees in coming generations.

*   *   *

Man too has roots, possesses a trunk and body, and produces fruit. In many aspects there is a remarkable degree of similarity between man's development — even his spiritual development — and that of a tree.

Man's roots are his faith. It is a person's faith that unites and binds him with G-d, the source and wellspring of his existence. Even after the Jew grows in Torah knowledge and in the performance of divine commandments, he still derives his life-force through his belief in G-d, Judaism, and Torah.

Conversely, a weakening in one's spiritual root system of faith can have dire consequences even on an otherwise spiritually well-developed individual.

Having achieved the level of striking viable roots of faith, a person may be inclined to rest on his laurels. Here the tree comes and teaches us that it is composed predominantly of trunk, branches and leaves. Man, too, should be predominantly composed of Torah study and good deeds. In spiritual terms this means that a Jew can never be satisfied with faith alone, for he would then be like a tree that laid down roots but never developed a trunk, branches and leaves. Such a "tree" is in reality no tree at all — its roots are there, but nothing else. In addition to healthy roots a Jew must have the full complement of trunk, branches, leaves, and so on.

A Jew's trunk, branches and leaves are the study of Torah, the performance of divine commandments, and good deeds. They should comprise the overwhelming majority of his activities. One can tell a Jew's "age" by measuring his "rings" as well — how many of his years have been spent in pursuit of spiritual knowledge and substantive deeds.

Furthermore, just as a tree's body grows constantly, so, too, should there be constant growth in the Jew's trunk, branches and leaves — in the study of Torah, and in the performance of divine commands and good deeds.

Yet as laudable as all these things are, man attains his state of wholeness only when — like a tree — he bears fruit, affecting his friends and neighbors in such a manner that they, too, fulfill the purpose of their creation. By doing so he bears an endless yield of fruit, generation after generation.

Based on *Likkutei Sichos*, Vol. VI, pp. 308-309.

Yisro   יתרו

A United People: A United World

The highlight of the Torah portion *Yisro* is *Matan Torah*, the moment at which G-d gave the Torah to the Jewish people at Mt. Sinai. A prerequisite for the giving of the Torah was the unity of the Jewish people — their shared desire to receive the Torah.

The Jews' remarkable state of unity prior to *Matan Torah* is alluded to in the phrase, "and Israel encamped there."[1] This verse is written in the singular, as if referring to one person — "Israel". The illustrious commentator, *Rashi*, notes[2] that this indicates that the Jewish people encamped "as one man, with one heart."

At the time of the Exodus from Egypt[3] there was revealed within the hearts of all Jews the quintessential aspect of their Jewishness, an aspect in which they were all equal. This aspect transcended the differences occasioned by their minds and hearts, enabling them to attain the state of being "as one man"; all Jews could be wholly united. In turn, this unity made it possible for them to be "of one heart" in their common desire to receive the Torah.

The world is composed of disparate entities; the connection between one component and the other is not readily apparent. Especially is this so regarding human beings, no two of whom are alike, either physically or intellectually.[4] Yet, with the giving of the Torah, unanimity was achieved within the whole world.

How was this unity achieved?

---

1. *Shmos* 19:2.
2. Commentary, *loc. cit.*
3. See *Likkutei Sichos*, Vol. XVI, end of p. 53 and footnotes.
4. See *Sanhedrin* 37b, 38a.

Unity within the world is brought about by the revelation of the One G-d who totally transcends the world's limitations and manifestations of individuality, thereby uniting seemingly disparate entities.

This revelation is brought about by means of the Torah and the Jewish people, the two entities that are spiritually superior to the world and for which the world was created.[5] When G-d united Himself with the Jewish people at *Matan Torah*, this unity trickled down to the world as a whole. It then became possible for the entire world to achieve a state of unity and harmony.

Before G-d gave the Torah this unity could not have possibly come about. For as our Sages tell us,[6] there then existed a heavenly decree that imposed a barrier between the physical world and G-dliness, making it impossible for this world to escape its mundanity. This decree was nullified at the time the Torah was given. G-dliness could then be revealed within this world, and physicality could be elevated to holiness.

Thus, at the time G-d gave the Torah it became possible for the One G-d to be revealed within the world, thereby enabling the world to achieve a state of unity and harmony with spirituality.

The giving of the Torah also made it possible for all humanity, including non-Jews, to be connected to G-dliness; they, too, could now attain a higher level of union with G-d than they could have previously attained. This spiritual advancement may be accomplished through the observance of the Seven Noachide Laws given to them in the Torah.[7]

Our Rabbis tell us, "Each and every individual is obligated to say: 'The world was created for my sake'";[8] i.e., every Jew has the ability to positively affect all portions of the world.

---

5. *Bereishis Rabbah* 1:4.
6. *Bereishis Rabbah* 12:3; *Tanchuma, Va'eira* 15.
7. *Rambam, Hilchos Melachim,* end of ch. 8.
8. *Sanhedrin* 37a.

Every Jew should therefore encourage non-Jews to observe their commandments, and see to it that they know that they are observing them because the Torah obligated them to do so.

Based on *Likkutei Sichos*, Vol. XXI, pp. 100-107.

Seeing Voices, Hearing Visions

With regard to G-d's giving the Torah to the Jewish people at Sinai, Scripture informs us: "All the people saw the sounds, the flames...."[1] Rabbi Akiva interprets this verse to mean that they then "saw that which is heard, and heard that which is seen."[2] Thus, "the sounds" which by nature are heard were literally seen, and "the flames" which are customarily seen were actually heard.

It is axiomatic that "G-d does not perform a purposeless miracle."[3] We must perforce say that the above-mentioned miracle was central to the theme of G-d's giving the Torah. In what possible way were these phenomena related to the revelation at Sinai?

There exist fundamental differences between sight and sound, both with regard to the viewer and hearer, as well as with regard to the object which is seen or heard.

With regard to the person: Sight has a more profound impact on the viewer than hearing has on the listener. Accordingly, the person who sees something is surer of the information conveyed to him by his sense of sight than the listener is of that which is conveyed to him by his power of hearing.

This fact results in the law that "a witness [to an event]

---

1. *Shmos* 20:15.
2. *Mechilta, ibid.*
3. See *Likkutei Sichos*, Vol. III, p. 966, and sources cited there; see also *Likkutei Sichos*, Vol. V, pp. 1124-1125.

may not serve as a judge,"[4] for, as the *Gemara*[5] explains, since he actually saw the person commit the misdeed, it will be impossible for him to find extenuating circumstances and deal leniently with the perpetrator. However, when a judge merely hears the testimony of witnesses, he is still capable of dealing leniently with the defendant by reason of extenuating circumstances, even when he is thoroughly convinced that the eye-witnesses are telling the complete truth, and that the person did indeed commit the misdeed of which he now stands accused.

The difference between sight and sound with regard to the object seen or heard is as follows. Sight discerns the actual physical matter, while hearing detects something more metaphysical in nature: sound waves are spiritual, so to speak, in comparison to the gross, material objects revealed to the naked eye.

These two differences between sight and sound, with regard to the person and with regard to the object, are interdependent.[6] As a physical being, man is naturally closer to the material than to the spiritual. It follows that he will grasp a material object — with his power of sight — more intimately and thoroughly than something spiritual, which he will only grasp from "afar" with his power of hearing.

*   *   *

This, then, is what is meant by "seeing that which is heard, and hearing that which is seen."[7] Spirituality is generally only "heard" by means of remote monitoring stations. When G-d gave the Torah to the Jewish people, however, He uplifted them to a level at which they became capable of "seeing" and grasping spirituality through direct perception.

Conversely, the physical world, which had always been clearly seen by them, now became distant from them. Their

---

4. *Rosh HaShanah* 26a.
5. *Ibid.*
6. See *Or HaTorah, Vaes'chanan*, p. 63.
7. See discourse entitled *Shlach Lecha* in *Hemshech 5672*.

heightened spiritual state caused them to be unable to "see" and fully grasp the corporeal; they were now only able to discern it with their weaker sense of "hearing."

We thus understand that this miraculous occurrence was an integral element of receiving the Torah. Since at that time the Jews were granted a revelation of G-d's Essence, they then grasped spirituality with the more intense power of "vision", while they lost sight of their own corporeal being; they were only aware of it through the less direct sense of "hearing".

Based on *Likkutei Sichos*, Vol. VI, pp.119-122.

Mishpatim   משפטים

Faith & Reason

The precepts of the Torah are divided into rational and suprarational commands. Rational commandments, termed *mishpatim*, are divine commands that are also understood, appreciated and dictated by human logic. Nonrational commandments are those that human beings would never have thought of alone — divine decrees that defy human logic.

The Torah portion of *Mishpatim*, as its name implies, deals mostly with rational commandments, both moral and civil. This passage immediately follows the portion of *Yisro* which tells of *Matan Torah*, G-d's giving of the Torah to the Jewish people.

The commandments unique to *Matan Torah* are those which are non-rational in nature; were it not for *Matan Torah* man would never have become aware of them. Why, then, does the Torah portion immediately following *Matan Torah* deal with the rational, social laws rather than with suprarational commands?

The Torah states: "This is my G-d and I will glorify Him, the G-d of my father and I will exalt Him."[1] This verse indicates that a Jew relates to G-d both as "*my* G-d" and "*my father's* G-d." What difference is there between the two?

A Jew is expected to relate to G-d in two ways. First, there is the belief in G-d ingrained in him because it is handed down from parent to child[2] — "the G-d of my father." However, a Jew is also expected to relate to G-d and to become united with Him through his own understanding — "my G-d."

In the first instance, since he only believes but does not

---

1. *Shmos* 15:2.
2. *Shaloh, BeAsarah Maamaros, Maamar Rishon* (40a).

know, his relationship to G-d is amorphous and distant — this is merely "the G-d of my *father*." Only when he comprehends G-d — to some limited degree — does this relationship permeate his mind. He can then say, "This is *my* G-d."[3]

Matan Torah made it possible for "that which is on high to descend below"[4] — it enabled spirituality to permeate the physical world, and for "those who are below to rise on high"[5] — it enabled physicality to cleave to the spiritual. This means that a physical entity itself, while retaining its physicality, should be able to become one with G-dliness.

Were only spirituality to descend below *without* the corresponding ability of this physical world to rise upwards, then this would merely entail the nullification of the physical within the spiritual. Since G-d intended that this physical world be sanctified and not nullified, it was necessary that physicality retain its identity.

This can be accomplished only when those who are "below" rise by dint of their own spiritual service. However, in order for them to accomplish this, G-d must first descend "below", and thereby empower them to rise through their own endeavors.

* * *

In terms of man's spiritual service these two levels correspond to faith in G-d and comprehension of Him. Absolute faith is a gift from Above. Thus, even when a person is blessed with faith — "the G-d of my father" — it does not permeate his own being, inasmuch as he did not toil for it. Only when a person strives himself to comprehend G-d — to the point that "this is my G-d" — can he be truly united with Him.

Nonetheless, faith is the bulwark of spiritual service, for

3. See *Likkutei Dibburim* II, 341b ff.; English translation (Kehot, N.Y., 1990), Vol. III, ch. 20, Section 25. See also *VeYadata*, 5693 (printed in *Sefer HaMaamarim Kuntreisim* I, p. 264a); *Hemshech 5672*, ch. 163.
4. *Shmos Rabbah* 12:3; *Tanchuma, Va'eira* 15.
5. *Ibid.*

intellect when left to its own devices may very well fail a man, whose self-love may ultimately blind him to the truth. By prefacing understanding with faith one guarantees that his subsequent comprehension will be on the mark.

The intent of *Matan Torah* in the portion of *Yisro*, which describes the events that imbued Jews with faith resulting from G-d's descent from Above, was that those "below" rise on high through their own service and reason; i.e., that Torah permeate and become one with man's reason, as expressed in the rational commands of the portion of *Mishpatim*.

This is why the Torah portion of *Mishpatim*, embodying the union of man's mind with G-d's, immediately follows *Yisro*, the passage that speaks of faith, and of the revelation of G-dliness from on high.

Based on *Likkutei Sichos*, Vol. XVI, pp. 243-247.

Torah & Secular Wisdom

The weekly Torah reading of *Mishpatim* begins with the verse, "And these are the laws that you shall set before them."[1] Our Sages comment: "Before *them*, and not before a secular court."[2]

The portion of *Mishpatim* deals mostly with civil laws whose counterparts are quite often found in secular law. Accordingly, our Sages interpret the opening verse of *Mishpatim* as an exhortation against litigating in non-Jewish courts when justice can be secured by going to a Jewish court of law *(beis din)*.

The ruling of a *beis din* is based on the Torah, while the ruling of a secular court is based solely on human intellect. Even when the outcome proves to be the same, there is something inherently superior in the ruling of a Jewish court of law.

---

1. *Shmos* 21:1.
2. *Gittin* 88b.

Wherein lies the superiority of Torah law?

Jews rightfully point with pride to the Torah as their fountainhead of wisdom and knowledge. Non-Jews too are aware of this, as the verse states: "For Torah is your wisdom and knowledge in the eyes of the nations."[3]

Torah, however, is much more than this: there is an element in Torah which simply cannot be found in any body of secular wisdom. It is for this reason that our Sages say, "[Should someone tell you that] 'wisdom exists among the nations,' believe him; [that] 'Torah exists among the nations,' do not believe him."[4] For Torah and secular wisdom are two distinct entities.

The word 'Torah' is etymologically related to the word horaah,[5] or directive. Torah, which is known as the "Torah of truth," not only explains the wisdom underlying every matter: it also teaches us its practical application — how we must conduct ourselves in our daily lives.

Secular knowledge, on the other hand, does not decree that a person must conduct himself in a particular fashion: it only points out that a particular manner of conduct will have specific consequences.

For example, medical science can demonstrate to an individual that caring for himself in a certain manner is healthful, while failure to do so may well prove detrimental. It does not, however, command him to act in a manner that will be beneficial to his health; if he so desires he is free to go ahead and harm himself. Torah, however, decrees[6] that it is forbidden to physically harm oneself.

Since every aspect of Torah wisdom has its practical application in a person's life, it follows that not only is Torah superior in its application of knowledge, it is also inherently superior in the realm of knowledge itself. When a person

---

3. *Devarim* 4:6.
4. *Eichah Rabbah* 2:13.
5. *Zohar* III, 53b.
6. *Bava Kama* 90b.

knows that the matter under study is not merely an intellectual exercise but will affect his behavior, he will then toil much more strenuously and think more deeply in order to ensure that he arrives at the intellectually true and practically relevant answer.

The reason for this difference between Torah and secular wisdom is rooted in the fact that Torah is the Divine will and wisdom — ultimate truth; by its very nature, therefore, it must penetrate every layer of one's existence. It is unthinkable that Torah should remain limited to one's understanding, and not be mirrored in one's actions, since "the essential thing is practice":[7] the *mitzvah* of Torah study stands supreme *"because it leads to action."*[8]

Based on *Likkutei Sichos,* Vol. III, p. 895; Vol. XXI, pp. 113-115.

---

7. Cf. *Avos* 1:17.
8. *Kiddushin* 40b.

Terumah   תרומה

Minutiae: An Entree to Holiness

The construction of the Tabernacle (the *Mishkan*) in the desert by the Jewish people is recorded in elaborate detail in the Torah portion of *Terumah*. Not only are the various building materials enumerated, but the Torah also takes great pains to provide an exact description of the Tabernacle's walls, coverings, columns, sockets, and so on, as well as its furnishings.

There is a saying of our Sages, "That which has passed is past."[1] This saying seems most appropriate when applied to the description of the Tabernacle's fine points. Unlike the Holy Temple (the *Beis HaMikdash*), the Tabernacle was never meant to be a permanent edifice; an elaborate recording of its specifications seems pointless.

The Tabernacle is referred to in the Torah[2] as a tent, a temporary dwelling. Its purpose was to serve as the religious focal point in the desert; when the people entered the Holy Land it was to be replaced by the Holy Temple.[3] Why does the eternal Torah describe the transitory Tabernacle at such great length?

The command to build the Tabernacle came soon after the Jewish people experienced the most awesome and meaningful event of their collective lives — the giving of the Torah on Mt. Sinai. At that time G-d revealed Himself in His full glory, and all Jews[4] saw and heard Him speak to them.

At that time the barrier[5] that had existed until then

---

1. *Yoma* 5b.
2. *II Shmuel* 7:6.
3. *Devarim* 12:9.
4. *Shmos* 20:15.
5. *Shmos Rabbah* 12:3; *Tanchuma Va'eira* 15.

between heaven and earth was lifted, and "G-d descended on Mt. Sinai"[6] — G-dliness was revealed in this world. Yet, for all the majesty and glory of Sinai, G-dliness did not permanently permeate the material world, the best proof of this being that after the Divine Presence departed from Mt. Sinai, the hallowed mountain reverted to its former non-holy status.[7]

The reason for this is that at Sinai the Jewish people were passive participants. It was G-d who descended; it was G-d who made Himself known to them; it was G-d's presence that allowed the physical world to be privileged to catch a glimpse of heaven.

Because of the non-participatory nature of the Sinai experience, the world was hallowed only temporarily; it was G-d presence alone that imbued the world with holiness, upon His "departure" the world reverted to its former worldly self.

There therefore followed a second stage in the revelation of G-dliness, a stage where it was incumbent upon man to actively draw G-dliness down into this world and to provide a dwelling place for G-d within it. This was done by the construction of the Tabernacle. Unlike the Sinai experience, the Tabernacle did not miraculously descend upon the Jewish people: they had to build it themselves.

The "hands on" experience of building the Tabernacle caused the material objects with which it was built to be permeated with *eternal* holiness. With the building of the Tabernacle the world was refined to the point that physicality itself became capable of becoming a vessel for holiness.

The very name of the Torah portion, *Terumah*, indicates how a Jew is able to take physical materials and turn them into something eternally holy. *Terumah* has two meanings, "separating" and "uplifting". By *separating* material objects from their mundanity, and consecrating and *uplifting* them to holiness, a Jew is empowered by G-d to transform the whole world into one vast Tabernacle. In such service, every object and

---

6. *Shmos* 19:20.
7. *Ibid.* 19:13.

every detail is important, as each object has its own manner of manifesting G-dliness.

There is a message in the above for us all: Even when we
feel that we are languishing in a spiritual desert, we can
always use the materials at hand and build a Tabernacle for
G-d's Presence.

Based on *Likkutei Sichos*, Vol. XXI, pp. 148-155.

A Matter of Give & Take

Among the various gifts presented for the construction
and maintenance of the Tabernacle and its offerings, was the
half-shekel, used to purchase communal sacrifices. Concerning these gifts the opening verse of the Torah portion of
Terumah says, "and you shall take for Me an offering
(terumah)."[1]

The famed commentator *Rashi* explains[2] that "for Me"
means "for My Name's sake," i.e., that these offerings had to
be suffused with the intent that they were being made for the
sake of fulfilling G-d's will.

Our Rabbis pose a number of questions. Firstly, why is the
word "take" rather than "give" used here? An offering is
generally said to be given rather than taken.[3] Secondly, unlike
the other gift-offerings alluded to in the beginning of this
Torah portion, the half-shekel offering was mandatory:
every Jew had to give it. How is it possible that this *forced*
donation was offered by every Jew "for Me," purely out of a
desire to fulfill G-d's will?

Actually, one question serves to answer the other. With
regard to the half-shekel the intent that it be "for Me" was
indeed not demanded of the giver but of the "taker": the

---

1. *Shmos* 25:2.
2. *Loc. cit.*
3. *Maskil LeDavid's* commentary on *Rashi, ibid.;* see also commentary on
   the *Maharik.*

appointed officials who collected the funds were obligated to have the intent that they were doing so "for Me."[4]

However, on a more spiritual level, a question still remains. As a mandatory gift, the half-shekel offering implied that the giver's intent was not of primary importance; it was of greater import that it reach the Sanctuary's coffers. Why was it then necessary for the officials who collected the moneys to have the intent that they were acting "for Me"?

The function of the various gifts for the Tabernacle and its sacrificial offerings was to make the Tabernacle, and through it the entire world, a dwelling place for G-d, King of the world.

There are two stages in making a dwelling fit for a king. First it is cleansed, and only then is it embellished with beautiful furnishings.[5]

In terms of the spiritual service through which a man transforms this world into a dwelling place for G-d, these two steps are: (a) refraining from doing evil, and (b) doing good. As in the case of an actual dwelling, clearing out the evil is but a preparatory step to doing good; the actual dwelling for G-d is fashioned through positive actions.[6]

There is therefore a major difference in the manner in which these two things are done. With regard to refraining from evil, what matters most is the deed itself; it is not so important *why* a person refrains from evil so long as he does so.

With regard to doing good, however, it is important that a person is motivated by the pure intent of fulfilling G-d's will, rather than by selfish reasons. Since his positive actions will reveal G-dliness in this world and make it a dwelling place for Him, it is vital that they be performed in the best manner possible.[7]

---

4. See commentaries of *Abarbanel* and *Sforno* on *Shmos, loc. cit.*
5. *Likkutei Torah, Balak* 70c; see also *Likkutei Torah, Shelach* 36d.
6. *Likkutei Torah, Balak, ibid.*
7. *Maamar VaYachalom,* 5708, ch. 3ff.

The above-mentioned two stages also relate to the actual materiality of the world as it is transformed into a dwelling place for G-d. At the stage in which materiality is to be separated from its mundane source, one's intention is not of primary importance. However, intention *is* important at the stage in which something is to be absorbed into holiness — the act of doing good. This is why the officials who received the half-shekels on behalf of the Sanctuary had to have the intention of doing so "for Me."

These two themes are alluded to in the very name of the Torah portion, *Terumah*. The word *terumah* has two meanings, "separating" and "uplifting". Separating material objects from their mundanity is its preparatory step. Then comes the second and more important aspect of *terumah* — the uplifting of these objects and their entry into the domain of holiness.

Based on *Likkutei Sichos*, Vol. XVI, pp. 288-290.

Tetzaveh   תצוה

Moshe & His People: A Unique Relationship

Moshe's place in the *Chumash* is truly unique. No other individual features so prominently, and is mentioned so often, as he. In fact, beginning with the Torah portion of *Shmos* where his birth is recorded, his name in mentioned in all subsequent portions[1] (until *Devarim*[2]) — except the Torah portion of *Tetzaveh*.

That Moshe is mentioned so often is no more than right, for the Torah as a whole is known as *Toras Moshe*,[3] Moshe's Torah. Moshe merited this distinction because, say our Sages, "His self-sacrifice for Torah knew no bounds."[4]

This being so, it is surprising that his name is not mentioned in the portion of *Tetzaveh*. If he had not been referred to in this portion it would be understandable; if he played no role in this particular portion there was no reason for his name to be mentioned.

This, however, was not the case. In the very opening verse of *Tetzaveh* G-d addresses Moshe, saying to him: "And you [Moshe] shall command the children of Israel...."[5] Later on in this portion G-d addresses him numerous times, and yet not once is he mentioned by name! Our Sages address themselves to this anomaly and explain that Moshe himself caused this omission.

After a small minority of the Jews had sinned with the Golden Calf, Moshe begged G-d to forgive them. Mincing no

---

1. *Zohar Chadash, Shir HaShirim* 60:3; *Baal HaTurim* on *Shmos* 27:20.
2. Commentary of the *Rosh* on beginning of *Parshas Tetzaveh*; supplement to *Baal HaTurim, ibid.*
3. *Malachi* 3:22.
4. *Mechilta* on *Beshalach* 15:1; *Shmos Rabbah* 32:32.
5. *Shmos* 27:20.

words, Moshe said to the Almighty: "And if [You should decide] not [to forgive them], then erase me from Your Book (the Torah) which You have written."[6] Say our Sages: "Even a conditional malediction uttered by a righteous person comes to pass."[7] Though he was successful in obtaining a pardon for the Jews who sinned, Moshe's name was omitted from the Torah portion of *Tetzaveh* as a result of these words.

Moshe was no doubt aware that even if G-d forgave the sinners his sharp words would have some lasting effect. Moreover, had G-d not forgiven them, Moshe's name would have been omitted from the *entire* Torah,[8] not just from one portion.

How is it possible that the selfsame Moshe who merited to have the Torah named after him because of his singular devotion to it, would eternally jeopardize his status in the Torah for a small group of individuals who had committed the most heinous sin of worshiping the Golden Calf?

As closely associated as Moshe was with the Torah, he was even more intimately bound up with the Jewish people. Indeed, it was impossible to separate him from them, whether collectively or individually. The illustrious *Rashi* states it beautifully: "Moshe *is* the Jewish people, and the Jewish people are Moshe."[9]

Moshe's bond with the Jews was thus even more intimate than his relationship with the Torah. His self-sacrifice on behalf of *all* the Jewish people, even for the greatest sinners among them, took precedence over his relationship with the Torah. In effect, Moshe said to G-d: "If there is no room in Your Torah to forgive these sinners then You may omit my name from it, for I have no place in a Torah that will not forgive even the most dastardly crime committed by one of my flock."

---

6. *Ibid.*, 32:32.
7. *Makkos* 11a.
8. *Shmos Rabbah* 47:9.
9. On *Bamidbar* 21:21.

Moshe, as our "faithful shepherd,"[10] enabled us to emulate him.[11] We too should love all Jews, whatever their status, with the greatest measure of self-sacrifice and without reservation, always striving to bring them closer to the Torah.

Based on *Likkutei Sichos*, Vol. XXI, pp. 173-180.

10. *Zohar, Shmos* 21a; *Tanchuma, Shmos* 7.
11. See beginning of *Tanya*, ch. 42.

A Tumult & a Still Small Voice

In describing the vestments of the *Kohen Gadol* the Torah states: "On the bottom [of his robe] place pomegranates... all along its lower border. In between [these pomegranates] all around, there shall be gold bells."[1] The purpose these bells served is enunciated a few verses later, when the Torah says: "and the sound [of the bells] shall be heard when he enters the Sanctuary...."[2]

Why was it necessary for the High Priest to enter the Sanctuary accompanied by the ringing of bells? Would it not have been better for him to enter silently, since "G-d is not [found] amidst a tumult"[3] but "within a still small voice"?[4] Indeed, when the *Kohen Gadol* would enter the Holy of Holies on Yom Kippur, he would wear a plain linen robe and not the one adorned by bells.

The *Kohen Gadol* served as a representative of all the Jewish people, acting on their behalf. When he entered the Sanctuary, all of Israel accompanied him, as it were.

Our Sages note[5] that the spiritual service of a penitent —

1. *Shmos* 28:33.
2. *Ibid.*, v. 35.
3. *I Melachim* 19:11.
4. *Ibid.*, v. 12.
5. See *Sifrei Maamarim 5699*, p. 2ff.; *5702*, p. 3ff.; *5710*, p. 4ff.

one who realizes that he is distant from G-d and seeks to flee
the evil that encumbers him — is characterized by tumult, as
with a person fleeing something or someone that seeks to kill
him.

To a certain extent, this approach to spiritual service
should be found within *all* Jews, even those who have not
actually been sinful. When a man realizes that he is distant
from G-d — whether because he has not yet eradicated the
evil within him, or because he has yet to achieve a state of
complete self-nullification before G-d — he cries out aloud in
his desire to escape his present spiritual state.

Parenthetically, this was the reason offered by the Baal
Shem Tov when asked why chassidim pray with so much
fervent clamor, movement to and fro, and the like. He
explained[6] that this was similar to the frantic sounds and
motions a drowning man makes in his efforts to reach safety.

This manner of service is in no way contradicted by the
verse that states that G-d can be found in a "still small voice."
When one attains the level of reaching out to G-d as He
transcends all worlds, as alluded to by His Ineffable Name, the
Tetragrammaton,[7] then the "still small voice" of complete
self-nullification[8] is indeed called for. When, however, one's
spiritual service is still bound up with fleeing from evil, or
with freeing oneself from being entirely separate from G-d,
then he is still generally cognizant of his own being, his
separate existence and distance from G-d. In such circumstances, crying out aloud is definitely in order.

Throughout the year, whenever the *Kohen Gadol* entered
the Sanctuary, he also (as it were) took along with him those
individuals who served G-d with a great hue and cry — those
who were still distant from Him. Such Jews, whose spirituality is of a lower order, are alluded to in the above-mentioned
verse as the "bells" found "along the lower border of the

---

6. Cf. *Keser Shem Tov*, Section 215.
7. *Hemshech Taf-Reish-Ayin-Beis*, ch. 399.
8. See also Introduction to *Tikkunei Zohar* (3b).

garment"; the "lower border" of their spirituality makes their divine service clamorous, like bells.

(This is only true during the regular days of the year, when the High Priest could enter the Sanctuary, but not the Holy of Holies. He would then enter wearing his robe with the bells. On Yom Kippur, however, all Jews attain the heights of complete unification with G-d[9] at the level of a "still small voice." The High Priest's entry on that day into the Holy of Holies therefore did not call for wearing the vestment that raised a clamor.)

This also explains why specifically in our times it is necessary to bring our people back to G-d in a clamorous manner — announcing loudly to all that Jews ought to put on *tefillin*, affix *mezuzos* on their doorposts, and so on.

We are now in the last and lowest stage of exile before the coming of *Mashiach* — the "lower edge of the robe." It is specifically there that the bells that arouse the clamor are to be placed. In other words, in our times the most effective manner of bringing Jews back to G-d is by ensuring that "the sound will be heard."[10]

Based on *Likkutei Sichos*, Vol. XVI, pp. 336-341.

9. See also *Likkutei Sichos*, Vol. IV, p. 1153ff.
10. See *Sefer HaMaamarim 5702* (beginning of p. 7): "Those who are in a profound state of slumber...must be wakened by loud sounds, etc."

Ki Sisa   כי תשא

Two Sides of a Coin

In the beginning of the Torah portion of *Ki Sisa* G-d tells Moshe that when taking a census of the Jewish people, he should direct them to give a half-shekel each as an "atonement offering." G-d indicated the exact type of half-shekel coin to be used by saying, "This is what they shall give...."[1] Our Sages comment: "He took out a sample coin of fire ... and showed it to Moshe, saying, 'Such a one shall they give.'"[2] *Tosafos*[3] explains that "Moshe was perplexed, thinking to himself, 'What can a person possibly give that will serve as atonement for his soul?' G-d therefore showed him a 'coin of fire.'"

Why did Moshe find it difficult to comprehend how a half-shekel coin could serve as atonement? Obviously, a Jew is amply rewarded for his performance of precepts. Consequently, it is eminently possible that a Jew should be granted forgiveness as a reward for fulfilling the precept of the half-shekel.

Moreover, how did the revelation of a "coin of fire" to Moshe answer his question as to how a half-shekel coin could possibly bring about atonement?

*   *   *

The reward for the performance of a *mitzvah* may emerge in one of two ways:[4]

(a) The performance of the precept itself is such that its

---

1. *Shmos* 30:13.
2. *Yerushalmi, Shekalim* 1:4; *Tanchuma, Sisa* 9, *Naso* 11; *Bamidbar Rabbah* 12:3, quoted in *Rashi* on this verse; see also *Likkutei Sichos,* Vol. XVI, p. 381, and sources cited there.
3. *Chullin* 42a *(Tosafos, s.v. Zos)*; see also *Midrashim* cited in *Likkutei Sichos, loc. cit.,* fn. 2.
4. See *Shaloh, Bayis Acharon* 12a-b.

intrinsic nature is the *cause* of a given reward — the reward is a direct consequence of the deed.

(b) The intrinsic nature of the precept has no direct correlation (at least rationally) to the given reward; it is only that G-d desired that a particular reward be granted for the performance of a specific *mitzvah*.

Just as there exists a whole category of commandments — suprarational precepts — that are not performed out of a logical imperative, so, too, there may exist various precepts that are suprarational in the sense that their *reward* is more than commensurate with the deed itself.

This is true of the reward for performing the precept of the half-shekel. Logically, there seems to be nothing within the *intrinsic nature* of donating a half-shekel to effectuate atonement for a spiritual entity as lofty and rarefied as the donor's divine soul. Moshe's intellect — the intellect of Torah — was therefore unable to fathom the logical connection between the precept itself and its subsequent reward.

On the other hand, he could not assume that the reward of atonement totally defied logic and was indeed suprarational, for the Torah does not designate this precept as a suprarational statute.

G-d clarified this to him by showing him a "coin of fire," and saying, "This is what is to be given." This revelation to Moshe stressed that the coins given by the Jewish people were *themselves* "coins of fire" — *spiritual* entities — capable of bringing about the soul's atonement.

*   *   *

This insight provides us with an invaluable lesson in our own daily spiritual service. When a Jew gives a coin to a pauper, he is not merely giving a physical coin, he is [also] giving a spiritual and holy "coin of fire." Indeed, this is true not only of charity, but of all other precepts as well. The object with which one fulfills any *mitzvah* is not merely physical but also spiritual — a "coin of [spiritual] fire."

The performance of *all* the precepts therefore demands the intensity and fervor associated with a coin of fire, so that ultimately this fire will burn constantly within the individual's heart,[5] never to be extinguished.

Based on *Likkutei Sichos*, Vol. XXVI, pp. 229-237.

---

5. See also *Likkutei Torah, Sukkos* 78c ff.

Tying the Knot

Forgetfulness has been the bane of humanity since creation. How often do we hear ourselves ruefully saying, "I forgot." No wonder, then, that for centuries man has tried to devise methods to help him jog his memory.

One of the earliest methods used — which obviously has worked, for it is used to this very day — is that of tying knots. In fact, commenting on *Parshas Ki Sisa,* the *Zohar*[1] relates that Rabbi Chiyya and Rabbi Yossi would tie knots in order to remember their Torah study.

An innate trait of every Jew in his belief that G-d constantly renews creation;[2] every moment of each day, G-d recreates the world anew. A Jew thus realizes that he is continuously dependent upon G-d for each and every moment of his existence.

Under these circumstances, it seems incredible that a Jew should be capable of sin; the knowledge that even as he is sinning his entire existence depends on G-d's creative spirit, should make sin an impossibility. The greatest hedonist will not indulge in forbidden desires while he is aware that G-d, to Whom he owes his continued existence, has forbidden them. Sin comes only as a result of our not realizing this, as a result of our unawareness. We forget.

In *Parshas Ki Sisa,*[3] Moshe asked G-d to reveal to him His

---

1. 190a.
2. *Tanya, Shaar HaYichud VehaEmunah,* ch. 1.
3. *Shmos* 33:17-23, and commentary of *Rashi.*

full glory. G-d replied that to reveal Himself completely to Moshe was an impossibility, for "man cannot have a vision of My Essence and still exist." Still, said G-d, He would reveal to Moshe a glimmer of His Essence, so to speak.

G-d did so by revealing Himself somewhat, in the guise of a leader of congregational prayer, garbed in a *tallis*, a prayer shawl, and wearing *tefillin*, phylacteries. He also permitted Moshe to catch a glimpse of the *tefillin*-knot placed behind His head, and to be privy to the Thirteen Attributes of Divine Mercy. G-d told Moshe that whenever Jews would beseech Him and mention the Thirteen Attributes, He would respond to their requests and when necessary, grant them forgiveness.

G-d's revealing Himself wrapped in a *tallis* and wearing *tefillin* is indicative of the importance of remembering. Both the *tallis* and the *tefillin* are worn — among other reasons — as an aid in remembering G-d, and the Torah and *mitzvos*.

Concerning the *tallis* it is written "And you shall see them (the fringes of *tzitzis* placed on the four corners of a *tallis*) and you shall remember and perform all My commandments."[4] Concerning *tefillin* too, the verse states, "It shall be a remembrance...."[5] Since sin is a result of spiritual forgetfulness, past sin is remedied and future sin is avoided through constant spiritual reminders.

There is also great significance in G-d's showing Moshe the *tefillin*-knot. When a cord is severed and then reknotted, the place of the knot is much stronger than it was before. Spiritually, a knot indicates a certain mode of repentance.[6] For as our Sages state: "A person who committed a sin and is liable to be put to death before the Almighty — what shall he do and live? If he was accustomed to study one page he should study two, to study one chapter, he should study two chapters."[7] In effect, the individual is tying a spiritual knot.

---

4. *Bamidbar* 15:39.
5. *Shmos* 13:9.
6. *Tanya, Iggeres HaTeshuvah*, ch. 9.
7. *Tanna Dvei Eliyahu*; cf. *Vayikra Rabbah*, ch. 25.

In our own daily lives it is most important that we constantly tie spiritual knots, to recall our continuous relationship with G-d, and to remember that He is constantly
responsible for our existence. These thoughtful reminders,
as well as those evoked by wearing a *tallis* and donning *tefillin*,
enable us to serve G-d in the spirit of the teaching that "All
your actions shall be for the sake of heaven,"[8] and "In all your
ways you shall know Him."[9]

Based on *Likkutei Sichos,* Vol. XXI, pp. 232-237.

---

8. *Avos* 2:12.
9. *Mishlei* 3:6.

Vayakhel ויקהל

To Light a Fire

Parshas Vayakhel begins with Moshe assembling the Jewish people and relating to them G-d's edict — that notwithstanding the supreme importance of building the Tabernacle, it may *not* be built on *Shabbos*.[1]

Although there are thirty-nine general categories of creative labor that the Torah prohibits on *Shabbos*,[2] yet when the Jewish people are exhorted here to observe the *Shabbos*, only the "labor" of creating fire is singled out.[3]

What is unique about the prohibition of creating a fire?

There are those who mistakenly believe that this Biblical prohibition was applicable only during those times when hard labor was involved, as was the case at the time of the Exodus. It was then necessary, they say, to rub two stones together to start a fire, and so on. Nowadays, they maintain, since all one has to do is merely flip a switch, no hard labor is involved, and creating a fire, or producing electricity, is permissible.

It goes without saying that this whole approach to *mitzvos* is misguided. *Mitzvos* are to be performed not because we necessarily understand, or even agree with their rationale, but because we were so Divinely commanded. Surely it is impossible for a human being, with his limited degree of comprehension, to understand the infinite wisdom of the Creator. Even the reasons found in the Torah for some *mitzvos* explain but a minute aspect of these commandments. This is why so many explanations are to be found concerning each *mitzvah:* each explanation grants us only a glimmer of its overall profundity.

---

1. *Shmos* 35:1, 2, and commentary of *Rashi*.
2. *Shabbos* 73a.
3. *Shmos* 35:3.

Apart from the above, those who think that lighting a fire should be prohibited only when it involves hard work, such as they assume it did during the times when the Jews received this command, err, both in their facts and in their reasoning.

G-d gave the Torah to the Jewish people soon after their Exodus from Egypt. It is a well-known fact, amply documented in all the books that deal with the history of that period, that the culture and technical expertise of the ancient Egyptians was most advanced. Their ability to move immense loads, erect buildings, compound various dyes, and so on, often defies explanation. During that period of Egyptian history, fires were not lit by rubbing stones together, but through much simpler means, most often from a pre-existing flame, involving little if any physical labor. Thus, to maintain that the prohibition against lighting a fire stemmed from the fact that to do so involved hard labor, is patently absurd.

Logically, as well, according to the simple meaning of the text, *Shabbos* is observed because "in six days G-d created heaven and earth, and on the seventh day He rested."[4] It takes no great degree of genius to understand that "G-d created the world without labor or toil."[5] It was from this *effortless* manner in which he created the physical world during the six weekdays, that He rested on the seventh day, on *Shabbos*. Jews were commanded to rest on the *Shabbos* in a similar manner. We are commanded to rest — not from toil, but from mundanity.

Based on *Likkutei Sichos,* Vol. XXI, pp. 500-501.

---

4. *Shmos* 20:11.
5. *Bereishis Rabbah* 3:2, 10:12.

Pekudei   פקודי

The Significance of a Name

The Pentateuch is divided into fifty-three portions, each having its own distinct name, which indicates its central theme.[1] *Pekudei*, the name of the final portion of the Book of *Shmos*, seems to defy the rule. Not only is the name *Pekudei* not consonant with the general theme of the Torah portion: it seems to contradict it.

The word *Pekudei* signifies *counting*.[2] Counting can only be done when each item counted exists as an individual and distinct entity. The central theme of *Pekudei* includes: (a) a comprehensive accounting of the *aggregate* of all the gold, silver and copper donated for the construction of the Tabernacle;[3] (b) a report of how all the materials necessary for the Tabernacle were *together* assembled before Moshe;[4] (c) G-d's command that *all* the components be utilized for building the Tabernacle;[5] (d) a description of how Moshe actually performed — in *totality* — the various tasks and services associated with the building of the Tabernacle.[6]

The central *theme* of the passage called *Pekudei* is, thus, how all the parts that made up the Tabernacle were amalgamated, while the *word* that gives it its name indicates how each item was counted and considered as a separate and distinct entity!

Indeed, the same question may be asked about the name of

---

1. See also *Likkutei Sichos*, Vol. V, p. 57ff.; Vol. XV, p. 145ff., *et passim*.
2. See *Targum Onkelos* and *Targum Yonasan ben Uziel*, beginning of *Parshas Pekudei*, and *Rashi* there.
3. *Shmos* 38:24ff.
4. *Ibid.*, 39:33ff.
5. *Ibid.*, 40:1ff.
6. *Ibid.*, 40:17ff.

the Torah portion called *Vayakhel*. This word signifies assembling and congregating — welding and merging separate parts into one whole. Yet, the primary subject of *Vayakhel* is an account of how all the parts and details of the Tabernacle and its furnishings were constructed individually![7]

When the construction of the Tabernacle was completed, a twofold manner of sanctification was achieved: "the glory of G-d filled the Tabernacle"[8] as a whole — signifying a pervasive and collective holiness; moreover, each individual entity that constituted part of the Tabernacle and its furnishings was hallowed individually.

The word *Vayakhel* thus alludes to the *manner* in which all the detailed parts of the Tabernacle and its furnishings were made. Though, as is recounted, each part was made separately, yet the intent was that all these parts form one collective entity, the Tabernacle. Prior to its completion as a whole, the individual parts could not be sanctified. And when the *amalgamation* of the parts into the one entity of the Tabernacle is recounted, the portion is called *Pekudei* — to indicate that even after the Tabernacle was a complete entity, each part was individually hallowed as well.

                    *   *   *

The Jewish people likewise are one collective congregation; all Jews together form one whole entity.[9] On the other hand, each individual Jew is a "complete world"[10] unto himself; so much so, that "each and everyone is obligated to say that the world was created expressly for me."[11]

A Jew may think that first and foremost he exists as a separate entity, with his own individual manner of divine service and purpose in life; additionally, he is part of the Jewish people.

---

7. *Ibid.*, 36:8ff.
8. *Ibid.*, 40:34-35.
9. *Likkutei Torah*, beginning of *Nitzavim*.
10. *Sanhedrin* 37a.
11. *Ibid.*

Herein lies the lesson of *Vayakhel*. When the vessels for the Tabernacle are about to be built, each of them has its own distinct shape and purpose, yet we must be aware that their importance lies in their becoming an integral part of the whole.

So, too, must each Jew realize that his individual being depends on his being part of the greater Jewish whole. It is for this reason that before praying for one's individual needs, each individual is to include himself in the collective Jewish congregation[12] by undertaking the performance of the command, "Love your fellowman as yourself."[13]

On the other hand, when someone devotes himself wholeheartedly to the collective good, he may believe that this does not enhance his attainments as an individual. *Pekudei* teaches him otherwise: erecting the Tabernacle for all Jews benefits the individual participant as well.

Based on *Likkutei Sichos*, Vol. XXI, pp. 250-257.

---

12. *Siddur Tehillas Hashem*, p. 12.
13. *Vayikra* 19:18.

Counting & Accounting

There is a general principle that "The end is wedged within the beginning, and the beginning [is wedged] within the end."[1] In the context of the Torah portions in the Book of *Shmos*, this rule points to a profound connection between the first passage, *Shmos*, and the final passage, *Pekudei*.

What is the connection between these two seemingly disparate passages, one of which deals with the enslavement and redemption of the Jewish people, while the other revolves around the construction of the Tabernacle?

One of the ways in which these portions are similar is that the theme of counting is alluded to in both titles.

---

1. *Sefer Yetzirah* 1:7.

The connection of the title of the portion of *Shmos* ("Names") to counting is readily understandable according to the commentary of *Rashi*.[2] In his comment on the opening words, "These are the names...," he states: "Even though He had counted [the Jews] during their lifetime by their names, He again counted them ...to make known His love for them...."

The title *Pekudei* ("Accounts") as the word itself indicates has to do with counting — "the enumeration of the weights of all the contributions to the Tabernacle."[3]

The general theme of the Book of *Shmos*[4] is the liberation of the Jewish people from Egyptian exile. Accordingly, liberation is related to the concept of counting — the concept that ties together the beginning[5] and end[6] of the Book.

This requires explanation, for "counting" and "liberation" are seemingly antithetical. When something is enumerated, it is clearly limited — there are only as many items as are counted and no more. True liberation, on the other hand, indicates *freedom* from limitation, constraint, and countable bounds. How can this paradox be resolved?

*   *   *

Although man's ultimate goal is to attain an "infinite state" that transcends counting — a state of liberation that soars beyond the bounds of this world — this does not mean that the ideal intent is to *nullify* the finite. Rather, the infinite must be *fused* with the finite.[7]

Since "G-d desired to dwell in the nethermost level,"[8] two things must be accomplished: (a) A dwelling place must be

---

2. *Shmos* 1:1.
3. *Rashi* on *Shmos* 38:21; see also *Rashbam* and *Ramban, loc. cit.*
4. In the words of *Ramban* (end of *Pekudei*), "The Book of Liberation."
5. Inasmuch as the beginning, or "head", of an entity encapsulates it entirely.
6. For "the final form is decisive."
7. Only through this union is G-d's truly limitless ability revealed. See *Likkutei Sichos*, Vol. III, p. 904ff.
8. *Tanya*, beginning of ch. 36, paraphrasing *Tanchuma, Naso* 16.

made for *G-d Himself*[9] (who totally transcends the world), and (b) this dwelling must be made specifically in this physically limited world.

These two goals find general expression in the difference that exists between Jewish souls and the world as a whole:

The essential goal of (a) making a dwelling place for G-d is effected mainly within Jewish souls, inasmuch as Jews are wholly united with G-d "so that they be a fit dwelling place for Him."[10] This indwelling in these souls is accomplished through (b) the divine service of Jews within this physical *nethermost* world, whose very physicality they transmute into a vessel for G-dliness. The inherent source of Jewish souls, their inherent union with G-d, is thereby revealed.

The Book of *Shmos*, dealing as it does with the birth of the Jewish people as a nation and the fulfillment of their mission of creating a "dwelling place" for G-d, likewise has both a "beginning" and an "end".

The "beginning", i.e., the main and *intrinsic* aspect of G-d's intent, is to be found within the Jewish people themselves, in their innate union with G-d. This is indicated by the count in the very first passage of *Shmos*, a count that took place in order "to make known His *love* for them."

The "end", i.e., the manner in which this intent actually manifests itself, is effected through the concluding count of *Pekudei*, the account of the weight of the objects of the Tabernacle — through (a) making a dwelling place for G-d (b) by transforming physical objects into holiness.

Based on *Likkutei Sichos*, Vol. XVI, pp. 476-478.

---

9. *Or HaTorah, Balak*, p. 997; *Hemshech Taf-Reish-Samach-Vav*, p. 3, *et al.*

10. *Hemshech Taf-Reish-Samach-Vav*, p. 468; see also *Torah Or, Mishpatim* 76d.

ספר ויקרא

Vayikra

Vayikra   ויקרא

A Small Alef

When the third Lubavitcher Rebbe, known as the *Tzemach Tzedek*, was a young child, he was due to start attending *cheder*, the local religious school. On his first day he was accompanied by his grandfather, the first Lubavitcher Rebbe, known as the Alter Rebbe, who asked the teacher to begin with the first section of the Torah portion of *Vayikra*.

After the lesson, the child asked his grandfather: "Why is the word *Vayikra* written with a small *alef*?" (This is one of the rare cases in which the Torah scroll includes a letter larger or smaller than the regular size.)

The Alter Rebbe lost himself in thought for quite a while, and then answered: "Adam was formed by G-d Himself,[1] Who testified that 'Adam's wisdom surpassed even that of the ministering angels.'[2] Aware of his sterling qualities, he became somewhat proud. He therefore succumbed to the sin of the 'Tree of Knowledge.'

"Moshe...was also aware of his singular qualities. However, not only was he not prideful, but on the contrary, this awareness brought him to be contrite of heart and utterly humble in his own estimation. Moshe thought to himself that any other Jew, not necessarily Amram's child and a seventh generation descendant of Avraham, would have surely been greater than he, had that person possessed such a lofty soul and such illustrious ancestry — qualities granted to Moshe without his having had to toil for them.

---

1. See *Bereishis Rabbah* 24:5; *Koheles Rabbah* 3:11(2); cf. *Avos deRabbi Nasan*, end of ch. 1.
2. *Bereishis Rabbah* 17:4.

"Adam, by being cognizant [and proud] of his qualities, succumbed to the sin of the 'Tree of Knowledge,' and that is why the word 'Adam' is written with a large *alef*.[3] Moshe, by being aware of his own unworthiness, attained the utmost level of humility. Accordingly, when he had to record in the Torah that G-d called him, he wrote the word *Vayikra* ('And He called') with a *small alef*."

Now why was it necessary for the Alter Rebbe to preface his remarks about Moshe with a lengthy and seemingly uncomplimentary exposition about Adam? Would it not have sufficed for him to say that the small *alef* alludes to Moshe's extraordinary degree of humility?

When the Alter Rebbe explained the above matter to his grandchild, he was interested not only in providing an answer to his question, but also in teaching him a lesson as to how one ought to serve G-d. This lesson could be learned only by prefacing his remarks about Adam.

Awareness of one's qualities is in itself not a fault. On the contrary, there is a well-known aphorism: "Just as one must be aware of his own faults, so too must one be aware of his own qualities."[4] One must know, however, that even so lofty an individual as Adam succumbed to sin by being *proud* of his singular gifts. Moshe's awareness of his own qualities did not lead him down the false trail of pride; rather, it caused him to be the most humble of men.[5]

*　　　*　　　*

On the one hand, every Jew must know that he possesses tremendous spiritual potential; so much so, that he is likened to Adam before his sin. Such knowledge enables him to overcome all doubts as to his spiritual worth, and to forge ahead. On the other hand, he must know that the sublime reaches of his soul were granted to him without toil; another individual

---

3. *I Divrei HaYamim* 1:1.
4. *Likkutei Dibburim*, Part IV, p. 1161; English translation (Kehot, N.Y., 1990), Vol. IV, ch. 31, Section 13. Cf. *HaYom Yom*, p. 107.
5. *Bamidbar* 12:3.

thus endowed could achieve even greater heights. This enables him to become truly humble.

Based on Likkutei Sichos, Vol. XVII, pp. 1-8.

Let the Pure Engage in Purity

The *Midrash* states: "Rabbi Asi said, 'Why do we begin a very young child's study of Torah with *Toras Kohanim* (the Book of *Vayikra*) and not with [the Book of] *Bereishis*? Because children are pure *(tehorim)* and *korbanos* (sacrificial offerings) are pure; let those who are pure occupy themselves with that which is pure.'"[1]

How are we to understand this statement of the *Midrash* that *korbanos* are themselves "pure"? Purity is not the attribute that the Torah normally associates with *korbanos*, which are usually qualified by the adjectives "whole" *(tamim)* or "choice".

With regard to the *korbanos* that were offered *before* the Giving of the Torah, our Sages state[2] that all animals, beasts and birds could be offered, so long as they were from species that were *"pure"*, i.e., kosher. We learn this from Noach's *korbanos* which were only of "pure" animals.[3]

Although at that time no difference existed between "pure" and "impure" animals with regard to the permissibility of their being eaten (i.e., their *kashrus*), a difference did exist in their intrinsic being, as would later be set out in the Torah.

Thus, beginning with Noach, *korbanos* before *Matan Torah* bore some relationship to the *korbanos* of the Jewish people after *Matan Torah*. This then is what is meant by saying that *korbanos* are pure — in the sense of Noach's use of kosher animals.

*   *   *

---

1. *Vayikra Rabbah* 7:3.
2. *Zevachim* 115b.
3. *Bereishis* 8:20.

The ultimate purpose of *korbanos* is to reveal G-d's essential love for the Jewish people, a love so great that it transcends His love for them as students of the Torah.[4]

This was expressed to a greater degree in the *korbanos* that preceded *Matan Torah*, which were not offered as a result of a directive of the Torah; once they became a specific *command* of the Torah it was harder to *reveal* that aspect within them that transcends Torah.

The Midrashic statement that children begin their study of the Torah with the Book of *Vayikra* because "those who are pure [should] occupy themselves with that which is pure," will be understood accordingly.

There are three general eras in the life of the Jewish people: (a) the era that follows *Matan Torah*, when Jews perform the Torah and *mitzvos* because they are so commanded by G-d; (b) the era that began with the Patriarchs (and lasted until *Matan Torah*), when they fulfilled the precepts "before being so commanded"; (c) even earlier on, beginning with Noach, when there was only a faint connection to the laws of the Torah (at the very least, insofar as it related to "pure" and "impure").

These three eras have their parallels in the spiritual life of each individual Jew in the following manner: (a) after becoming *bar* or *bas-mitzvah*, when he is obligated to perform the *mitzvos*; (b) the time a child reaches the age of *chinuch*, the age at which he can be educated in the ways of Torah and *mitzvos*, preparing for the time he will be obliged to perform them; (c) when he is still at a very tender age and cannot conduct himself according to the Torah and *mitzvos*.

Even in the last-mentioned instance, the tender Jewish child has a relationship with Torah and *mitzvos*. This is his rightful inheritance. He possesses it in its totality, and its framework is relevant to him.

Furthermore, as a child who has no connection to the practical service of Torah and *mitzvos*, his essential relation-

---

4. See the essay that follows.

ship to G-d is more readily *apparent*; G-d's intrinsic and essential love for the Jewish people is *revealed* to a greater extent within a very young child than within someone older.[5]

This, then, is the meaning of "letting those who are pure occupy themselves with that which is pure." The intent of *korbanos* is to reveal G-d's essential love for the Jewish people, who are essentially pure, inasmuch as they are rooted in a Source that cannot be tainted by impurity.

Therefore, these very young and pure children within whom G-d's love is palpably revealed should engage in the study of that which is itself pure — the study of *korbanos*.

Based on *Likkutei Sichos*, Vol. XXII, pp. 1-6.

---

5. See the *maamar* beginning *Ki Naar Yisrael*, 5666; see also *Likkutei Sichos*, Vol. XXI, p. 20ff.

Tzav   צו

A Jew's Relationship with G-d

The passage entitled *Tzav* deals with various types of sacrificial offerings, or *korbanos*, as does most of the Book of *Vayikra*, which is also known as *Toras Kohanim*, "the Book of Priestly Laws."

Although *korbanos* comprise but a few of the 613 precepts of the Torah, their effect — and thus their essence — *transcends* the Torah and its commandments. It is for this reason that they are able to act as atonement and compensate[1] for one's failings in Torah and *mitzvos*.

To state this in a slightly different form: When a Jew brings an offering to G-d, he thereby expresses his inherent connection and closeness with Him. Every Jew enjoys this intrinsic relationship with Him, a relationship that is not at all dependent on Torah and *mitzvos*. Just as this relationship is not brought into being by the performance of Torah and *mitzvos*, it is likewise not diminished by their non-performance; the essential bond of a Jew with G-d is loftier than Torah and *mitzvos*. This echoes the teaching of the Sages on the verse, "You are children to the L-rd your G-d"[2] — "[Although they have sinned,] they are still My children."[3]

For this reason *korbanos* have the ability to atone for sins. When a Jew transgresses, heaven forbid, he impairs his bond with G-d. This connection, forged through his performance of Torah and *mitzvos*, may now be repaired through *korbanos*.

This is done by arousing and revealing — through *korbanos* — his *essential* bond with G-d, which is not subject to impairment. This has the effect of bringing about atonement — it

---

1. See *Iggeres HaTeshuvah*, ch. 2.
2. *Devarim* 14:1.
3. See *Kiddushin* 36a; *Sifri, Haazinu* 32:5.

cleanses the blemish away, and repairs his relationship with G-d at the level of Torah and *mitzvos*.

This dynamic deepens our understanding of the whole theme of *korbanos*, which would otherwise be subject to the following very powerful question.

Why did G-d see fit that Jews achieve a level of Divine service through *korbanos*, which involve slaughtering an animal and offering it upon the altar? Would not a more spiritual form of service, such as prayer, be more fitting, inasmuch as it makes the Jews' relationship with G-d more manifest?

Moreover, since *korbanos* are not unique to Jews — *korbanos* may also be offered by non-Jews, even in the Holy Temple[4] — how, then, do they reveal the singular relationship Jews enjoy with G-d?

According to the above, this may be clearly understood. It is specifically because the intrinsic bond of Jews with G-d is loftier than their connection to Him through Torah and *mitzvos*, that this bond finds expression through the service of *korbanos*.

The reason for this is that G-d freely chose[5] to bind himself with the Jewish people — "I love Jacob[6]" — even though "Esav is Jacob's brother,"[7] i.e., He could have chosen Jacob's brother, Esav.

This is expressed specifically with the service of *korbanos*, wherein one does not see — when it is viewed superficially — the spirituality of a Jew. Though it is difficult to perceive the spirituality inherent in *korbanos*, it is expressly the *Jews'* service of *korbanos* that is able to activate the innate unity with G-d that results from His freely choosing specifically the Jewish people.

Based on *Likkutei Sichos*, Vol. XXII, pp. 3-4.

---

4. See *Menachos* 73b.
5. See *Likkutei Sichos*, Vol. IV, pp. 1309, 1341.
6. *Malachi* 1:2.
7. *Ibid.*

Transforming Quantity into Quality

The Book of *Vayikra*, or Leviticus, is also known by the name *Toras Kohanim*, "The Laws of the Priests." It is known by this name since so much of this third Book of the Pentateuch deals with laws that relate to the *Kohanim*, particularly the laws of the sacrificial offerings that they were to bring in the Tabernacle and Holy Temple.

In the first portion of *Toras Kohanim*, the portion of *Vayikra* (this being the name of the whole book as well as the name of its first weekly portion), we find that the Torah states the regulations which apply to three categories of offerings: the *Olah*, the burnt offering that was wholly consumed upon the altar; the *Minchah*, the gift offering; and the *Chatas*, the sin offering.

The second portion of *Toras Kohanim*, the portion of *Tzav*, speaks of five categories of offerings. Not only does it provide additional details regarding the offerings already mentioned in *Vayikra*, but it also speaks of two new types of offerings: the *Asham*, the guilt offering, and the *Todah*, the thanksgiving offering.

Providing additional details concerning those offerings that were previously mentioned in *Vayikra* is a *qualitative* addition; the new laws regarding a previously known offering change the quality of the offering. Mention of the two new categories of offerings is a *quantitative* addition.

Thus, the Torah portion of *Tzav* indicates that increases with regard to quality alone do not suffice; quantity must be increased as well.

When comparing the worlds of materiality and spirituality, we observe that by and large the material world is measured quantitatively and the spiritual world is measured qualitatively. The Torah portion of *Tzav* indicates that there are times when increased quality, i.e., increased spirituality, can only come about through an increase in dealing with matters that are quantitative, i.e., the physical world.

Judaism teaches that great spiritual heights are not attained by closing oneself off from the world and dealing only with strictly spiritual matters. Rather, spirituality is attained by making physical matters ever more fit to be offered upon the altar of holiness. Only by enabling "form" to prevail over "matter",[1] which is achieved by transforming the mass of corporeality into the form of spirituality, and by changing quantity into quality, is it possible to reach truly lofty levels in the soul's service of G-d.

When nine men over the age of *bar-mitzvah* gather together they are as yet unable to form a *minyan*, the religious quorum of ten adult males which is necessary for the recitation of congregational prayers and Torah reading. As soon as the "tenth man" appears, they are then able to form a *minyan*. Clearly, the additional person causes not only a quantitative change, but a qualitative change as well. We thus have not only an addition of quantity, an additional person, but also a metamorphosis of quantity into quality.

In a broader sense, an increase in quantity includes seeing to it that as many Jews as possible are drawn closer to Torah and *mitzvos*, until even those who superficially seem to be blemished and unfit for the altar of holiness, are also elevated. Furthermore, they ought to be drawn close in a manner that ensures that their elevation will last.

Based on *Likkutei Sichos*, Vol. XVII, pp. 48-49.

---

1. See *Kuntreis Toras HaChassidus*, chs. 11, 12.

Shabbos HaGadol   שבת הגדול

A Truly Great Shabbos

The *Shabbos* that precedes Passover is known as *Shabbos HaGadol*, the "Great *Shabbos*." The Alter Rebbe, Rabbi Shneur Zalman of Liadi, author of the *Tanya* and founder of *Chabad* Chassidism, cites the following reason in his *Shulchan Aruch*[1] for its being so named:

"The *Shabbos* before Passover is called *Shabbos HaGadol* since a great miracle occurred on the day. For...when the Jews took the lambs for their Paschal offerings on that *Shabbos*, the Egyptian firstborn assembled before them and inquired why they were doing so. The Jews responded: 'This is our Paschal offering, for G-d shall slay the Egyptian firstborn.'

'[Thereupon] the firstborn went to their fathers and to Pharaoh, and demanded that they liberate the Jews. When they refused to do so, the firstborn declared war against the rest of the Egyptians and killed many of them. This is the meaning of the verse, 'Who struck Egypt through their first-born....'[2] It was instituted that this miracle be remembered in future generations on this *Shabbos*, which is therefore known as *Shabbos HaGadol*."

Many other momentous events which occurred on this day are mentioned by other Sages as appropriate explanations for its name. Yet the Alter Rebbe only gives the reason mentioned above. Why? It is because the Alter Rebbe's reason identifies so strongly with the concept of *Shabbos* as a whole. When this particular miracle occurred on *Shabbos*, it underscored the fact that this was not a common *Shabbos*, but a "Great *Shabbos*."

*   *   *

---

1. *Hilchos Pesach*, beginning of Section 430.
2. *Tehillim* 136:10.

After the six days of creation, say our Sages, "What was the world lacking? It was lacking [nothing but] *repose*. When *Shabbos* arrived, repose arrived."[3]

Time is a creation just as are all other created things;[4] prior to the world's creation time simply did not exist, inasmuch as time and space are inexorably related. During each of the six days of creation, then, time was constantly being created anew. Just as during each of these six days new creatures came into being, so too, during each of these days a different span of time came into existence.

This being so, before the seventh day the world lacked not only *repose,* it lacked the entire seventh day as well: the framework of time of the seventh day had yet to be brought into existence. Clearly, then, *Shabbos* and repose are so closely intertwined that we cannot differentiate between the two; when repose was created, the time of *Shabbos* was created together with it.

All six days of creation share a certain similarity. In the framework of time, all of them consist of past, present and future — the basic elements of time. What is novel about the framework of time during *Shabbos* is that while it retains time's basic dimension, still it is repose; it transcends past, present and future. During *Shabbos*, time is transformed and elevated to a level that *transcends change.*

A similar transformation occurred on *Shabbos HaGadol*. The firstborn of Egypt, the mightiest[5] Egyptians and the greatest oppressors of the Jewish people, were suddenly and miraculously transformed by G-d into people who — while remaining Egyptians — took up the Jewish cause. The similarity to time, which on *Shabbos* retains its basic composition yet at the same time transcends it, is striking.

Based on *Likkutei Sichos,* Vol. XVII, pp. 57-62.

3. *Rashi* on *Bereishis* 2:2; see also *Bereishis Rabbah* 10:9.
4. See *Siddur im Dach, Shaar HaKerias Shema* (75d ff.); cf. *Likkutei Sichos,* Vol. X, p. 176.
5. See *Targum Onkelos* on *Bereishis* 49:3.

Pesach   פסח

Matzos, Freedom & Passover

The festival of Passover is known by three names: (a) initially, in the Pentateuch, it is referred to as the Festival of *Matzos*;[1] (b) in the text of the holiday prayers it is also known as the Season of our Freedom; (c) later on our Sages referred to it, as do most people, as the Festival of Passover (Pesach).

The prophet Ezekiel speaks of the Exodus from Egypt as the time of the Jewish people's birth.[2] He does so not only because the Jewish people then attained nationhood, for were this the sole reason the term would also apply to other nations who won their freedom. Rather, it is because at that time the Jews became an entirely new entity.

The ultimate purpose of the Exodus was consummated when the Jews received the Torah, as the verse states: "When you shall take out the nation from Egypt, they shall serve G-d on this mountain (Sinai)."[3] Thus, the birth of the Jewish people is bound up with their becoming a Torah-nation. The essential quality of a Jew, both as an individual and as part of the collective whole, is Torah.

The three names mentioned above, and their respective order, emphasize the three distinct stages necessary for the Jewish people to become a wholly new entity.

This is analogous to a teacher imparting knowledge to a pupil — knowledge so profound that the pupil could never attain it on his own. The first thing the pupil must do is to arrive at a state of *self-nullification*, abandoning all preconceptions, and thereby becoming a fit receptacle for his master's

---

1. *Shmos* 23:15, 34:18; *Vayikra* 23:6; *Devarim* 16:16.
2. *Yechezkel* ch. 16 and commentaries.
3. *Shmos* 3:12.

teachings. After attaining this state, the pupil must, however, also make an effort to *comprehend* the knowledge imparted to him. This he does by utilizing his own intellect.

During the initial stages of learning, the student's knowledge of the subject can in no way compare to his master's, and is constricted by his intellectual capacity. Ultimately, it is to be hoped that his comprehension will equal his teacher's.[4] But in order for him to attain this state he must *transcend* the limitations of his intellect and elevate himself to the intellectual state of his teacher.

*   *   *

The birth of the Jewish people as a nation was dependent on three similar stages. In order to receive the Torah they first had to attain a state in which they could fulfill the injunction, "You shall *serve.*" Like a servant who nullifies himself before his master, they first had to expend effort to nullify their previous state, which was contrary to Torah. This level of service — like the first stage in the attainment of knowledge — is reflected in the name, the Festival of *Matzos,* for the flat *matzah* bespeaks the nullification of one's bloated ego.

This manner of service, far from being restrictive, leads to a second state that truly *frees* a Jew, for it is in keeping with his essence, inasmuch as "a Jew and Torah are one." This level of freedom — like the second stage of attaining knowledge — is celebrated in the Festival of our Freedom, for "only a Jew who studies Torah is truly free,"[5] and such a desire is part of a Jew's essential being. (Conversely, when a Jew leads a life "free" of the constraints of Torah and *mitzvos* he is in reality in a state of "slavery", for he is straining against the grain of his very essence.)

For our forefathers, the second level of freedom led to the final stage — receiving the Torah. This changed them radically, just as in the final stage of intellectual growth, the

---

4. Cf. *Avodah Zarah* 5b.
5. *Avos* 6:2.

student's level of comprehension is radically transformed into the level of his master. So great is this metamorphosis that even the former level of "you shall *serve*" — a finite level — is thereby transformed into a level of service that transcends limitation. This level is termed the Festival of Passover, for — as implied by its name — *Pass-over* means to transcend, to leap[6] from the bounds of the finite to the realm of the infinite.

Based on *Likkutei Sichos*, Vol. XVII, pp. 71-76.

---

6. *Rashi* on *Shmos* 12:11, 13.

Celebrating the First & Final Redemptions

The third Lubavitcher Rebbe, the *Tzemach Tzedek*, once said: "The last day of Passover is known as *Acharon shel Pesach*, the 'Final Day of Passover.' This day marks the conclusion of the theme begun on the first day of Passover.

"We celebrate the *first* night of Passover in order to commemorate the first redemption, when G-d liberated us from Egyptian exile through Moshe, the first redeemer. However, this was only the beginning. On *Acharon shel Pesach* we celebrate the final redemption from the final exile, which G-d will bring about through our Righteous *Mashiach*...."[1]

The relationship of *Acharon shel Pesach* to the final redemption is also apparent from the *Haftorah* recited on that day,[2] which describes in detail the promises that will then be fulfilled.

It is also known[3] that the Baal Shem Tov was accustomed to partake of three festive meals on *Acharon shel Pesach*, the

---

1. Quoted by the Previous Rebbe in *Sefer HaSichos 5700*, p. 72.
2. *Yeshayahu* 10:32-12:6.
3. See *HaYom Yom*, p. 47.

final meal being called "the Meal of *Mashiach*," for *Acharon shel Pesach* is illuminated by a ray of the light of *Mashiach*.

What, indeed, is the difference between the first and final redemptions, celebrated respectively on the first and final days of Passover?

With regard to the Exodus from Egypt Scripture states, "...for the people had fled."[4] They had to *flee* the evil and impurity of Egypt because "the evil in [their] souls was still in its strength."[5]

Regarding the final redemption, however, the prophet states, "You will not depart in haste";[6] there will be no need to flee in haste inasmuch as evil and impurity will then cease to exist; as the verse testifies, "I will cause the spirit of impurity to depart from the world."[7]

Furthermore, during the time of the final redemption evil will not only cease to exist, but will actually be transformed into good. This is stated in the *Haftorah* of *Acharon shel Pesach*: "the weaned child will stretch out his hand over the viper"; i.e., even the viperous evil inclination will be overcome by a metamorphosis. And an anticipatory glimmer of this era may be sensed on *Acharon shel Pesach*.

In a more general sense this is also the difference between the first two and last two festive days of Passover: the first two days are related to the first redemption, while the last two days — the Seventh Day of Passover included — are connected with the forthcoming redemption.

The latter parallelism finds expression in the fact that the unholy Egyptians met their complete annihilation — "not a single one remained"[8] — during the Seventh Day of Passover, at the time the Jews crossed the Red Sea. This foreshadows the eradication of evil that will take place during the final redemption.

---

4. *Shmos* 14:5.
5. *Tanya*, ch. 31.
6. *Yeshayahu* 52:12; see also beginning of *VeKacha 5637*; *ibid.*, ch. 129.
7. *Zecharyah* 13:2.
8. *Shmos* 14:28.

There are other similarities as well. Concerning the time
of the final redemption Scripture[9] states: "And I shall pour
forth My Spirit upon all flesh (including 'servants and hand-
maidens'[10]) and they shall speak prophecy...." At the time of
the crossing of the Red Sea, too, "A handmaiden beheld at the
sea that which was not revealed even to the prophets."[11]

Additionally, just as the final redemption will occur at the
time when evil and darkness are transformed into goodness
and light — "the night will be as bright as the day"[12] — so, too,
with regard to the events that took place at the time of the
crossing of the Red Sea. For at that time, "there was the cloud
and *darkness,* and it *illuminated* the night."[13] The very darkness
was transformed into a luminary.

Based on *Likkutei Sichos,* Vol. XXII, pp. 34-37.

---

9. *Yoel* 3:1.
10. *Ibid.,* v. 2.
11. Commentaries of *Mechilta* and *Rashi* on *Shmos* 15:2.
12. *Tehillim* 139:12.
13. *Shmos* 14:20.

Shemini   שמיני

Eighth: More than Just Another Number

The opening words of the Torah reading of *Shemini* — "It was on the *eighth* day..." — are related to the first *seven* days of installation of the *Kohanim* ("priests"), described at the conclusion of the previous passage, *Tzav*. However, the name itself, *Shemini* ("Eighth"), does not indicate this (because it does not include the connecting words). Furthermore, inasmuch as the reading is called *Shemini* and not *BaYom HaShemini* ("On the Eighth Day"), this would seem to indicate that what is most important is the very fact that it is the "eighth". Why is this deemed to be so important?

There are two underlying and antithetical concepts contained within the number "eight".

On the one hand, the cardinal number "eight" signifies a concept that transcends by far the preceding digits one through seven, for as the *Keli Yakar* explains,[1] all aspects of creation fall within the category and cycle of "seven", while "eight" is "unique to G-d Himself." As further elucidated by our Sages,[2] this means to say that "seven" includes not only those things encompassed by creation, but also the G-dliness that is vested within creation. "Eight", however, alludes to G-dliness insofar as it transcends creation.

On the other hand, the ordinal number *shemini* ("eighth") indicates that it is not an entity unto itself; rather, it is related to the "seven" that preceded it, and is a continuation of them.

Thus, the novelty of *shemini* ("eighth") is the fact that it expresses the Omnipotence of G-dliness, in that the selfsame

---

1. Beginning of *Shemini*; see also *Rabbeinu Bachya, loc. cit.*
2. See *maamarim* entitled *Vayehi BaYom HaShemini* of the years 5704 and 5705; see also *Likkutei Sichos*, Vol. III, p. 974.

G-dliness ("eight") that transcends creation is drawn down and revealed *within* creation ("eighth") — it is connected to the preceding "seven" which indicate creation.

For this reason our Sages state that the "harp of Messianic times will be of *eight* strings."[3]

During the Messianic era "G-d's glory will be revealed for all flesh to behold";[4] G-d's glory, which infinitely transcends flesh, will be palpably perceived by creatures of flesh. So much so, that this perception will then be an entirely natural phenomenon.[5]

If man's flesh would then be able to perceive G-dliness not because of his corporeal ability to do so, but only because it is enabled to do so by G-d's infinite capacity to transcend the bounds of finitude, then this perception would not become one with the world itself; it would be innovative, not a natural phenomenon.

However, during the Messianic era G-dliness will truly be perceived as naturally as we now perceive physical things. This comes about as a result of a transformation within the nature of man himself, making it possible then for him to perceive G-dliness naturally.

Thus, the revelation of G-dliness during the Messianic era is also related to the concept of "eighth", for it, too, is composed of two opposites: G-d's glory which totally transcends creation — and the order of "seven". Both of these elements will be revealed within the world in such a way that perceiving G-dliness will be entirely natural — the "eighth" will be conjoined with the "seven".

*   *   *

This, too, was the accomplishment of the "eighth" day of priestly installation. During the first *seven* days of installation, Aharon, the *Kohen Gadol*, and his sons accomplished all that could be done through man's service. This included the reve-

---

3. *Arachin* 13b; see also *Likkutei Torah, Tazria* 21d.
4. *Yeshayahu* 40:5.
5. See *Toras Chayim, Tetzaveh*, 482ff.; see also *Shaar HaEmunah*, ch. 25.

lation of G-dliness that is encompassed within the aspect of "seven".[6]

However, all this merely served as an *introduction* to the indwelling of the Divine Presence in the Sanctuary on the eighth day of installation. At that time the level of *"shemini"* was revealed; on the *eighth* day, G-dliness that totally transcended creation — "eight" — was bound up with creation — "seven".

Based on *Likkutei Sichos*, Vol. XVII, pp. 92-97.

---

6. See *Likkutei Sichos*, Vol. XII, p. 62ff.

Offerings & the Divine Presence

Water and fire have always symbolized opposite forces. In classical Jewish thought, water alludes to *Chesed*, beneficence; like water, it flows from the giver above, to the recipient below. Fire, on the other hand, alludes to *Gevurah*, severity and withdrawal; it resembles fire, whose searing flames rise upwards.

The offerings brought in the Tabernacle and the Holy Temple expressed both *Chesed* and *Gevurah*, as too did the manner in which they were accepted by G-d. The very word *korban*, Hebrew for "offering", means to draw close and raise up to G-d that which is being offered, similar to fire and *Gevurah* which rise upwards. The effect of an offering was to give G-d pleasure,[1] this pleasure manifesting itself even in this world — as a downward flow of *Chesed* and benevolence from above.

The offerings themselves were consumed by a heavenly fire[2] — *Gevurah*. This descended — an act of *Chesed* — in the

---

1. *Rashi* on *Vayikra* 1:9; *Sifri* and *Rashi* on *Bamidbar* 28:2.
2. *Vayikra* 9:24.

form of a lion.[3] A lion is, of course, symbolic of strength and ferocity, which are expressions of *Gevurah*. Yet a lion comprises aspects of *Chesed* as well.[4]

Inasmuch as all sacrificial offerings combine both of these elements, it seems strange that during the first seven days of initiation and consecration of the Tabernacle, when Moshe erected it daily and brought the offerings, the Divine aspect of *Chesed* associated with them was lacking. For during these days the *Shechinah*, the Divine Presence, had yet to reside in the Tabernacle.[5] This manifestation of *Chesed* came only on the eighth day (the details of which are described in the Torah portion of *Shemini*), when the *Shechinah* resided in the Tabernacle as a result of the offerings.[6]

Since the consecration of the Tabernacle and the sacrificial offerings brought during the first seven days affected offerings for all time,[7] it stands to reason that during these days too there was an element of the *Shechinah* present, albeit in a different manner from that which was manifest during the eighth day and later.

*   *   *

There are two general levels in the revelation of the *Shechinah*:[8] (a) a revelation brought about by man's spiritual service, similar to the attribute of *Gevurah* that ascends from below; (b) a revelation brought about from above, and which transcends a man's service, similar to the beneficent attribute of *Chesed*.

The first seven days of consecration and initiation served as man's preparatory service to the revelation of the *Shechinah* in the Tabernacle.[9] This level of service drew down only that

---

3. *Yoma* 21b.
4. Cf. *Yechezkel* 1:10.
5. *Rashi* on *Vayikra* 9:23; *Toras Kohanim*, beginning of *Shemini*.
6. *Vayikra* 9:23.
7. See *Torah Or* 29d ff.
8. See *Tanya*, ch. 53.
9. Explained at length in *Likkutei Sichos*, Vol. XI, p. 182ff.; Vol. XII, p. 58ff., *et passim*.

level of *Shechinah* which was consonant with man's spiritual service. On the eighth day, however, there was revealed the far loftier level of *Shechinah* brought about from above.

Still, G-d does not desire that we eat "bread of shame,"[10] i.e., that He grant us a gift of which we feel unworthy, not having earned it. For this reason it was necessary that on the eighth day itself, before the *Shechinah* came to reside in the Tabernacle, Aaron had to bring the offerings of that day.

The revelation of the eighth day was so great that it affected *"all* the people."[11] It was an emanation so potent that it was able to reach down and affect even those who were on the lowest of levels.[12]

It was for this reason that in blessing the Jewish people on the eighth day, Moshe said: "May it be G-d's will that the *Shechinah* reside in the actions accomplished by your hands."[13] Action, unlike thought, speech, emotions, etc., is the lowest faculty possessed by man. Once an action is done by an individual, the result exists as a separate and distinct entity. The revelation of the *loftier* level of *Shechinah* is such, that it penetrates even as far as this far-removed state of being, and elevates it to holiness.

Based on *Likkutei Sichos*, Vol. VII, pp. 237-238; Vol. XXII, pp. 16-20.

---

10. See *Likkutei Torah, Shemini* 7d.
11. *Vayikra, loc. cit.*
12. Discourses beginning *Vayehi BaYom HaShemini*, appearing in *Sefer HaMaamarim 5704* and *5705*.
13. *Rashi* on *Vayikra* 9:23.

Tazria   תזריע

Circumcision: A Family Affair

When an infant is brought into the room or synagogue where his circumcision is to take place, a married couple is customarily honored to carry him to the place of the *bris*. The couple so honored are known in Yiddish as *kvaters*. The female *kvateren* carries the infant to the entrance of the room, and her husband, the male *kvater*, takes him from her and brings him to "Eliyahu's Chair."[1]

Inasmuch as "a Jewish custom is Torah,"[2] we may deduce from the weekly reading of *Tazria* that there is a relationship between a Jewish woman and the precept of circumcision, which accounts for this custom which insists that a woman must take part in a ceremony relating to circumcision.

The commandment of circumcision[3] is stated in the verse, "And on the eighth day, the child's foreskin shall be circumcised."[4] This verse appears in the passage that begins, "When a *woman* conceives," that deals with the specific laws applying to a woman after childbirth.

The duty to circumcise is actually the father's obligation: women are not commanded to see to it that their sons are circumcised. Nevertheless, this commandment is stated in the passage that deals almost exclusively with the laws that apply to a woman soon after she gives birth.

All this seems to indicate that a woman has some relationship with the precept of circumcision, and this finds expression in her serving as a *kvateren* at a *bris*.

---

1. See *Magen Avraham* 551:3; *Pri Megadim* and *Shaarei Teshuvah, loc. cit.*
2. See *Tosafos, s.v. Nifsal,* on *Menachos* 20b; see also *Maharil,* quoted in the *Rama, Yoreh Deah* 376:4.
3. See *Yerushalmi, Kiddushin* 1:7; *Sheiltos, Acharei* 93.
4. *Vayikra* 12:3.

In many communities, moreover, a pregnant woman does not act as *kvateren*. Being a widely accepted custom, this, too, is governed by the rule that "a Jewish custom is Torah." What is the reason for it?

With regard to the custom of *kapparos* (expiatory fowl which are circled above a person's head on the dawn of the day before Yom Kippur) the *Shulchan Aruch* states[5] that a pregnant woman uses at least one additional fowl in this ceremony on behalf of the fetus, for it is seemingly regarded as an additional entity.

Since the custom is for the *kvaters* to be limited to two people — one couple — a pregnant woman does not customarily serve as a *kvateren*, inasmuch as there would then be yet another entity involved — the fetus, and there would be three people participating in the ceremony rather than the customary two.

Actually, a closer examination of the custom of *kapparos* will lead to the conclusion that the fetus is not considered to be a *separate* entity, for if it were why would it be necessary for a sinless fetus to require expiation?

Rather, the fetus in its mother's womb serves to change the status of the *mother*, adding to her an aspect which makes her count for more than one individual. More than one fowl is thus required for her expiation.

The reason why a pregnant woman does not act as *kvateren* will be understood accordingly; it is not because the fetus, in and of itself, is a third participant in the ceremony, but because in her present state the woman herself is considered to count for more than one individual.

Based on *Likkutei Sichos*, Vol. XXII, pp. 56-60.

---

5. *Orach Chayim* 605 (subsection 3 in *Shulchan Aruch Admur HaZaken, loc. cit.*).

Metzora   מצרע

The Effect of a Candle

The Torah portion of *Metzora* opens with a discussion of
the purification offerings that are to be brought by an individual afflicted with *tzaraas*, a leprous-like malady — nowadays
extinct — resulting from a person's spiritual failings. The
ritual impurity resulting from *tzaraas* affected not only the
individual, but also the dwelling in which he found himself.[1]

If a person with *tzaraas* enters a friend's house without
permission, Rabbi Yehudah declares in the *Mishnah*[2] that the
owner is granted a period of grace which extends "as long as it
takes to light a *[Shabbos]* candle," during which time he is to see
to it that the person with *tzaraas* leaves his home.

Candle-lighting just before *Shabbos* differs from other
forms of candle-lighting. It brings "peace and tranquillity in
the home,"[3] by ensuring that the family members "do not
stumble over wood and rocks";[4] i.e., it averts untoward
occurrences. In a spiritual sense, too, the sanctity of the
Shabbos candles prevents the spreading of the ritual impurity
of *tzaraas*.

Although all illumination prevents one from stumbling,
only *Shabbos* candles offer spiritual protection. Other forms of
light do not guarantee to further peaceful and harmonious
relationships within the household. The very opposite may
result: subjecting someone to the merciless glare of objective
illumination may shed an uncomplimentary light on him,
leading to the very opposite of peace and harmony.

---

1. *Toras Kohanim* on *Vayikra* 13:46; *Rambam, Hilchos Tumas Tzaraas* 10:12.
2. *Nega'im* 13:11.
3. *Shabbos* 23b.
4. Commentary of *Magen Avraham* on *Shulchan Aruch, Orach Chayim*
   263:12-13; *Shulchan Aruch Admur HaZaken, Orach Chayim, ibid.*

Truly peaceful and harmonious relationships will result only when others are viewed in the light of the verse that teaches that "a *mitzvah* is a candle and Torah is illumination."[5] Since "the entire Torah was given in order to bring peace to the world,"[6] viewing others in the light of Torah surely leads to family unity and peace. Although all of Torah and *mitzvos* lead to peace, that peace is mainly spiritual. The illumination of *Shabbos* candles, however, has the additional merit of leading to interpersonal peace.

Our Sages tell us that one of the causes of *tzaraas* is slanderous and evil gossip[7] — the very antithesis of peaceful and harmonious relationships. It can therefore best be prevented and remedied by *Shabbos* candles, whose purpose is peace and harmony.

*   *   *

It is thus abundantly clear that nowadays, when the darkness of the world is so dense, the light radiated by *Shabbos* candles is the need of the hour. It is extremely important that every Jewish girl begin lighting *Shabbos* candles as soon as she is old enough to understand their significance.

The radiance of the *Shabbos* candles, coupled with the blessing recited over the kindling, will illuminate the life of the young girl who lights them. She will be ever mindful of what she recites in the blessing over the candle-lighting — that G-d is "King of the world." Her candle-lighting will also ensure that when she matures she will follow the path of the verse that promises that "G-d shall be your guiding light in [your journey through] this world."[8] And when she marries and becomes the "foundation and mainstay of the home," the life of her home will be conducted on the foundation of Torah and *mitzvos*.

Our Sages tell us that *Shabbos* candle-lighting blesses one

---

5. *Mishlei* 6:23.
6. *Rambam*, end of *Hilchos Chanukkah*; cf. *Likkutei Sichos*, Vol. VIII, p. 349ff.
7. *Arachin* 16a.
8. *Yeshayahu* 60:20.

with scholarly children and sons-in-law.[9] Nowadays, when —
for better or worse — it is the daughter who decides whom
she will marry, her candle-lighting will assure her of a good
match as well.

Based on *Likkutei Sichos*, Vol. XVII, pp. 141-147.

---

9. *Shabbos, loc. cit.,* and commentary of *Rashi.*

Acharei   אחרי

To Come before G-d

At the beginning of *Parshas Acharei*,[1] G-d tells Moshe to instruct his brother Aharon, the high priest, that he is to wear linen vestments when he enters the innermost chamber of the Tabernacle, the Holy of Holies, on Yom Kippur. Ordinarily the *Kohen Gadol* (the high priest) would wear vestments that included gold. Upon entering the Holy of Holies, however, he was to wear plain linen vestments like those of an ordinary *Kohen*.[2]

Rashi[3] explains the reason for this as follows: "A prosecutor cannot become an attorney for the defense." Since gold had been used to make the Golden Calf, which some of the Jews had worshiped, it was inappropriate that the *Kohen Gadol* should wear gold when entering the Holy of Holies to gain forgiveness for all the Jewish people; it would serve as a reminder of their sin.

When the *Kohen Gadol*, the saintly representative of the Jewish people, entered the most sacred place in the world, the Holy of Holies, on the holiest day of the year, Yom Kippur, there was a conjoining of the most sacred aspects of the three elemental dimensions — time, space, man. All other aspects of the service of the *Kohen Gadol* during Yom Kippur were but a prelude to this epochal event, at which time he was able to gain pardon for the sins of his people.

For the high priest to wear vestments interwoven with gold during the rest of Yom Kippur was inoffensive; wearing

---

1. *Vayikra* 16:1-4.
2. *Shmos* 28:40-42.
3. On *Vayikra* 16:4.

these golden vestments — reminiscent of the Golden Calf — in the Holy of Holies, at the very moment that he was striving to obtain pardon for all past sins, was unthinkable.

The service of the high priest on Yom Kippur, like Yom Kippur itself as a whole, brought about not only atonement, but also a state of purification before G-d, as the verse states, "For on this day shall atonement be made for you, to purify you; you shall be cleansed of all your sins before G-d."[4]

The spiritual cleansing of sin and achieving a state of standing "before G-d" is, of course, not limited to Yom Kippur. While that day is more conducive than other days to achieving a lofty spiritual state, a Jew is able to affect both himself and others every day of the year. All Jews, on every single day of the year, may attain the level of being "before G-d" — drawing closer to Him, and to His Torah and *mitzvos*.

However, in order for this state to be achieved, a Jew must know that he must first enter into a spiritual "Holy of Holies" — a state of internalization, of *inwardness*. The individual must seek to plumb the depths of his soul and have it illuminate his whole being. When this is achieved, atonement and purification may be obtained both for himself and for others.

How is one to achieve such a state? — By divesting oneself of self-aggrandizing garments, the garments of gold. So long as one is preoccupied with banalities such as self-importance, one cannot be sensitive to one's innermost dimension, nor enter the innermost chamber — the true and ultimate purpose and G-dly intent of Creation.

Only after a person clothes himself in the linen garments of a *simple Kohen,* i.e., only after achieving a state of true simplicity and humility,[5] can he enter the state of the Holy of Holies, and thereby effect atonement and purification on his own behalf and on behalf of others. Ultimately, he may then reach such a lofty state that, like the *Kohen Gadol,* he secures

---

4. *Loc. cit.*, v. 30.

5. See *Likkutei Torah* on *Acharei* 28b ff.; cf. *Ateres Rosh, Shaar Yom HaKippurim*, ch. 5ff. (30a), where this matter is discussed at length.

"pardon for himself, his household, and for the whole congregation of Israel."[6]

Based on *Likkutei Sichos,* Vol. XXII, pp. 89-95; Vol. XVII, p. 172.

---

6. *Vayikra* 16:17.

Mastery of Self

The concluding chapter of the Torah portion of *Acharei* enumerates the prohibited incestuous relationships. The section begins with the following exhortation: "G-d said..., I am the L-rd your G-d. The deeds of the land of Egypt...and the land of Canaan...you shall not do.... You shall follow My commands and observe My statutes.... You shall guard My statutes and laws...."[1]

Rashi, commenting on the words "I am the L-rd your G-d," notes: "It was revealed and known to Him that eventually [the people] would become severed from Him through the sin of illicit relationships.... He therefore decreed, 'I am the L-rd your G-d': Know Who it is that has decreed this to you; He is sure to punish [transgression], (lit., "He is a Judge who will mete out retribution) and is faithful in providing reward [for obedience].'"[2]

How does *Rashi* know that "I am the L-rd your G-d" means *both* "Know Who it is that has decreed this to you," *and* "He is sure to punish, and is faithful in providing reward"?

In almost all instances[3] where *Rashi* comments on the words "I am the L-rd," and explains that "He is faithful in providing reward" or "He is sure to punish," he does not preface this by stating, "Know Who it is that has decreed this to you."

---

1. *Vayikra* 18:1-5.
2. *Ibid.,* v. 2.
3. See *Rashi* on *Vayikra* 18:5-6; 19:10, 16, 25, 36; 22:33; 23:22.

Furthermore, in those instances where *Rashi* explains "I am the L-rd" to mean "I have decreed this; you may not shirk it,"[4] or "Know Who has decreed this; do not take it lightly,"[5] he does not add that "He is faithful in providing reward," and the like.

How, then, does *Rashi* know that the verse "I am the L-rd your G-d" stated here, refers *both* to "Know Who it is that has decreed this to you" *and* "He is sure to punish, and faithful in providing reward"?

* * *

The section dealing with illicit relationships is unique in that before the Torah even begins to enumerate the specific prohibitions, it first provides a general introduction: "The deeds of the land of Egypt...and the land of Canaan...you shall not do.... You shall follow My commands and observe My statutes.... You shall guard My statutes and laws...."[6] This general introduction is prefaced by the verses, "G-d said..., I am the L-rd your G-d."[7]

The reason such a lengthy introduction is needed is evident: Illicit relationships are something that "a person strongly desires." So much so, that after all of G-d's warnings there still exists a strong potential for transgression and G-d knew that "eventually [the people] would become severed from Him through the sin of illicit relationships." All these exhortations and warnings are therefore necessary in order to ensure that one will not succumb to temptation.

Since "I am the L-rd your G-d" prefaces this general introduction, it is to be understood that each of the three Hebrew words, (a) *Ani* — "I am," (b) *"HaShem* — "the L-rd," (c) *Elokeichem* — "your G-d," warns and exhorts the Jew in a distinctive manner.

When seeking to help a Jew refrain from something he

---

4. *Ibid.*, 18:4.
5. *Ibid.*, 22:30.
6. *Ibid.*, 18:3-5.
7. *Ibid.*, verses 1- 2.

finds very tempting it is necessary that he first be told to "know Who it is that has decreed this to you." He must know that inasmuch as a particular decree emanates from his Creator, he cannot possibly benefit if he succumbs to his own selfish desire and acts contrary to G-d's Will. This warning is the message of the first word, *Ani*.

However, a person may be ready to suffer the eventual consequences so long as he is able to satisfy his transitory lusts. The Torah therefore gives the second warning: "He is a Judge who will mete out retribution"; i.e., the "return" will be such that it will negate all the previous pleasure, so that the person remains with nothing but unpleasantness. This warning is alluded to by the word *Elokeichem*, which refers to G-d in his capacity as stern Judge.

But why does G-d present us with temptation that is so difficult to withstand?

This is answered by the promise that He is "faithful in providing reward." Since G-d *(HaShem)* desires to *reward* the Jew, he tests him. And the more difficult the test, the greater the ensuing reward.

Based on *Likkutei Sichos*, Vol. XXII, pp. 97-99.

Kedoshim   קדושים

Fruits of the Fifth Year

In the Torah reading of *Kedoshim* we learn that one may not eat the fruits of a tree during the first three years after it was planted, while the fruits of the fourth year are holy.[1] They are to be eaten only in Jerusalem. The Torah proceeds: "But in the fifth year you may eat its fruit [in all places], *so that* it may yield you more produce...."[2] Thus, the objective of the first four years is the increase in yield during the fifth year.

The fifth year's increase in physical yield resulted from the fact that in a spiritual sense,[3] too, the fruits of the fifth year possessed a quality that was lacking — not only during the first three forbidden years, but also during the fourth year when the fruits had to be eaten in Jerusalem. Why, then, could these more spiritually elevated fruits be eaten wherever one desired? Why were they not restricted to the confines of the Holy City of Jerusalem, as were the less spiritual fruits of the fourth year?

Before the Baal Shem Tov, the founder of *Chassidus*, became renowned, it was his custom to wander from town to town and village to village, because one of his approaches to divine service was to inquire among Jews as to their welfare, and elicit responses of praise to G-d for their well- being.

He was most gratified to hear the loving phrases with which they responded to his queries: "Blessed be His Name," "Praise the L-rd," "The loving G-d does not forsake," and so on.

It once happened that the Baal Shem Tov visited a certain town where there lived an aged and eminent scholar who for the past fifty years had been piously abstemious, studying

---

1. *Vayikra* 19:23-24.
2. *Loc. cit.*, v. 25.
3. See *Likkutei Torah, Kedoshim* 29c.

Torah day and night in holy isolation. He would sit garbed in his *tallis* and *tefillin* until the very late afternoon, and fast until after the evening prayer. He would then break his fast with a crust of bread and some water.

The Baal Shem Tov once entered this scholar's "seclusion chamber," which was in a corner of the synagogue, inquired after his health, and asked him whether his needs were being met. The recluse ignored him. After the Baal Shem Tov repeated his questions a number of times the scholar became angry and showed his visitor the door. Said the Baal Shem Tov to the scholar: "Rebbe, why don't you provide G-d with His sustenance? You will starve Him, G-d forbid, and He will depart from the world."

Hearing these words the scholar was perplexed: a Jew, a villager, speaking such strange words about seeing to G-d's needs so that He should not starve?! The Baal Shem Tov noticed the scholar's bewilderment and explained himself: "Jews exist by virtue of G-d's sustenance, but what sustains *Him*? This is answered by King David in *Tehillim*,[4] wherein he says: 'And You, Holy One, are enthroned upon' — i.e., You are sustained by — 'the praises of Israel,' by the words of praise that Jews give You for their health and sustenance."[5]

To make this world a "dwelling place for Him,"[6] so that G-d be immanent in this world, is the purpose of all creation. Accomplishing this requires more than Torah study. It requires — as indicated by the Baal Shem Tov's conduct — that we praise and acknowledge G-d for even the simple things in life, for all things are to be imbued with holiness.

So, too, regarding the fifth year's fruits. The highest state of holiness is attained not by eating the fruits in Jerusalem; it is achieved by transforming the whole world into the Holy City of Jerusalem.

Based on *Likkutei Sichos*, Vol. VII, pp. 134-138.

---

4. 22:4.
5. This encounter is recorded in *Sefer HaMaamarim Yiddish*, p. 138ff.
6. *Tanchuma, Naso* 16; cf. *Tanya*, ch. 36.

Lag baOmer   ל"ג בעומר

Rabbi Akiva's Disciples

Lag baOmer, the thirty-third day of the counting of the *Omer*, is a Jewish holiday. One of the reasons for this holiday is that on this day the fatal plague that struck down many of the students of the illustrious Rabbi Akiva came to an end.[1]

Rabbi Akiva's scholarship and holiness were such that he attracted twenty-four thousand devoted disciples, and the epidemic partly resulted from their not properly respecting one another.[2]

Rabbi Akiva is known for his aphorism: "'Love your fellowman as yourself' — this is a cardinal principle of the Torah."[3] How is it possible that those who are deemed by the "Torah of truth" to have been his disciples, should act in a contrary manner, and not have properly respected one another?

Since no two people's personalities and opinions are ever entirely alike,[4] it is to be understood that each of Rabbi Akiva's disciples understood his master's teachings in a slightly different manner. Accordingly, each placed particular emphasis on his own manner of divine service which he derived from his own comprehension; one stressed the love of G-d, another the fear of Him, and so on.[5]

All of Rabbi Akiva's disciples, of course, based their conceptions and approach to divine service on Rabbi Akiva's

---

1. *Meiri* on *Yevamos* 62b, quoting the *Geonim; Tur* and *Shulchan Aruch* (and *Shulchan Aruch Admur HaZaken*), *Orach Chayim* 493: 2.
2. *Yevamos* 62b.
3. *Sifra* on *Vayikra* 19:18.
4. See *Berachos* 58b; *Sanhedrin* 38a.
5. See also *Likkutei Sichos*, Vol. VII, pp. 342-3.

teachings. However, so permeated were they by their own individual conceptions, and with their own approaches based on these teachings, that each student felt that whoever did not follow his particular path was deficient both in understanding and in divine service.

As faithful disciples of Rabbi Akiva, who placed so much emphasis on loving one's fellowman as oneself, they were not satisfied with merely attaining great heights themselves. Each disciple also endeavored to prevail upon his peers to serve G-d according to what he understood to be the proper path — his individual path.

The other students did not accept the path of their fellows for they, too, were completely preoccupied with their own manner of service. This led to their not treating each other respectfully. As honest individuals they could not possibly act in a two-faced manner, honoring their friends — who they thought were not following the proper path — externally, while inwardly disagreeing with their manner of service. It was therefore impossible for them to harbor true feelings of honor towards friends whose comprehension and divine service they held to be deficient.

As faithful disciples of Rabbi Akiva, their attitude surely mirrored in some way Rabbi Akiva's philosophy. Indeed, Rabbi Akiva had told his disciples[6] that throughout his life he had intensely desired to attain a state of *mesirus nefesh*, total self-sacrifice and martyrdom on behalf of G-d. Such a state permeates the entire individual: there is no part of him insensitive to this state, involving as it does one's entire existence. Rabbi Akiva's disciples, too, shared his desire. While in this state, their manner of divine service did not leave room for anything or anyone else.

The greatness of this service notwithstanding, it leaves something to be desired. To crave martyrdom, i.e., to flee the world and be absorbed in holiness and in G-d, must be accompanied by an equal desire to secure an indwelling of G-dliness

---

6. *Berachos* 61b.

within the world. Only Rabbi Akiva was able to combine the relentless drive for *mesirus nefesh* with the calm performance of Torah and *mitzvos*, thereby permeating this physical world with holiness.[7] Those of his students who passed away before Lag baOmer, unfortunately were not equal to the task.

Based on *Likkutei Sichos,* Vol. XXII, pp. 138-140.

---

7. See *Chagigah* 14b; cf. *Torah Or* 25b; *Maamar Acharei Mos,* 5649; *Likkutei Sichos,* Vol. III, p. 990.

Emor   אמור

What's in a Name?

The Torah passage of *Emor* is replete with laws and descriptions of the various Jewish festivals. Only two of them, however, are given specific names: the Festival of Matzos and the Festival of Sukkos.

With regard to the Festival of Matzos, Scripture states: "And on the *fifteenth* day of this month is the Festival of Matzos to the L-rd...,"[1] thus implying that the designation Festival of Matzos does not apply to the entire seven-day holiday period. However, concerning the Festival of Sukkos the Torah speaks of "the *Festival of Sukkos for seven days* to the L-rd."[2]

On the other hand, after the designation of Festival of Matzos the verse *immediately* concludes, "for seven days you shall eat *matzos*," while with regard to the Festival of Sukkos the injunction that "you shall dwell in *sukkos* for seven days"[3] is mentioned only at the end of the section and not in close proximity to the festival's name.

How are we to understand these differences?

There is yet another difference between these festivals: The Festival of Matzos is most often referred to in Rabbinic literature as well as in common speech as "Passover". However, we do not commonly find the Festival of Sukkos alluded to by any name other than "Sukkos".

All this tends to indicate that the theme of Passover is not strictly limited to its being the Festival of Matzos, while the theme of Sukkos is delineated by its name — the Festival of Sukkos.

---

1. *Vayikra* 23:6.
2. *Ibid.*, v. 34.
3. *Ibid.*, v. 42.

Therefore, when the Torah states that "on the fifteenth day of this month is the Festival of Matzos...," it immediately concludes that "for seven days *you shall eat matzos.*" This emphasizes that Passover is called the Festival of Matzos only because of the requirement to eat *matzah;* this is, however, not the exclusive theme of the festival and the entire seven-day period. This is not so with regard to the holiday of Sukkos. In this instance "the *Festival of Sukkos for seven days* to the L-rd" is indeed the total theme of the seven-day holiday period.

Were the Torah to state that "you shall dwell in *sukkos* for seven days" immediately after the phrase "Festival of Sukkos," we might erroneously conclude that — similar to the "Festival of Matzos" — the holiday of Sukkos is so designated only by virtue of our actually dwelling in the *sukkah.*

But why is it that the theme of the Festival of Sukkos is exclusively what is implied by its name, while the theme of Passover is not merely that of the Festival of Matzos?

* * *

The fifteenth day of the month of Nissan — the first day of Passover — is distinctive because it is the occasion of the Exodus from Egypt. The liberation of the Jewish people from slavery is of such great import that the day on which it happened became a holiday, as Scripture states: "And this day shall be unto you for a remembrance; you shall celebrate it for all coming generations as a festival to the L-rd."[4] It is precisely because of its being a singular day that we are commanded to do special things during this day, which include the eating of *matzos.*

This is not the case with regard to Sukkos. "The fifteenth day of this seventh month" is not unique in its own right; it is the obligation to dwell in the *sukkah* for seven days that gives rise to the Festival of Sukkos.

Based on *Likkutei Sichos*, Vol. XXII, pp. 126-128.

---

4. *Shmos* 12:14.

The Four Kinds

In *Parshas Emor* we read: "On the first day [of Sukkos] you shall take for yourselves the fruit of a beautiful [*esrog*] tree, a bound branch of palm trees, boughs of thick-leaved [myrtle] trees and willows of the brook, and you shall rejoice before the L-rd your G-d for seven days."[1]

Concerning the first three kinds, the conditions given in the Torah have to be met exactly in order to fulfill the command. The *esrog* must be a completed[2] fruit, beautiful to behold;[3] if it has dried out it is unfit for use.[4] The palm branch must be *bound*,[5] i.e., its leaves must be closely attached to its spine.[6] The myrtle, too, must be thick-leaved — three leaves growing from the same place on the stem.[7] However, the "willows of the brook" do not necessarily have to grow near a brook;[8] even if they grow somewhere else they are also fit for use, as long as they are the type of willow that *generally* grows by a brook.[9] Why the difference?

The *Midrash* says[10] that the four kinds of vegetation which are taken on Sukkos are symbolic of four types of Jews: an *esrog*, which possesses both a good taste as well as a fragrant odor, is symbolic of the Jew who possesses both Torah learning and good deeds. The palm branch [which must come from a date-palm] has a good taste but has no fragrant odor, signifying Jews who have obtained Torah knowledge but lack good

---

1. *Vayikra* 23:40.
2. See *Shulchan Aruch Admur HaZaken, Orach Chayim* 648:29.
3. *Sukkah* 31a.
4. *Ibid.,* 34b.
5. *Ibid.,* 31a.
6. *Shulchan Aruch, ibid.,* par. 3.
7. *Sukkah* 32b.
8. *Ibid.,* 33b.
9. See *Rambam, Hilchos Lulav* 7:3; *Rosh,* commentary on third chapter of *Sukkah,* Section 13; *Tur* and *Shulchan Aruch* (and so too that of *Admur HaZaken), Orach Chayim* 647:1.
10. *Vayikra Rabbah* 30:12.

deeds [commensurate with their knowledge]. Those individuals who possess good deeds but are lacking in Torah knowledge are likened to the myrtle, which has a fragrant odor but lacks taste. The willow, which is inedible and lacks aroma as well, represents thos people who lack both Torah and good deeds.

The *mitzvah* of taking these four kind on Sukkos mirrors the ideal state in which Jews of all kinds are bound together.

Thus, there is a cardinal difference between the first three kinds of vegetation and the willow. The first three kinds of vegetation, i.e., the first three types of Jews, are similar to one another in that they all possess certain qualities which are clearly revealed. Consequently, their unity is also much more easily perceived.

Achieving a state of unity with the willow — with the Jew who lacks both Torah and good deeds — comes about not as a result of that Jew's *revealed* quality, but rather because of his *essence*; essentially he, too, is a Jew. This quality of being Jewish is intrinsic to every individual who is a descendant of Abraham, Isaac and Jacob, and it is present even when the individual lacks both Torah and good deeds. Even if a person is unaware of his Jewishness, he still retains his essential quality.

For this reason, in the halachic perception as well, there is a difference between the first three kinds and the willow. The first three kinds must openly reveal their qualities, while the willow is fit for use even if it did not grow by the brook; even then it may be bound up, without question, with the other three kinds.

Even when a Jew does not grow up among fellow Jews, like a willow that was not nurtured amongst its brother willows, — as long as he is of the same *kind*, a descendant of Abraham, Isaac and Jacob, he is an inseparable part of the Jewish people and bound up with them all.

Just as all four kinds together are necessary for the performance of the *mitzvah*, so, too, must all Jews unite; if the "willow" is missing, then Jewry as a whole is lacking an essential component. Similarly, just as the willow need not possess revealed qualities for it to be utilized, so must our approach to the "willow Jew" be without pre-conditions. It suffices that he is a Jew.

Based on *Likkutei Sichos*, Vol. XXII, pp. 132-136.

Behar   בהר

The Loftiness of Humility

The Torah portion of *Behar* begins by stating: "G-d spoke to Moshe at Mount Sinai...."[1] The Hebrew word for "at Mount" is *behar*, giving rise to the accepted title of this Torah portion — *Behar*.

Choosing the word *Behar* for the title is truly perplexing. The emphasis in the verse is not that G-d spoke to Moshe on a mountain, but that He spoke to him at Mount *Sinai* — the mountain upon which He chose to give the Torah to the Jewish people. Surely the passage should therefore be called *"Sinai"*, or at the very least *"Behar Sinai."* Why was the title *"Behar"* chosen?

The question becomes even more acute in relation to the spiritual lesson we are to derive from "Mount Sinai." Our Sages tell us[2] that G-d chose to give the Torah on Mount Sinai because it was the "lowest of all mountains."

Choosing this mountain thus carried the following two-fold message.[3] On the one hand, it was chosen because of its modest height, thus teaching us the quality of humility. On the other hand, Sinai was still a *mountain*, thereby imparting that while humility is of the greatest import, nevertheless a person should not allow this to turn him into a doormat to be trodden upon by all; humility is to be accompanied by a measure of self-esteem and self-assertion, such as are needed to enable a man to stoutly face his spiritual trials and challenges.

These two teachings are alluded to in the two words

---

1. *Vayikra* 25:1.
2. See *Midrash Tehillim* (Buber) 68:17.
3. See *Likkutei Torah, Bamidbar* 15b, c; *Likkutei Sichos,* Vol. I, p. 276ff.

"Mount Sinai." "Mount" is symbolic of loftiness, "Sinai" symbolizes the nullification of self.

Clearly, humility and self-nullification — "Sinai" — are of primary importance. "Mount" is a lesson that serves only to buttress one's "Sinai," in order to ensure that one will not allow his humility to turn him into a Milquetoast. This being so, how can it be that the Torah portion is only titled *Behar* — the secondary aspect of loftiness and exaltation — while the main aspect of "Sinai" — humility and self-nullification — is not mentioned at all?

* * *

Self-nullification and humility are a result of being cognizant of G-d's greatness;[4] a man grows humble and feels truly insignificant when he realizes that G-dliness is the true essence of all being.

Ultimate nullification of self can only be arrived at when the state of nullity is imperceptible, i.e., when the person himself does not perceive his degree of nullification. An individual's cognizance of his nullification indicates that there still exists an independent entity in need of nullification.[5] Upon attaining true self-nullification, *nothing* other than G-dliness is perceived.

It is readily understandable that when a person reaches such an altruistic state, his feelings of insignificance do not clash with his feelings of esteem and importance, for it is not he who is esteemed and important but G-d.[6] This recalls the saying of our Sages, "The servant of a king is *himself* a king."[7] Surely this does not cause the servant to become conceited, for his privileged status merely reflects the king's importance, and not his own.

---

4. See *Rema, Orach Chayim* 98:1.
5. See *Sefer HaMaamarim 5672*, ch. 214; the *maamar* beginning *Mi Yitein,* 5706, ch. 4.
6. See *Sefer HaMaamarim 5564,* p. 106; *Or HaTorah, Vayechi,* p. 359ff.; *Sefer HaMaamarim 5666,* p. 159; *5688,* p. 43.
7. *Shevuos* 47b; *Sifri, Devarim* 1:7.

And for this reason the Torah portion is titled *Behar* alone. The sign of true humility and self-nullification is the point at which a person is able to feel as elevated and self-assured as a mountain — and yet know that this feeling does not stem from haughtiness; it stems solely from his complete nullification to G-dliness.

Based on *Likkutei Sichos*, Vol. XXII, pp. 159-162.

Bechukosai   בחקתי

Nullification of Self

Parshas Bechukosai enumerates the rewards received for performing the *mitzvos*, as well as the punishments incurred for their non-observance. This being so, it seems puzzling that the name of the Torah portion, which indicates the content of the portion as a whole, is *Bechukosai*.

This title is rooted in the word *chukim*, which refers to divine commands that are superrational. They are not performed out of any logical imperative — indeed logic finds them pointless and perplexing — but only because G-d has so commanded. It is difficult to understand how a passage which is entitled *Bechukosai* — signifying nonrational commands — should then proceed to address itself to the logical imperative of performing commands because of their subsequent rewards.

An obvious prerequisite to the proper performance of *chukim* is self-nullification before G-d.[1] When man ponders his own insignificance[2] in relation to G-d's greatness he attains a state of self-abnegation, for he realizes that G-dliness is the true and ultimate existence.

True self-nullification before G-d only comes about when the state of nullity is imperceptible, i.e., the person himself is unaware of his nullification. An individual's cognizance of his nullification indicates that here still exists an independent entity in need of nullification.[3] When one attains true self-nullification, *nothing* other than G-dliness is felt.

---

1. See *Bamidbar Rabbah,* beginning of *Parshas Chukas;* cf. *Tanchuma, ad loc.,* and *Rashi, ad loc.*
2. See *Rama, Orach Chayim* 98:1.
3. *Hemshech Te'erav,* ch. 214; cf. *maamar* begining *Mi Yitein,* 5706, ch. 4.

Attaining such an altruistic state is alluded to both in the word *Bechukosai* as well as in the performance of *mitzvos* in the spirit of *chukim*, for, as explained by the Alter Rebbe, R. Shneur Zalman of Liadi, the word *Bechukosai* also derives from a root meaning to hew out, or engrave.[4]

There is something quite remarkable about letters that are hewn out of stone. Not only are such letters united with the material from which they are hewn out, but they also do not exist as a separate and independent entity.

Indeed, herein lies the difference between written letters and engraved letters. Written letters are also united with the paper upon which they are written, but they exist as a separate entity. The entire existence, however, of engraved letters is the material in which they are engraved: they cannot possibly exist as a separate and distinct entity.

The word *chukim* — meaning as it (also) does to engrave — thus indicates that the person who performs the divine commands is so nullified before G-d, that he ceases to exist as a separate and independent entity, just like letters engraved on a precious stone. Such a person then fulfills the divine will as a matter of course.

When an individual attains such a state, his individual being — i.e., his intellect, emotions, and so on — does not impede his self-nullification. For having attained this level, he has ceased to exist independently; he exists only as an extension of G-dliness.

The same holds true with regard to the reward received for performing *mitzvos*. Attaining such a lofty state of nullity leads a person to perceive the goodness[5] of *G-dliness*, rather than his *personal* good. He will thus perform *mitzvos* in a truly selfless manner, rather than seeking *his* reward and benefit from their performance.

---

4. *Likkutei Torah*, beginning *Parshas Bechukosai;* cf. *Likkutei Sichos*, Vol. III, *Parshas Bechukosai; ibid.,* Vol. IV, p. 1056; *ibid.,* Vol. VIII, p. 127ff., *et passim;* cf. *maamar* beginning *Zos Chukas,* 5665, p. 224.

5. Cf. *Tehillim* 34:9.

Nevertheless, since G-d is the ultimate source of goodness, it also follows that the performance of His *mitzvos* leads to all manner of good, up to and including material goodness as well.[6]

Based on *Likkutei Sichos*, Vol. XXII, pp. 159-165.

---

6. Cf. *Likkutei Sichos*, Vol. XV, p. 312.

ספר במדבר
Bamidbar

Bamidbar   במדבר

Counting the Jews: A Countdown to Shavuos

The portion of *Bamidbar* is always read before the festival of Shavuos.[1] The reason for this is that the matters discussed in it directly relate to the preparations[2] one should make before receiving the Torah on Shavuos.

The general content of *Bamidbar* is the census that was taken of the Jewish people during the second year of their sojourn in the desert. So important was this event, that the whole fourth book of the Torah is known as the "Book of Counting."[3]

Specifically, the portion relates three manners of counting the Jewish people. Initially all Jews were counted, with the exception of the tribe of Levi.[4] Afterward, the tribe of Levi was counted separately.[5] Levites who had reached the age of one month were included in the count.[6] The portion concludes with the counting of the Levite family of Kehos. They were counted from the age of thirty years, at which age they became fit to carry the furnishings of the Tabernacle's Holy of Holies.[7]

As part of the people's preparation for receiving the Torah, Moshe related to them G-d's words, that upon receiving the Torah they were to become His "beloved treasure from among all the nations, for all the earth is Mine; a kingdom of rulers, and a holy nation."[8]

---

1. *Tur* and *Shulchan Aruch, Orach Chayim* 428:4.
2. See *Rambam, Hilchos Tefillah* 13:2.
3. *Yoma* 68b.
4. *Bamidbar* 1:49.
5. *Rashi, loc. cit.*
6. *Bamidbar* 3:15.
7. *Ibid.,* 4:2-3, and *Rashi.*
8. *Shmos* 19:5-6, and *Rashi.*

Firstly, says the verse, the Jewish people were chosen by
G-d to become a "beloved treasure," separated from all other
nations.[9] Thereafter, the verse implies, they were to reach an
even higher degree, that of "rulers"; they were to rule over
their surroundings. The verse then concludes with the additional merit of being "a holy nation." They would become so
lofty that they would be entirely removed from the mundane,
and become a "holy nation" unto G-d.

Thus, three successive stages of elevation are mentioned
in the Torah. These three stages are remarkably similar to the
underlying themes and reasons for the three systems by
which the Jewish people were counted.

The *Shaloh* states[10] that this counting enabled them to
become "an object that is worthy of numeration and cannot
become nullified."[11] Were the Jews not to have been counted
we would not have known their importance. Spiritually, this
relates to that level at which they superficially seem to be no
different from other nations. By G-d's counting them, His
special love for them — even as they exist in this unexalted
state — is revealed.

This general count recalls G-d's promise regarding the
first state that the Jewish people would achieve through
receiving the Torah: "You will be My beloved treasure *from
among all the nations*." Although other nations exist alongside
the Jewish people, still G-d chooses the Jewish people; they do
not become nullified among other nations, notwithstanding
the outward similarities.

The second count, that of the Levites, was intended not
only to make them "an object worthy of numeration" and
hence "not subject to nullification," but also for the purpose
of "ruling"[12] over Israel. This is similar to the second stage of
elevation that the Jews achieved by receiving the Torah: "a
kingdom of rulers."

---

9. *Rashi, ibid.*
10. 347a ff.
11. *Beitzah* 3b, and references there.
12. *Bamidbar* 1:50, and *Rashi.*

Counting the family members of Kehos for the purpose of carrying the furnishings of the Holy of Holies, is similar to the third objective accomplished by the giving of the Torah — totally removing the Jewish people from the mundane and transforming them into "a holy nation."

Each year, before the festival of Shavuos, when "these days are remembered,"[13] Jews prepare themselves spiritually to receive the Torah anew[14] and to attain the three accompanying levels mentioned above. This is actualized during Shavuos, when Jews receive the Torah afresh, and merit to become "a beloved treasure from among all the nations...; a kingdom of rulers, and a holy nation."

Based on *Likkutei Sichos*, Vol. XVIII, pp. 18-27.

---

13. *Esther* 9:28; cf. *Ramaz* in *Sefer Tikkun Shovavim.*
14. See *Maamar* beginning *Ve'asisa Chag Shavuos*, 5705, ch. 45.

Shavuos   שבועות

A Time to Eat & Rejoice

Judaism offers many opportunities for rejoicing, gladness and delight, chief among them being the three pilgrim festivals of Pesach, Shavuos and Sukkos. Concerning these festive days G-d commands us: "You shall rejoice in your festival...."[1]

Passover commemorates the Jews' physical exodus from Egypt; Shavuos — their receiving the Torah; Sukkos — their protection in the desert from the sun's searing heat by the Clouds of Glory.[2] Of the three festivals, Shavuos is obviously the most spiritual in nature, commemorating, as it does, an entirely spiritual event.

The Three Festivals are supposed to be celebrated not only with prayer and study but also with fine food and drink.[3] In certain circumstances, however, the delight of Pesach and Sukkos may be expressed in a wholly spiritual manner, foregoing food and drink. Such would be the case when one fasts during these holidays on account of a distressing dream.[4]

This is not so with regard to Shavuos. On Shavuos we are obliged to "eat and rejoice, demonstrating that Jews are pleased and gratified with the day on which the Torah was given";[5] fasting on Shavuos because of a disturbing dream is prohibited.[6]

It seems paradoxical that Passover and Sukkos, the two

---

1. *Devarim* 16:14.
2. *Shulchan Aruch Admur HaZaken, Orach Chayim,* Section 625.
3. *Rambam, Hilchos Yom Tov* 6:19; *Tur* and *Shulchan Aruch,* beginning of Section 529; *Shulchan Aruch Admur HaZaken, ibid.,* sub-section 10.
4. *Shulchan Aruch Admur HaZaken,* 494:18.
5. *Ibid.*
6. *Ibid.*

festivals that commemorate mainly physical events, may be celebrated in a totally spiritual manner, while Shavuos, which commemorates an event that is completely spiritual, must be celebrated not only spiritually, but also physically. Why must Shavuos be so celebrated?

Shavuos is unique in that the revelation of G-dliness that accompanied the giving of the Torah penetrated all of creation. In the words of our Sages: "The sound of G-d's giving the Torah emanated from all four sides as well as from above and below."[7] So awesome and all-encompassing was this event that "no bird twittered; ... no cow lowed; ... the world was silent and held its peace."[8]

Moreover, the sound of G-d's giving the Torah infused everything, even the inanimate. Therefore, say our Sages, this sound did not produce an echo.[9] An echo results when sound waves are not absorbed by an object, but bounce off it. Since the sound of G-d's giving the Torah penetrated all matter, it was impossible for the sound to be echoed.

This was so, because when the Torah was given G-d's quintessential Essence was revealed, for G-d imbued the Torah with His Essence.[10] Since G-d is the one entity that is truly infinite, it follows that at the time the Torah was given — when His Essence was revealed — nothing was impervious to this revelation; it penetrated and infused all of creation, even the grossest of corporeal matter.

A holiday that celebrates the ultimate in spiritual revelation and which also infuses all of creation without limitation, must itself be celebrated in a truly revealed manner and without limitation, up to and including celebration that is manifested in eating and drinking.

If fasting because of a distressing dream were permitted on Shavuos, this would indicate that there remained a level

---

7. *Tikkunei Zohar, Tikkun* 22 (64b); *Tanya,* ch. 36.

8. *Shmos Rabbah,* end of ch. 29.

9. *Ibid.,* end of ch. 28.

10. See *Tanya,* ch. 47.

in the universe that was impervious to the joy of Shavuos. This would be contrary to the spirit of the festival as a whole, which proclaims that even the nethermost level is "pleased and gratified" with receiving the Torah.

Thus, Shavuos affects even an individual who is so distressed that at any other time of the year it would be impossible for him to derive pleasure from food. Shavuos and its accompanying joy transform even this troubled individual, for he, too, is "pleased and gratified" with receiving the Torah.

Based on *Likkutei Sichos*, Vol. IV, pp. 1092-1096; Vol XXIII, pp. 27-32.

Eternal Torah in a Changeable World

When G-d gave the Torah to the Jewish people, He invested His very "soul" and essence in its written words,[1] for the Torah is a manifestation of G-d's essential wisdom and will. Hence, just as G-d and His will are immutable, the Torah and its commandments are likewise not subject to change.[2]

This eternity and immutability apply not only to the Written Torah but to the Oral Torah as well, for "even that which a distinguished scholar will one day propound before his master was already said to Moshe at Sinai."[3]

Thus, all subjects found in the *Talmud*, including references to the healing arts and the like, are an integral part of the eternal Torah which is not subject to change. Accordingly, we must understand why our Rabbis tell us that many remedies and forms of healing found in the Oral Law no longer apply because of the physiological and other changes that man has undergone since Talmudic times.[4] How can we

---

1. *Shabbos* 105a; see also *Likkutei Torah, Shelach* 48d.
2. *Rambam, Hilchos Yesodei HaTorah*, beginning of ch. 9.
3. *Yerushalmi, Peah* 2:4; *Megillah* 4:1.
4. See *Rema, Even HaEzer* 156:4; *Magen Avraham, Orach Chayim* 173:1; *Shulchan Aruch Admur HaZaken, Orach Chayim*, end of ch. 179.

possibly say that these cures which are part of the eternal and immutable Torah do not apply today?

Our Sages have stated: "Essentially the Torah addresses itself to things as they are on high, and alludes in a secondary manner to these things as they are found down below."[5] Thus, the Torah speaks *directly* of things as they exist in a spiritual state and only hints at these matters as they are found in this world.

It goes without saying that "the verse is not to be taken out of its literal context";[6] i.e., every verse in the Torah retains its literal meaning as well. Nevertheless, this literal meaning comes only after the verse has addressed itself to the subject as it exists in its spiritual state above. Our Sages explicitly state this concept in their comment on the verse, "He tells *His* words [Torah] to Yaakov, *His* statutes and ordinances to Israel."[7] They note: "That which *He does*, He tells Israel to do and observe."[8]

The above in no way contradicts the axiom that "*deeds* are the essential thing,"[9] for G-d desired that the commandments be performed in a literal manner in this physical world. However, with regard to Torah and its commands *in and of themselves*, the opposite is true: their source and beginning exists spiritually above. They then descended from their spiritual heights and were enclothed in physicality.[10]

The changes regarding various remedies, healing techniques, and the like, may be understood accordingly.

When the Torah speaks of remedies and means of healing it "essentially addresses itself to things as they are on high." I.e., first and foremost the Torah refers to a subject as it exists in the spiritual realms; only afterwards does it filter down

---

5. *Asarah Maamaros* [by Rabbi Menachem Azariah da Fano], *Maamar Chikur Din*, III, ch. 22.
6. *Shabbos* 63a.
7. *Tehillim* 147:19.
8. *Shmos Rabbah*, 30:9; see also *Yerushalmi, Rosh HaShanah* 1:3.
9. *Avos* 1:17.
10. See *Tanya*, ch. 4.

into our world. As these remedies exist in their *spiritual* state they are truly eternal; spiritually, their benefit exists constantly.

Simply stated: All things relating to a person's body — its diet, health, and so on — descend from their spiritual counterpart as they exist within his soul. These various remedies for the soul are as relevant today as they were in the past. However, as these things descend to the level of the physical it is possible that a change may occur.[11]

When the world is in a proper spiritual state then the selfsame things work in this physical world just as they do in the loftier spiritual worlds. These remedies and means of healing are therefore effective.

When, however, this world alters and degenerates, this spirituality cannot descend wholly. A change therefore occurs with regard to the physical effectiveness of these remedies; they are then efficacious only in their spiritual sense.

Based on *Likkutei Sichos*, Vol. XXIII, pp. 33-39.

---

11. See *Likkutei Sichos*, Vol. XVI, p. 98ff.

Naso   נשא

A Modern-Day Levitical Tally

There is an axiom that "the Torah is eternal."[1] This, of course, applies to the entire Torah, even to those things which are not *physically* applicable nowadays; they, too, continue to exist in their spiritual state.[2]

Thus, this principle also applies to the tally of the Levite families, Gershon and Merari, mentioned in the Torah portion of *Naso*, as well as to the tally of the family of Kehos, which is described at the conclusion of the preceding portion of *Bamidbar*. Although the tally was a physical, one-time event, nevertheless in a spiritual sense these tallies and their resulting lessons exist eternally.

What possible lesson can we derive in terms of our own spiritual service from the above-mentioned censuses?

We are told in the Torah that the sin of the spies caused a forty-year delay in the entry of the Jewish people into *Eretz Yisrael* — "one year for each day."[3] While it is true that because of this sin forty years had to pass before they could enter, why was it necessary for them to remain in the desert? Could they not just as easily have spent that time in an inhabited place, albeit not the Land of Israel?

Chassidus explains that "the reason for their journeying through the desert with the Tabernacle and its vessels was in order to subjugate the forces of evil, whose roots are specifically in the desert."[4] Furthermore, by subjugating the forces of evil, the Jews drew down G-dliness into this world.[5] It was

---

1. *Tanya*, beginning of ch. 17.
2. See preceding essay.
3. *Bamidbar* 14:34.
4. *Likkutei Torah*, beginning of *Naso*.
5. *Likkutei Torah*, ibid., 22b.

in order to accomplish all this that they were forced to remain in the desert for forty years.[6]

This is also the deeper reason for the separate census of the Levites, who were counted before being assigned to their service of carrying the Tabernacle and its vessels. It was this service that effected the spiritual transformation of the desert into a place fit for divine habitation.

The special count of the Levites for the sake of carrying the Tabernacle enabled them to attain a marked degree of spiritual eminence,[7] for "that which is subject to numeration cannot be nullified." This ensured that they would not be detrimentally affected by the spiritual desolation of the desert; on the contrary, they would be able to transform it into holiness.

*   *   *

The ability to transform a spiritual desert into a place of habitation and to derive the strength for this by "being counted," applies to all Jews in every generation. For, as mentioned earlier, the Torah and its lessons are eternal.

When a person contemplates his environs he may sometimes conclude that he exists in a spiritual wasteland, inasmuch as the people surrounding him know little of G-dliness, or of the Torah and its commandments. He may despair of ever being able to successfully change his surroundings, and he could decide to flee to some other place.

Herein lies the above-mentioned lesson. Just as the Jews found themselves in the desert because G-d had so dictated, so, too, every individual Jew has his own specific mission in the place he inhabits, even if it happens to be a desolate wasteland. Since "G-d directs the footsteps of man,"[9] it is by an act of Providence that he finds himself specifically there, in order to transform it into a place fit for G-dly habitation.

---

6. Had the spies not sinned, the Jews' spirituality would have been such that they could accomplish the above without its taking forty years.
7. See *Shaloh* 347a; *maamar* entitled *Tzohar Taaseh LaTeivah*, 5673.
8. *Beitzah* 3b; *Rema, Shulchan Aruch, Yoreh Deah* 110:1.
9. *Tehillim* 37:23; see also *HaYom Yom*, pp. 69, 104.

This lesson also applies to a person's *own* spiritual service.[10] It is quite possible that when a person makes a truthful accounting of his own spiritual state, he will realize that it resembles a vast wasteland. Furthermore, he may despair of ever making his personal desert blossom, when he realizes that he has become habituated to acting in a less than desirable manner.

Should a person find himself in such a spiritually desolate state, he may take heart from the lesson of counting the Levites. The Levites' service of carrying the Tabernacle only began at the age of thirty. G-d nevertheless enabled them — through their being counted — to transform the desert into a place of divine habitation.

So, too, G-d grants every single Jew the ability — notwithstanding his present spiritual state — to rid himself of all evil and to draw down G-dliness upon himself, so that he himself is transformed into a Tabernacle in which G-d resides.[11]

Based on *Likkutei Sichos,* Vol XIII, pp. 16-19.

---

10. See also *Likkutei Torah, Naso* 20b ff.
11. See *Tanya,* ch. 34.

Princely Offerings

In the portion of *Naso* we read that beginning on the day that Moshe finished setting up the Tabernacle, the twelve tribal princes of Israel brought dedicatory offerings for the altar, each on his appointed day. The gifts of all the princes were the same, each offering one silver dish, one silver bowl, one golden spoon, and so on.

The Torah then records the total number of dishes, bowls, spoons, and so on, dedicated by the princes: "This was the dedication offering for the altar, on the day on which it was anointed, from the princes of Israel: twelve silver dishes, twelve silver bowls, twelve golden spoons...."[1]

---

1. *Bamidbar* 7:84.

180 NASO

In answer to the question that on the *day* the altar was anointed only one of each kind of vessel was offered, not twelve, the *Midrash* comments:[2] "The Torah credits them (the princes) as if they had *all* brought their offerings on the first day...." The manner in which the princes offered their gifts was such, that they were credited with bringing their gifts collectively on the first day.

Korban, the Hebrew word for "offering", is rooted in the word *kiruv* — meaning to draw close.[3] The purpose of all offerings, like the purpose of spiritual service as a whole, was to draw the individual who brought the offering closer to G-d.

There are twelve general paths by which a Jew may draw closer to G-d, corresponding to the twelve tribes of Israel. Each tribe followed a unique path in the service of G-d.[4]

Accordingly, it is understandable why the altar was dedicated by the twelve tribal princes:[5] each prince dedicated it according to his unique manner of spiritual service. Thus, each of the twelve days of dedicatory offerings saw a new manner of offering being brought. Although the princes brought the selfsame objects, the spiritual intentions that accompanied these offerings differed,[6] in accordance with the spiritual path of each individual tribe.

Notwithstanding the uniqueness of each of the princely offerings, they were considered to be "communal offerings,"[7] intended to represent not only the individual concerned, but all of Israel as well. It was this collective intent within each of these offerings that enabled them to be considered as if they had "all been [collectively] brought on the first day."

---

2. *Bamidbar Rabbah,* end of 14:13; cf. *op. cit.,* 13:9.
3. *Sefer HaBahir* 109 (46); cf. *Zohar* III, 5a; *Rabbeinu Bachya* on *Vayikra* 1:9.
4. See *Pri Etz Chayim,* Introduction to *Shaar* 1; Introduction to *Shaar HaKolel;* cf. also notes *ad loc.;* cf. *Likkutei Sichos,* Vol. VI, p. 11, footnote; *ibid.,* p. 304; *ibid.,* Vol. X, p. 97ff.
5. See *Likkutei Torah, Berachah* 98c.
6. *Bamidbar Rabbah* 13:14; *op. cit.,* 14 (1-11).
7. Commentary of *Yedei Moshe* to *Bamidbar Rabbah* 14:13; cf. *Likkutei Sichos,* Vol. XXIII, p. 42ff.

The commingling of the uniqueness of the individual and the oneness of the collective whole was mirrored in the fact that the individual spiritual intentions of the tribal princes were unique, while their actual, physical offerings were the same. This is also true of the Jewish people: each Jew is unique and yet all Jews are equal.

There are certain qualities shared equally by all Jews. This results from the fact that "we all have one Father."[8] Furthermore, Jewish souls rooted in their Source are indeed one entity and thus completely united.[9] There are also specific qualities found within all Jews that are uniquely personal.[10]

Yet even these individual and personal qualities may lead to unity among the Jewish people. This comes about when all individuals realize that all Jews need each other, and can be complete only when they bind themselves with their fellows.[11]

Ultimately, both these qualities should merge. Even when Jews are aware of their singular qualities, they should also feel that not only do they need other Jew for the qualities possessed by others and which they themselves lack, but that all Jews are truly one entity.

The dedicatory offerings of the tribal princes were offered in a similar manner. Each prince brought his tribe's unique offering on a separate day. However, each of these unique offerings was accompanied by the feeling that it was also a communal offering — at one with all the other princes and tribes.

Based on *Likkutei Sichos*, Vol. XXIII, pp. 53-59.

---

8. *Tanya*, ch. 32.
9. *Ibid.*
10. *Likkutei Torah*, beginning of *Nitzavim*.
11. *Ibid.*

Behaalos'cha   בהעלתך

Why Lose the Privilege?

In the portion of *Behaalos'cha* the Torah relates how the
Jewish people sacrificed the Paschal offering on the fourteenth day of Nissan, one year after their Exodus from
Egypt.[1] This was the only Paschal offering they were commanded to bring during the 40 years they spent in the desert.[2]

There were certain people who were ritually impure at
that time and consequently could not bring the offering.
They came before Moshe and Aharon and said: "Why should
we lose the privilege of bringing the offering?" G-d there-
upon told Moshe to tell the people that those who were unable to bring the offering at the appointed time could do
so one month later, on the fourteenth of Iyar.[3]

The purpose of the Torah is not to serve as a history book,
but to teach us how to live our lives. The events it records are
therefore not necessarily listed in chronological order.[4] However, when *dates* of events are specified and at the same time
the events themselves are not listed in chronological order,
there must be a reason for it.

The Book of *Bamidbar* begins by describing the census of
the Jewish people that took place a year and a month after the
Jewish people left Egypt, as the Torah itself indicates. The
events surrounding the Paschal offering, described in *Behaalo-
s'cha*, the *third* portion in the Book of *Bamidbar*, took place one
month earlier. This is also explicitly stated in the Torah.
Nevertheless the Book of *Bamidbar* does not begin with this
event, as it seemingly should.

---

1. *Bamidbar* 9:1-5.
2. *Rashi* on *Shmos* 12:25.
3. *Bamidbar* 9:6-12.
4. *Pesachim* 6b.

Why, indeed, does the Book of *Bamidbar* not begin, in chronological order, with the events surrounding the Paschal offering the Jews brought in the desert?

Rashi[5] explains that "this is because this [event of bringing the Paschal offering] bespeaks the shame of the Jewish people; during all of the forty years that the Jews were in the desert they brought the Paschal offering only once." The Torah seeks[6] to begin a new Book with "praises of Israel" and not with their shame; beginning the Book of *Bamidbar* in chronological order would have defeated this purpose.

The following objection to *Rashi's* explanation may be raised: The reason the Jewish people brought the Paschal offering only once during their entire forty-year sojourn in the desert was simply that they were never again commanded by G-d to do so (while in the desert)! How, then, was their failure to bring additional Paschal offerings an act that "bespeaks their shame"?

Although the Jews were indeed not commanded to bring additional Passover offerings in the desert, this command was unlike other commands that *could* only be fulfilled in *Eretz Yisrael*: G-d simply *did not command them* to bring additional Paschal offerings in the desert. Furthermore, when the few individual Jews who lacked the opportunity to bring the offering at its appointed time requested a chance to offer it they were given the opportunity to do so a month later — something not found concerning any other command or offering.

This being so, the Jewish people should have requested and demanded the privilege of bringing the Paschal offering in the subsequent thirty-nine years of their sojourn in the desert! That they did not do so *points* to their "shame". Had the Jewish people stated: "Why should we lose the privilege," G-d would have acceded to their request.

But why did Moshe and Aharon and others of similar

---

5. On *Bamidbar* 9:1.
6. See *Rashi,* beginning of *Shmos, Vayikra, Bamidbar.*

stature not request that the people be allowed to bring the Paschal offering during these years?

Jewish leaders are entirely dedicated to the good of all of Israel.[7] The "shame" of the Jewish people by not taking a lesson from those who said, "Why should we lose the privilege," was — up to that point — not especially great. After all, we only find that G-d acceded to the requests of those who desired to bring a *compensatory* offering.

Had the petitioning of Moshe and Aharon given rise to a *new* Paschal offering, the shame of the Jewish people would have been *heightened:* Why had the people themselves not requested this? Moshe and Aharon were ready to forego their own spiritual advancement (through 39 Paschal offerings) for the sake of the Jewish people. They did not want the Jewish people to be shamed any more than they already were.

The "Eternal Torah"[8] here teaches us an eternal lesson: Jews may always request, "Why should we lose the privilege?" This request is especially apt now, in relation to our ultimate desire for the coming of *Mashiach*.

Based on Likkutei Sichos, Vol. XXIII, pp. 62-72.

---

7. See *Shmos* 32:32; cf. *Likkutei Sichos*, Vol. XXI, p. 173ff.
8. *Tanya*, ch. 17.

Sounding the Trumpets

In the Torah portion of *Behaalos'cha* we learn of G-d's command to Moshe to make two silver trumpets.[1] The Torah goes on to say: "When you go to war in your land against an enemy who oppresses you, you shall sound a staccato on the trumpets. You will then be remembered before G-d your L-rd, and will be delivered from your enemies. And on your days of rejoicing [when you celebrate your victories], on your

---

1. *Bamidbar* 10:1-2.

festivals, and on your new-moon celebrations, you shall sound a note with the trumpets for your burnt offerings and your peace offerings...."[2]

How are we to understand these verses in terms of man's personal spiritual service at all times and in all places?

"When you go to war... against an enemy who oppresses you..." alludes to the constant war man wages against his evil inclination[3] — the "enemy who oppresses you"; for "no other enemy oppresses us as he does."[4] This is especially true during the time of prayer, for "the time of prayer is the time of battle."[5] At that time, both the divine and animal souls strengthen themselves to the utmost, each one trying to overcome the other.[6] The evil inclination then engages the good inclination in battle, and endeavors to unsettle the individual by invading him with all kinds of alien thoughts.

One can achieve victory, the Torah teaches us, by "sounding a staccato," i.e., by humbling oneself to the point of weeping with the brokenhearted, staccato sobs of contrition. Standing humbled and nullified before G-d, he can sincerely beseech "that He have mercy upon his soul and save it from the 'turbulent waters.'"[7] Doing so will ensure the promise of the verse — that "you will then be remembered before G-d your L-rd, and will be delivered from your enemies."

A person may mistakenly think that this manner of service is necessary only at the beginning of his spiritual quest — that once victory over the enemy has been secured and he serves G-d intellectually and pleasurably, then self-nullification and subservience are no longer necessary.

To correct this misconception Scripture tells us: "And on your days of rejoicing ...you shall sound a note with the

---

2. *Ibid.,* verses 9-10.
3. *Shaloh, Cheilek Torah Shebichsav, Behaalos'cha,* 351a.
4. *Shaloh, ibid.;* see also *Tzror HaMor* on this Torah portion, quoting *Midrash HaNe'elam.*
5. *Zohar,* quoted and explained in *Likkutei Torah, Teitzei* (34c, 35c) *et al.*
6. *Tanya,* ch. 28 (p. 69).
7. *Ibid.* (p. 70).

trumpets for your burnt offerings and your peace offerings...." Even after having vanquished the enemy and having
attained a state of closeness to G-d — as indicated by the
bringing of offerings — the trumpets must still be sounded;
i.e., self-nullification and self-abnegation are still a necessary
ingredient of one's divine service.

With regard to the offerings themselves, the Torah indicates that burnt offerings — offerings wholly consumed
upon the altar — are to be presented first, and only afterwards are peace offerings to be brought. In terms of man's
spiritual service this implies that one must first totally negate
("consume") himself; only then can he bring the peace offering from which personal pleasure may be derived — by serving G-d intellectually and pleasurably.

In a more general sense, the burnt offering indicates
prayer, wherein one totally cleaves to G-d, while the peace
offering represents man's labor throughout the day. Concerning his personal labor it is necessary that it, too, be done
in such a way "all *your* actions should be for the sake of
heaven,"[8] and "in all *your* ways you shall know Him."[9] Furthermore, the fact that the burnt offering precedes the
peace offering alludes to the principle that one may not
engage in one's personal affairs before prayer.[10]

Based on Likkutei Sichos, Vol. XIII, pp. 24-29.

---

8. *Avos* 2:12.
9. *Mishlei* 3:6.
10. *Shulchan Aruch Admur HaZaken* 89:4.

Shlach   שלח

Faithful Understanding

The passage entitled *Shlach* relates at length how Moshe sent twelve fine and upstanding individuals[1] to spy out *Eretz Yisrael.* This was done in order to find out the best and easiest way[2] of conquering the land,[3] and also to obtain more information about the land itself.[4] They were to demonstrate the quality of the land to their brethren by returning with some of the fruits of the land.[5]

While faith is of extreme importance, and is the basis for the observance of the Torah,[6] faith itself does not suffice. After prefacing pure and simple faith, G-d desires that Jews exercise their understanding as well.

The same was true about entering *Eretz Yisrael.* Although G-d had already told the people that the land was good, He desired that they not only *believe* that it was good, but that they see (comprehend) this for themselves. "Hearing [and believing] cannot compare to seeing [and understanding]."[7]

So vital was it that the Jewish people should desire to enter the land as a result of the positive impressions they would gain of its goodness, that it was felt that for this purpose it was even worthwhile to endanger the lives of the spies.[8]

So, too, regarding the first phase of their mission — to

---

1. *Rashi* on *Bamidbar* 13:3, based on *Tanchuma, Shlach* 4; *Bamidbar Rabbah* 16:5; *Zohar* III, p. 158a.
2. *Ramban* on the beginning of *Shlach.*
3. *Bamidbar* 13:18-19.
4. *Loc. cit.,* 19-20.
5. *Ibid.*
6. See *Shabbos* 88a.
7. See *Mechilta* on *Yisro, Shmos* 19:9.
8. *Ramban* and *Sforno* on *Bamidbar* 13:20.

seek out the easiest way of conquering the land, so that the people would comprehend with their own intelligence that this was definitely possible.

Upon their return, these find and upstanding individuals committed the grave sin of telling the Jewish people that the land would be impossible to conquer.[9] Inasmuch as they had witnessed "mighty people"[10] and "descendants of the giants,"[11] the spies felt in their own minds that they were correct to logically *conclude*, in their presentation before the Jewish people, that the land would be impossible to conquer.

In this they misunderstood Moshe. He had never asked them *whether* the land *could* be conquered; he had sent them in order to ascertain *how* it would be *easiest* to conquer. On the contrary, since he sent them to find out the best way the land could be conquered, it was evidently conquerable by natural means. [If it could be accomplished only in a miraculous manner, spies would be superfluous.] Thus, the spies' testimony that the land was unconquerable opposed the whole thrust of their mission.

The spies committed this grievous error because they were too much aware of their own selves and their own logical conclusions, and not sufficiently bound and subservient to Moshe, whose whole being was truth.[12] Had they been more attached to Moshe and less concerned with themselves, they would not have been so fearful of the "descendants of the giants," in whose eyes they felt themselves to be "mere grasshoppers."[13]

Moshe knew that the land was conquerable; their faith in him would have caused them, too, to rightfully understand that "the land which the L-rd our G-d is giving us, is good."[14]

*　　　*　　　*

---

9. *Loc. cit.*, v. 31.
10. *Loc. cit.*, v. 28, 32-33.
11. *Ibid.*
12. See *Sanhedrin* 111a; cf. *Shmos Rabbah* 5:10.
13. *Bamidbar* 13:33.
14. *Devarim* 1:25.

A Jew would do well to remember that even when he is involved in matters that require his own comprehension, he is doing so as Moshe's messenger; i.e., he must seek to understand the subject at hand not out of his own individual desire, but because G-d desires him to do so.

He will then be assured of understanding matters truthfully, rather than foisting his own subjective and erroneous interpretations on the truth — something that easily happens when one is blinded by self-love.

Based on *Likkutei Sichos,* Vol. XXIII, pp. 92-95.

Challah: A Negation of Idolatry

In the Torah portion of *Shlach* we learn of the precept of *challah.* This entailed separating the first portion of the kneaded dough as an offering and consecrating it to G-d, by giving it to the *Kohanim.*[1] The *Midrash* states: "Why does the passage in the Torah describing the *mitzvah* of *challah* appear next to the laws concerning idolatry? This is to teach us that whoever fulfills the precept of *challah* is considered as if he had negated idolatry; whoever fails to fulfill it is considered as if he had reinforced idolatry."[2]

At first glance the words of the *Midrash* seem to be truly perplexing. What possible connection is there between the simple act of separating a piece of dough with the negation of idolatry? This is especially troubling, since negating idolatry is fundamental to the Jewish faith, a bastion of the whole Torah, while the dough offering is just one particular *mitzvah.*

All of man's needs may be termed "dough", for nourishment, which is symbolized by bread — the "staff of life" — is essential to his existence. In order to obtain his daily bread, man must plow, sow, reap, and so forth — all in accordance

---

1. *Bamidbar* 15:17-21.
2. *Vayikra Rabbah* 15:6.

with the laws of nature. This being so, one may possibly err and think that his sustenance is not dependent upon G-d, but rather upon the laws of nature. Even if he is aware that it was G-d who established the laws of nature, he may still miscalculate and think that these principles are no longer dependent upon Him.

Herein comes the lesson of *challah*. Before a person benefits from his dough he must recognize (and actualize the thought) that the very *first* portion, i.e., its very being, is derived from G-d. And the same is true of his other needs as well. Thus, *challah* teaches us that it is not man's laboring according to the established rules of nature that provides him with his sustenance. Rather,[3] "it is He who gives you the power to become prosperous,"[4] and "it is G-d's blessing that assures wealth."[5]

Additionally, since G-d continuously[6] renews Creation, His blessing does far more than merely clothe itself in nature and in man's actions. For all aspects of nature and all that a person does have no intrinsic existence: they exist solely because they are constantly recreated and revivified by G-d. The sin of idolatry consists not only of actually serving idols — G-d forbid — and recognizing them as deities. Even if the forces of nature are acknowledged to possess independent power and dominion, this, too, constitutes idolatry.[7] And this is so even when one acknowledges that the forces of nature were originally created by G-d and by Him were endowed with their might.[8]

In truth, all the forces of nature possess no free will at all; they are but the tools through which G-d conducts the world. No one asks the ax whether wood is to be chopped. The forces

---

3. See introduction to *Derech Chayim; Kuntreis U'Maayan, maamar 17, et al.*
4. *Devarim* 8:18.
5. *Mishlei* 10:22.
6. Beginning of *Shaar HaYichud VehaEmunah* (*Tanya*, p. 152).
7. See *Rambam*, beginning of *Hilchos Avodah Zarah.*
8. See *Rambam, ibid.:* "...and this was the main form of idolatry."

of nature are but channels through which G-d's beneficence flows.[9]

In a more refined sense, maintaining that there is true existence other than G-d's is a subtle form of idolatry, for nothing at all truly exists apart from Him.

When a Jew fails to fulfill the precept of *challah*, i.e., he fails to recognize that all his sustenance and needs are provided him by G-d, "he is considered as if he *reinforced* idolatry." For by negating the principle of *challah* he reinforces the mistaken notion that nature has the ability to provide for him, and that it possesses a will, ability and existence of its own. Conversely, by performing the *mitzvah* of *challah*, one *negates* idolatry, for he demonstrates that everything in this world is wholly dependent on G-d, and owes its existence to Him.[10]

Based on *Likkutei Sichos*, Vol. XVIII, pp. 183-185.

---

9. See also *Sefer HaMitzvos* of the *Tzemach Tzedek*, *Mitzvas Milah*, ch. 3; *Mitzvas Tiglachas Metzora*, ch. 3; *Kuntreis U'Maayan*, *maamar* 23, ch. 1; *maamar* 24ff.

10. See also *Likkutei Torah*, *Shir HaShirim* 64d; *maamar* entitled *Veyadata*, in *Sefer HaMaamarim* 5657; *maamar* entitled *LeOlam Yehei Adam Zahir*, 5691.

Korach   קרח

Unity vs. Uniformity

In this portion we read of Korach's rebellion against Moshe and Aharon. Underlying his revolt was his charge: "All the people in the community are holy and G-d is in their midst; why are you setting yourselves above G-d's congregation?"[1] Korach thus desired that there should not be any differences between Jews; it goes without saying, that no single Jew should lord over the rest. He was obviously intent upon bringing unity within the ranks of the Jewish people. How is it then that his actions led to so much discord and dissent — the very antithesis of what he was seeking?

This may be understood by analyzing Moshe's answer to Korach, as explained in the *Midrash*:[2] Moshe said, "In the *morning* G-d will make known...."[3] Explains the *Midrash*: "Moshe said to them, 'G-d has placed boundaries in His world'.... Can you possibly intermingle night and day?... So, too, has He separated Aharon.... You have the same chance of negating Aharon's separate sanctity as you have of undoing G-d's separation of night and day.'"

The *Midrash* may be understood as follows. G-d created the world in a manner wherein each created being is different and distinct from the other. Only when each aspect of creation fulfills its own purpose can it unite with the rest of creation in implementing the total purpose of the greater whole. When a created being does not accomplish its appointed task but rather performs the task of another, it causes a disruption in G-d's orderly creative process.

---

1. *Bamidbar* 16:3.
2. *Midrash Tanchuma, Korach* 5; *Bamidbar Rabbah, Korach* 7.
3. *Bamidbar* 16:5.

Just as each creature performing its appointed task leads to a state of peace and harmony within creation, so, too, with regard to the various states of sanctity found within the world: tranquillity and harmony in the spiritual realm can be best achieved when each level achieves its exclusive objective.[4]

However, acting in the above manner has yet to achieve complete peace and true harmony, for while these levels do not encroach on one another, neither do they yet help each other. Ultimate peace and harmony only come about when each level supports the other, helping it achieve what it could not accomplish on its own.

For example: The Alter Rebbe explains[5] how all Jews are part of one whole and need each other, like the different parts of the human body which when taken together as a whole constitute a complete human being. Just as each limb possesses its own characteristic and unique quality that benefits the body as a whole, so, too, are the Jewish people divided into different spiritual "limbs"; each Jew has his own mission and task and every Jew benefits all other Jews by accomplishing his distinctive function.

Understandably, this level of peaceful unity can be achieved only when the boundaries of each individual limb and Jew are clearly delineated, for unity is achieved by joining disparate entities into one whole. A body cannot possibly be a composite solely of heads, hands, or whatever. However, as holiness exists in its divine *source*, i.e., within G-d, it exists as truly one entity, for G-d is true and simple Unity. This level of unity will be revealed only during the era of *Mashiach*.

Korach maintained that "all the people are holy"; he desired that the peace and unity of the Jewish people should exist during his lifetime — in the same manner as it exists within its source, and as it shall indeed be in the time to come, when there will be no disparate levels, all being utterly united

---

4. See *Likkutei Sichos*, Vol. XVII, p. 227ff.
5. *Likkutei Torah*, beginning of *Nitzavim*.

with G-d. However, this desire was foolish, for within the time frame of temporal existence and within the levels in which sanctity is achieved through practical deeds, differences in intensity of performance and levels of sanctity are indeed necessary. Negating this can only lead to strife.

Based on *Likkutei Sichos,* Vol XVIII, pp. 203-209.

The Desire to be a High Priest

The Torah portion of *Korach* describes how Korach led a band of 250 men in a rebellion against Moshe and Aharon. They all desired to become high priests and be like Aharon the high priest, who was always able to "stand before G-d and serve Him."[1]

The *Midrash*[2] tells us that in trying to dissuade them from their folly, Moshe said to them: "We have but one G-d...and but one high priest; the 250 of you all desire to be high priests?! I, too, desire to be one!"

Moshe was telling them that while their desire was proper and laudable, and was in fact shared by Moshe himself, it was also unrealistic, since there could only be one high priest at any given time.

When G-d gave the Torah to the Jewish people He said to them: "And you shall be to Me a kingdom of priests and a holy nation."[3] The *Baal HaTurim* comments:[4] When G-d gave the Torah to the Jewish people they all were on the level of high priests. Korach's band desired to attain this lofty level once again.

With regard to the tribe of Levi, the *Rambam*[5] states that

---

1. *Devarim* 10:8.
2. *Tanchuma* on *Parshas Korach* 5; *Bamidbar Rabbah* 18:8; cf. *Rashi* on *Bamidbar* 16:6.
3. *Shmos* 19:6.
4. *Ibid.*
5. *Hilchos Shemitah VeYovel* 13:12-13.

"they were singled out for divine labor and service, and to teach His just and righteous paths and laws.... They were therefore isolated from worldly affairs...they are G-d's army." He goes on to say: "Not only the tribe of Levi, but all individuals whose spirit moves them...are sanctified [i.e., are deemed] to be 'holy of holies.'"

Thus, we have an anomaly: any Jew, if he so desires, *may* attain the level of the tribe of Levi; he is however not obliged to do so. However, Jews could aspire to the level of high priest, though it is impossible to become one.

*   *   *

There are three general degrees in divine service: *mitzvos,* Torah study, and *mesirus nefesh,* total self-sacrifice for G-d. Performing *mitzvos* involves interaction with the physical world and elevating it to holiness. Torah, however, always remains aloof from physicality[6] — "Torah is not subject to spiritual impurity."[7] According to the Torah itself, *mesirus nefesh* transcends the bounds and limitations of Torah and *mitzvos,* enabling the individual to unite with G-d without restriction.

Most Jews serve G-d in the first manner — that of "those who do good deeds,"[8] although, they, too, must also fix times for daily Torah study. The tribe of Levi, and those who choose their lifestyle, are more concerned with the study of Torah. The service of the high priest, however — that of cleaving to G-d in a manner of *mesirus nefesh* — is not a manner of daily service for every Jew.

Service of G-d with *mesirus nefesh* is so powerful, that it is unrealistic that an individual should serve G-d in such a manner on a daily basis and still be able to keep his soul from fleeing the encumbrances of the body. Indeed, if the soul did flee the body, this would be contrary to G-d's desire.

G-d desires that in this physical world the soul shall be

---

6. See *Likkutei Torah, Re'eh* 20a.
7. *Berachos* 22a.
8. See *Iggeres HaKodesh,* Epistle 5 (p. 109a).

clothed in the body, serving Him and transforming the world into a dwelling place for Him through the service of *mitzvos* and Torah. Still, all Jews should desire to reach the high-priestly state of *mesirus nefesh*. For this *desire* leads to selfless dedication to G-d, enabling the individual to perform *mitzvos* and study Torah, utterly without qualification.

Based on *Likkutei Sichos*, Vol. XVIII, pp. 188-195.

Chukas   חקת

The Red Heifer: A Foundation of Torah

The commandments of the Torah are divided into three general categories: *eidos*, testimonies; *chukim*, decrees; and *mishpatim*, laws.[1]

Eidos are those commandments that recall and/or testify to past significant events. Examples are *Shabbos*, Pesach, Shavuos and Sukkos.

Mishpatim are those commands that are also dictated by mortal understanding. Examples are the obligation to honor one's parents or give charity, and the prohibition against stealing.

Chukim are commands that have no rational explanation. In commenting on the verse, "This [law of the Red Heifer] is the *chukah* of the Torah...,"[2] *Rashi*[3] notes the following: "Satan and the nations challenge Jews, 'What kind of *mitzvah* is the Red Heifer, and what rationale is there for it?' The Torah therefore prefaces this *mitzvah* with a declaration that uses the term *chukah*: this is a decree ordained by G-d....'"

Indeed, among *chukim* themselves, the most puzzling of all is the command of the Red Heifer. Even King Solomon, the wisest of men, who could understand the divine rationale underlying other *chukim*, could not fathom the reasoning behind the command of the Red Heifer, which brought purity to the impure and rendered the pure impure.[4] Concerning this decree, he admitted: "I said, 'I will gain wisdom,' but it is

---

1. See *Devarim* 4:45.
2. *Bamidbar* 19:2.
3. *Loc. cit.*
4. *Bamidbar Rabbah* 19:3.

far from me."[5] The command of the Red Heifer transcended even the superior intellect of King Solomon.

The terminology, "This is the *chukah of the Torah,*" rather than "This is the *chukah* of the Red Heifer," indicates that the inexplicable decree of the Red Heifer *is the Torah:* it is a foundation for the whole Torah,[6] including its commandments. Even the commandments of *eidos* and *mishpatim,* the rational commands, are essentially expressions of the divine will,[7] and as such they transcend logic — they, too, are *chukim,* just like the law of the Red Heifer. However, G-d desired that the divine will underlying these commands descend and become clothed in intellectual categories.

The same is true with regard to Torah.[8] Even those matters in Torah that are comprehended by human intellect are, in fact, suprarational. After all, Torah is *G-d's wisdom;* just[9] as no created being can comprehend his Creator,[10] likewise it is impossible for any created being to comprehend His wisdom.

Knowledge of this matter is basic to one's spiritual service of Torah and *mitzvos.* The performance of all *mitzvos,* the rational as well as the suprarational, ought to be motivated by *kabbalas ol,* accepting the heavenly yoke upon oneself, and performing the commandments because G-d has so decreed. This is mirrored in the text of the blessing made for all *mitzvos* — "…and He has *commanded* us." The same is true with regard to Torah study.

This is why the rationale for the commandment of the Red Heifer remained concealed even from King Solomon; it was necessary that at least one command of the Torah remain in a state of *chukah,* thus indicating that the rest of the Torah and *mitzvos* were essentially similar — they, too, were *chukim.*[11]

---

5. *Koheles* 7:23.
6. *Likkutei Torah,* beginning of *Chukas.*
7. See commentary of *Or HaChayim* on this verse.
8. Cf. *Likkutei Sichos,* Vol. IV, p. 1056ff. and notes *ad loc.;* Vol. VIII, p. 129ff.; Vol. XIII, p. 67.
9. See *Likkutei Sichos,* Vol. XVII, p. 319ff.
10. See *Shaar HaYichud VehaEmunah,* chs. 4 and 8.
11. See *Rambam, Hilchos Yesodei HaTorah* 1:5-10; *op. cit.,* ch. 8, *et passim.*

Furthermore, if all Torah matters were to have descended to a rational level it would be impossible for us to perform *mitzvos* with the feeling that we were doing so solely because they voice G-d's will. Additionally, inasmuch as the performance of *mitzvos* would then be limited to rational understanding, it would be impossible for a Jew to reach the level of *mesirus nefesh*, total self-sacrifice for G-d, a level that defies and transcends the limitations of intellect.

*   *   *

An individual who exemplified this latter manner of service was the previous Lubavitcher Rebbe, Rabbi Yosef I. Schneersohn, who was known as the "man of *mesirus nefesh*." The 12th of *Tammuz*, the day on which we read the Torah portion(s) of *Chukas* (and *Balak*) this year, marks the date of his liberation in the year 1927 from Communist imprisonment. He was incarcerated for upholding Judaism under the most trying circumstances — a paradigm of utter *mesirus nefesh*.

Based on *Likkutei Sichos*, Vol. XVIII, pp. 229-237.

The Bond between Body & Soul

The passage entitled *Chukas* begins by setting out the laws for the purification of an individual who has become ritually defiled by coming in contact with a corpse. This defilement is called *tumas meis*.

In relation to this the *Midrash*[1] recounts the following incident. When Moshe became aware of the degree of defilement that comes about through *tumas meis*, he asked G-d: "If a person becomes so defiled, how is he to attain purification?" Even after G-d answered him, "They shall take for the impure person from the ashes of the burnt atonement offering...," Moshe was still not completely satisfied, asking G-d, "Is this indeed purification?"[2]

---

1. *Bamidbar Rabbah* 19:4; *Tanchuma* (end of) 6.
2. *Koheles Rabbah* 8:1(5).

Why was Moshe so troubled by the difficulty of achieving purification from *tumas meis*? We find that there are a number of other types of defilement such as *tumas zav* and *tumas metzora*[3] which in many aspects are even more severe than *tumas meis*. Why did Moshe feel that securing this particular purification should be so difficult?

*   *   *

All other ritual defilements of a Jew are related to a living body. Even after it has become defiled, it still houses a soul which is "truly a part of G-d above."[4] Since G-d's ability is limitless, it may be readily understood that the soul is able to rectify the impurity, so that ultimately (e.g., through immersion in a *mikveh*) the person will become purified.

However, this is not the case regarding *tumas meis*, wherein the very impurity stems from the fact that the body — having become sundered from the soul — has ceased to live; a body separated from its soul is but an inanimate object.

Moshe was therefore perplexed: "How is purification possible," he thought, "from such a severe manner of defilement?"

G-d relieved his anxiety by saying, "These are the laws of the Torah": the effect of the Torah and its *mitzvos* is so powerful that it can bring about purification even after the soul departs from the body.

*   *   *

On a deeper and more esoteric level: The spiritual aspect of defilement refers to a blemish on a Jew's relationship with G-d. Jews are considered to be "alive" as a result of their cleaving to Him.[5] When a Jew sins, this bond with G-d is weakened; he is thus less "alive" and becomes defiled. The further his relationship with G-d diminishes, the greater is his state of defilement.

Even when there is a serious breach in his relationship

---

3. See *Pesachim* 67b ff.; *Rambam, Hilchos Biyas Mikdash* 3:2ff.
4. *Tanya,* beginning of ch. 2 (p. 11).
5. *Avos deRabbi Nasan,* conclusion of ch. 34.

with G-d, causing his defilement to be quite severe, nevertheless, so long as the relationship is not severed, the Jew retains his innate ability to become pure again by firming up his commitment to G-d and to His Torah and *mitzvos*. However, when a Jew transgresses so severely that his cleaving to G-d is severed, then this results in the impurity of *tumas meis*.[6]

Moshe was baffled when it came to the means of purification from so forbidding a defilement. He could not understand how it could be possible to achieve purification from *tumas meis*. G-d resolved his perplexity by assuring him that a Jew's relationship to G-d is never totally sundered. The innate relationship of a Jew with G-d and the effect of his previous fulfillment of Torah and *mitzvos* is so great, that even *tumas meis* is subject to purification.

Based on Likkutei Sichos, Vol. XVIII, pp. 232-234.

---

6. See *Iggeres HaTeshuvah*, chs. 4-6; *Kuntreis U'Maayan, maamar* 7.

Balak   בלק
Yud-Beis Tammuz   י״ב תמוז

The Ultimate Miracle

The *Shaloh* states[1] that all Jewish festivals, including those of Rabbinic origin, are related to the Torah readings of the weeks in which they occur. Understandably, this also applies to the Festival of Liberation of the 12th-13th of Tammuz, which celebrates the release of the Previous Lubavitcher Rebbe from Soviet incarceration and exile, to which he had been sentenced for his selfless dedication to the propagation of Judaism. The festival is thus related to the Torah portion of *Balak*, during which week it falls this year. But how?

Our Sages tell us[2] that Balak hated the Jewish people with a passion. He therefore endeavored to harm them in every imaginable way, including the hiring of the sorcerer Bilam.[3]

The same was true with regard to those who arrested the Previous Lubavitcher Rebbe. As he himself wrote in a letter,[4] his religious work was "permitted according to the laws of the land." The arrest resulted from the efforts of those who sought to disrupt "those who observe the laws of Moshe and Israel," although this disruption was *"in opposition* to the laws of the land." The hatred of these people to Judaism and to observant Jews was — like Balak's — so great that they were ready to contravene the laws of the land, so long as this would hinder the Previous Rebbe's sacred work. And just as Balak and Bilam were dismally unsuccessful in their quest, so much so, that instead of cursing them, as he was hired to do,[5] Bilam ended up blessing the Jews, so, too, regarding the liberation of the Previous Lubavitcher Rebbe: the very same people

---

1. *Cheilek Torah Shebichsav,* beginning of *Vayeishev* (p. 297a).
2. *Tanchuma, Balak* 2; *Bamidbar Rabbah* 20:2.
3. *Bamidbar* 22:5ff.
4. *Sefer HaMaamarim 5688,* p. 263ff.
5. *Bamidbar* 22:6.

responsible for his arrest were forced to assist in his release, expending efforts to allow the Rebbe to leave the country.[6] This highlights the fact that his miraculous release took place in a manner that could even be clothed in nature. Rather than nullifying the bounds of nature, the miracle of his release was so lofty that it took place in a natural way.

* * *

Generally speaking, there are three paths of divine conduct in relation to this world:[7] (a) the natural day-to-day conduct of this world; (b) miraculous conduct that transcends and negates the bounds of nature; (c) miraculous conduct in so high an order of divine revelation, that rather than negating nature it is able to clothe itself *within* nature.

Concerning the latter manner, nature itself is so permeated with spirituality that it agrees and lends itself to the miracle. Such was the miracle of Purim. Although clothed in nature, it was clear to all that its impelling causes transcended nature by far. Such too was the miracle of the 12th-13th of Tammuz, wherein the same people who ordered that the Rebbe be arrested had to later order that he be released.

The Previous Rebbe merited this manner of miracle because his very being was permeated with actual and total self-sacrifice. Indeed, his work of spreading Judaism in "that country" necessitated self-sacrifice for each and every aspect of Torah and *mitzvos*.

Our Rabbis tell us[8] that divine service infused by self-sacrifice reaches so lofty a level that it transforms nature itself into a vessel for G-dliness. The Previous Lubavitcher Rebbe's unstintingly self-sacrificing service thus resulted in a miracle of the highest order.

Based on *Likkutei Sichos*, Vol. XVIII, pp. 237-238, 300-306.

---

6. See *Likkutei Sichos*, Vol. VIII, p. 120ff.; Vol. IV, p. 1065ff.
7. See *Or HaTorah, Acharei*, p. 564; *Or HaTorah, Bereishis* 18b ff.; *maamar* entitled *HaChodesh HaZeh*, 5666.
8. See *Torah Or* 99d ff.

# Pinchas					פינחס

Pinchas' Reward: Peace & Priesthood

The portion of *Pinchas* begins with the statement of G-d to Moshe: "Pinchas...has turned My wrath away from the Children of Israel, when he displayed anger among them in My behalf, so that I did not wipe out the Children of Israel in My anger. Therefore say: I grant him My covenant of peace. Unto him and his progeny after him, will be granted the covenant of everlasting priesthood, for he displayed anger and brought atonement for the children of Israel."[1]

Although Moshe himself had turned away G-d's wrath from the Jewish people not once, but on numerous occasions,[2] as related in the Torah,[3] we do not find that he was granted the "covenant of peace unto him and his progeny after him." Moreover, even though Moshe specifically expressed the desire that his sons should succeed him to the leadership of the Jewish people,[4] his wish was not granted.

Moshe and Pinchas assuaged G-d's anger in divergent ways. Moshe accomplished this by praying; his prayers were heeded, and G-d nullified numerous decrees. Pinchas, however, accomplished this through his *actions* — by displaying zealous anger among the people, thereby bringing them to repentance.

There is another difference between the two in their manner of intercession on behalf of the Children of Israel.

1. *Bamidbar* 25:11-13.
2. See *Zohar* on *Parshas Pinchas*, p. 320a.
3. At the time of the sin of the Golden Calf — *Shmos* 32:11ff.; when the Jews were "as murmurers" — *Bamidbar* 11:2; after the return of the spies — *ibid.* 14:13. See also *Rashi, ibid.,* 16:4.
4. *Tanchuma* on *Pinchas* 25:11; *Bamidbar Rabbah* 21:14; *Rashi* on *Bamidbar* 27:16.

After the sin of the Golden Calf, Moshe said to G-d: "...and if You will not [forgive the Jewish people], then erase me from the book that You have written (i.e., the Torah)."[5]

Moshe's self-sacrifice[6] on behalf of the Jewish people was spiritual in nature. Pinchas, on the other hand, placed his physical life in jeopardy, arousing the ire of the tribe of Shimon who sought to kill him[7] when he sought to stave off G-d's anger against the Jews; this was physical self-sacrifice.

The difference between Moshe and Pinchas also manifested itself in their *personal* manner of divine service.[8] Moshe's service was at the level of the soul,[9] while Pinchas' service was more at the level of bodily service. Therefore, when it came to their self-sacrifice, Moshe's self-sacrifice was spiritual in nature, while the self-sacrifice of Pinchas was physical in nature.

When a person's spiritual service comes as a result of divine illumination permeating the physical world, as was the case with Moshe, there is no guarantee of its lasting effect. This is because the spiritual illumination does not purify and elevate the physical level in which it is manifest.[10] It is therefore possible that as soon as the divine illumination ceases, materiality reverts to its earlier state.

Thus we find that though G-d's gift of the Torah to the Jewish people freed them of spiritual taint,[11] nevertheless it was still possible for them to soon afterwards commit the grave sin of the Golden Calf.

However, when spiritual illumination results from *man's* service, as was the case with the spiritual service of Pinchas — elevating and purifying the material world itself, and leading

---

5. *Shmos* 32:32.
6. See *Zohar, ibid.*
7. See *Sifri* and *Tanchuma,* end of *Parshas Balak; Sanhedrin* 82b.
8. Cf. end of *maamar* beginning *Vaydaber...Pinchas,* 5675.
9. See *Hemshech Taf-Reish-Samach-Vav* (5666), pp. 158ff., and p. 558, *maamar* beginning *VeHar Sinai,* 5708.
10. See *Likkutei Torah, Vayikra* 2d.
11. *Shabbos* 146a; *Zohar* I, p. 52b; *Zohar* II, p. 193b.

the people to repentance — then the effect is lasting and the atonement is permanent.[12]

This is why the blessing of the "everlasting covenant of peace and priesthood unto him and his progeny after him," was granted specifically to Pinchas. Because Pinchas succeeded in obtaining everlasting atonement for the Jewish people, he was rewarded — measure for measure — with the "everlasting covenant of peace and priesthood."

Based on *Likkutei Sichos*, Vol. XVIII, pp. 344-347.

---

12. *Sifri* on *Bamidbar* 25:13.

Personal & General Refinement

During the three weeks between the fast of the Seventeenth of Tammuz and the fast of Tishah beAv, the *Haftoros* do not reflect the contents of the weekly Torah readings, but deal instead with the tragic "times and events"[1] — the destruction of the Holy Temples and the subsequent Jewish exiles. Nevertheless, since all aspects of Torah are meticulously exact, it stands to reason that these *Haftoros* relate to the content of the weekly Torah readings as well.[2]

What is the connection between the Torah portion of *Pinchas* which relates — in part — how Pinchas upheld G-d's honor, and the *Haftorah*, which relates how Yirmeyahu became a prophet and then goes on to foretell the destruction of the Holy Temple?

Concerning the difference between the prophecies of Yirmeyahu and Yeshayahu, we find the following statement in the *Talmud:* "Yirmeyahu is all destruction ... and Yeshayahu is all consolation."[3] Yirmeyahu's prophecy concerned the de-

---

1. *Tur, Orach Chayim* 428.
2. See *Likkutei Sichos*, Vol. IX, p. 61 and fn.
3. *Bava Basra* 14b.

struction of the Holy Temple and the subsequent exile; Yeshayahu's prophecy revolved around the Jews' eventual redemption and consolation.

The difference in their prophecies was a direct result of the respective times in which they prophesized: "Yirmeyahu lived during a period in which Divinity was seemingly unapproachable and concealed; Yeshayahu lived during a time when Divinity was revealed."[4] Consequently, Yirmeyahu's prophecies relate to darkness and destruction, while Yeshayahu's prophecies bespeak revelation, consolation and redemption.

While it is true that Yeshayahu's prophecies contain many admonitions of the Jewish people for their sinful behavior, nonetheless they are considered to be "all consolation" since they led to repentance in a spirit of revelation and redemption. Yeshayahu inspired his brethren by dwelling on the consolatory theme of redemption, assuring them that this would be achieved through their repentance. Yirmeyahu, however, aroused Jews to repentance in a spirit of darkness and Divine self-concealment — by warning them of the terrible destruction that would overwhelm them should they not repent.

The *Midrash* informs us[5] that both Pinchas and Yirmeyahu descended from "foreign families." Because of their less than illustrious ancestry, both of them were treated disparagingly by their contemporaries. This gave rise to similar approaches in their spiritual service: both Pinchas and Yirmeyahu elevated the lower levels of creation and incorporated them into higher levels of holiness. This they did by elevating themselves, i.e., refining their own lower aspects — their "foreign families" — as well as their surroundings. Though they were both treated with contempt, they aroused and uplifted their fellow Jews to repentance.

The service of elevating the lower levels of creation,

---

4. *Sefer HaSichos 5703*, beginning of p. 140.
5. *Pesikta deRav Kahana* (Buber), ch. 13; *Yalkut Shimoni, Remez* 257.

whereby the worldly here and now is purified and refined, has the salutary effect of transforming those very levels — the levels of those who disparage holiness — into the realm of holiness.

In terms of man's personal spiritual service, the service of Pinchas — who refined both himself and the Jewish people — involves the purification and refinement of one's body and animal soul, as well as the portion of the world which G-d entrusted to him.

In a more general sense, this approach to divine service is the universal spiritual task of the time of exile: not to be fazed by the darkness, by the self-concealment of the Divine, and by the difficulties of exile. Rather, to transform this very darkness into illumination and into holiness — as in the divine service of Yirmeyahu, who thus addressed the issue of exile.

Based on *Likkutei Sichos*, Vol. XVIII, pp. 342-348.

Matos & Masei   מטות־מסעי

Of Staffs & Journeys

The readings of *Matos* and *Masei* are always read during *Bein HaMetzarim*,[1] the three-week period of quasi-mourning for the destruction of the *Beis HaMikdash*, the Holy Temple in Jerusalem. This year, these two portions are combined and read on the same *Shabbos*.

The name of a Torah portion indicates the theme of the portion as a whole.[2] This, or course, is also true of *Matos* and *Masei*. The literal meaning of the word *Matos* is "wooden staffs," and *Masei* means "journeys".

With respect to their tribal affiliations, the Jewish people are often referred to by the terms *shevatim* and *matos*, "branches" and "staffs".[3] A branch is a limb that — even when cut off — still retains some of the sap and nourishment of the original tree; it is therefore still moist and supple. A staff, however, is a thoroughly dried piece of wood; it is thus strong and firm. So, too, regarding these terms as appelatives of the Jewish people: *shevatim* and *matos* both signify that Jewish souls are rooted in the "divine tree"[4] of G-dliness. *Shevatim* denotes a revealed connection with G-dliness, while *matos* alludes to a connection that is not readily apparent.

In a general sense, *shevatim* intimates the pristine state of the soul before it descended into the corporeal world and into a physical body, while *matos* suggests the soul's coarsened state, after its descent. The title *Matos* thus implies the seem-

---

1. See *Shaloh*, p. 366a; cf. *Likkutei Sichos*, Vol. IX, p. 61, footnote 3.
2. See *Likkutei Sichos*, Vol. V, p. 57ff.
3. *Maamarei Admur HaZaken 5562*, p. 237ff; notes to *maamar* in *Or HaTorah*, *Matos*, p. 1294ff.; cf. *Or HaTorah*, *Beshalach*, end of p. 415; *Hemshech Te'erav* I, p. 322ff.
4. *Maamarei Admur HaZaken 5562*, ibid.

ing separation of souls from their source as a result of their descent into the physical world.

The title *Masei*, "journeys", referring as it does to the journeys of the people as they drew ever closer to the Promised Land, indicates — in terms of man's divine service — the journeys and advances achieved by the soul after its descent into a body, this descent having been in a manner of *matos*. Only through this descent is the soul able to attain a higher spiritual plane than it enjoyed before its descent. For by descending into a physical body, a state of *matos*, and utilizing physical reality in performing Torah and *mitzvos*, which are G-d's Will and Wisdom, the soul attains the state of *masei* — the dynamic of advancement through true spiritual "journeys".[5]

More specifically, both the soul's descent and its resultant spiritual advancement are alluded to in each of these two Torah portions.

The strength and firmness of *matos* not only alludes to the soul's descent, but also suggests the firmness in his spiritual service[6] that a Jew must possess in order to overcome the hindrances of the body and the corporeal world. It is necessary to have the firmness and strength of a mighty "staff", if one is not to be fazed by the impediments or blandishments of physicality.

The same is true with the Torah portion of *Masei*. The term *masei*, "journeys" (in the plural), not only refers to the soul's advance and "upward journey" achieved through the performance of Torah and *mitzvos*, but also indicates the soul's prior "downward journey" into the world.[7]

The connection between these two Torah portions and the period of *Bein HaMetzarim* now becomes clear. Both the ultimate descent of the soul — *matos*, and the soul's ultimate

---

5. See *Likkutei Torah*, pp. 38d, 67d; cf. *Torah Or*, p. 30a ff.; *Sefer HaMaamarim 5562*, p. 117ff.
6. See *Or HaTorah, Beshalach*, p. 417; *Or HaTorah, Matos* p. 1300.
7. See *Likkutei Torah, maamarim* on *Parshas Masei*.

ascent — *masei*, can only occur during the time of exile[8] which is brought about by the destruction of the Sanctuary, commemorated by the period of *Bein HaMetzarim*.

During exile,[9] when G-dliness is not revealed, as it was when the Sanctuary stood, the soul must strain itself to the utmost and, more than ever, use the firm and strong staff of *matos* to overcome the darkness of exile. When it ultimately succeeds in doing so, the advances and "upward journey" of the soul — *masei*, are realized to a much greater extent than was possible even during the time of the Temple's existence.

Based on *Likkutei Sichos*, Vol. XVIII, pp. 378-384.

---

8. See *Or HaTorah, Seitzei*, pp. 900, 910; cf. beginning of the *maamar* entitled *Ki Imcha*, 5700.
9. See also *Likkutei Torah* 98b; *Or HaTorah, Masei*, pp. 1358, 1365; *maamar* beginning *Kol Dodi*, ch. 2ff., ch. 11ff.

Masei   מסעי

A Tale of Two Journeys

There is a famous statement of the *Shaloh*[1] that the weekly
Torah readings are related to the time of year in which they
are read and studied. Since the Torah portion of *Masei* is
always read during *Bein HaMetzarim*, the three-week period of
quasi-mourning for the destruction of the Holy Temples and
the exile of the Jewish people, it follows that *Masei* and *Bein
HaMetzarim* are related.

In what lies this relationship?

Beyoned its description of the wanderings of the Jewish
people in the desert, *Masei* ("journeys") also alludes to the
downward journey of the soul from its source on high into
this lowly world.[2] In the words of our Sages, this Odyssey is
"truly a state of exile."[3] As the soul descends into this *Bein-
HaMetzarim*-world, this world of spiritual constriction,
fraught as it is with evil forces and temptations that may
draw it away from G-dliness, it becomes fearful. It wonders
how it can possibly fulfill its task — to remain holy and to
bring holiness into this worldly exile.

The reassurance given to the soul is found in the very
beginning of the first *Haftorah* of *Bein HaMetzarim*, which sets
the tone for all of man's divine service during this period. At
the very beginning of the soul's descent it is fortified and
encouraged by G-d's words to the Prophet, so that it will be
successful in fulfilling its *Bein-HaMetzarim*-mission.

In that *Haftorah*[4] the soul is told: "Before I formed you in

---

1. *Cheilek Torah Shebichsav,* beginning of *Vayeishev* (297a).
2. See *Likkutei Torah,* discourses on this Torah portion.
3. *Tanya,* ch. 37 (p. 96).
4. Beginning of *Yirmeyahu.*

the womb, I knew you, and before you left the womb, I sanctified you; I have made you a prophet unto the nations."⁵ In effect, the soul is told that it has nothing to fear about its mission to be "a prophet unto the *nations*"; to purify and elevate the "[alien] nation that dwells within you" — the body, the animal soul and its personal portion of the world which is to be elevated to the realm of holiness.

The reason there is no need to be apprehensive is twofold: (a) "*Before I formed you* in the womb, I knew you*," i.e., the soul is "truly a part of G-d above,"⁶ and it *transcends* the immediate source of its descent; (b) "Before you *left* the womb, I sanctified you": In addition to the innate loftiness of the soul, it was also prepared and given strength to fulfill its mission.

However, the soul puts its plaint before G-d: "I know not how to speak for I am but a lad"⁷ — as if to say that while it is true that all this potential power was invested and concealed within it, yet on a *revealed* level it is "but a lad." While these internal powers may indeed suffice — so it argues — to overcome the vicissitudes of the world insofar as they impinge upon itself, yet with regard to transforming its body, its animal soul and its portion in the world, it is "but a lad": it lacks the necessary strength.

G-d responds to the soul's plaint in these words: "Do not say 'I am but a lad,' for to all that I shall send you, you will go.... Do not fear them for *I am with you*...."⁸ Thus, in addition to all the innate qualities and powers given to the soul before its descent, G-d reassures it that when it descends within the body and is in a state of exile, it is given further reinforcement — "I am with you" — to successfully tackle the mission with which it was entrusted.

And when the soul utilizes its qualities and strengths during its exile and descent into this world of *Bein HaMetzarim*,

---

5. *Yirmeyahu* 1:5.
6. *Tanya*, beginning of ch. 2.
7. *Yirmeyahu* 1:6.
8. *Ibid.*, verses 6-8.

it transforms this journey into a journey — *Masei* — of elevation. Moreover, it ultimately reaches a level that would have
been impossible for it to attain without its descent into spiritual exile within the corporeal world.

Based on *Likkutei Sichos*, Vol. XVIII, pp. 349-350, 378, 383.

ספר דברים

Devarim

Devarim   דברים

Oil for a Silent Flame

In the Torah portion of *Devarim*, Moshe relates how the
Children of Israel defeated "Og, the King of Bashan and all his
people.... We captured all his cities... [including] Chevel
Argov...."[1]

Concerning the importance of Chevel Argov (i.e., the
region of Argov) we find in the *Mishnah*:[2] "Tekoa is first for
[olive] oil." (The choicest quality oil for use in the Holy Temple came from Tekoa.[3]) "Abba Shaul says: 'Second to it is [the
oil of] Regev in *Ever HaYarden* [Trans-Jordan].'" My father
explains:[4] "Regev is Chevel Argov, located in the land apportioned to [the tribe of] Menashe, in *Ever HaYarden*."

Oil stands for the total nullification of self.[5] We therefore
observe that oil is produced through pressing. Also, when oil
is lit it is "drawn after the wick and is burned and wholly
consumed..., none of it remaining."[6] Oil also burns quietly,[7]
without tumult. All these traits are symbolic of complete and
total nullification of self.

On his own, it is impossible for man to reach such a state
of nullity. As much as a person may ponder "G-d's greatness
and man's insignificance,"[8] he will be unable to reach a state
of complete and total abnegation of self.[9] Since it is *he* that is

---

1. *Devarim* 3:3-4.
2. *Mishnah, Menachos* 8:3.
3. Commentary of *Bartenura, loc. cit.*
4. *Toras Levi Yitzchak* on *Middos*, p. 284; cf. note on *Gilyon HaMishnayos,
   Menachos, ibid. (Yachin* and *Boaz* edition).
5. *Torah Or* 81c ff.; *ibid.,* 104d ff.; *Shaarei Orah* 35b ff., 37a ff.
6. *Torah Or* 81d.
7. *Zohar* III, p. 39a; *Torah Or, loc. cit.*
8. See *Rama, Orach Chayim* 98:1.
9. See *Likkutei Torah, Berachah* 98b.

217

doing the nullification, based on his own limited comprehension, the best he can hope to achieve is a limited state of nullity; it is impossible for a being to achieve a state of non-being.

Complete and total nullification must therefore come as a result of revelation from Above,[10] for before G-d there is no true being other than He. When this divine illumination is revealed within an individual, he will then achieve a state of non-being as a matter of course. However, in order for this G-dly state to permeate the individual, he must cultivate himself in order to become a fit *vessel* to absorb this illumination.

The difference between *Eretz Yisrael*, where the town of Tekoa was located, and *Ever HaYarden*, where Regev was located, with regard to the oil most fit fro the Holy Temple, will be understood accordingly.

Eretz Yisrael was chosen by G-d to be given to the Jewish people as an eternal inheritance. *Ever HaYarden*, however, is not in *Eretz Yisrael*, and originally was not meant to be apportioned to the Jews. Rather, the children of Reuven and Gad "took it on their own,"[11] by successfully petitioning Moshe to request of G-d that the land be granted to them.

There is therefore a fundamental difference between the sanctity of *Eretz Yisrael* and *Ever HaYarden*. The sanctity of *Eretz Yisrael* is not dependent on the Jewish people and their spiritual service, inasmuch as its holiness was granted from Above. As such its sanctity is limitless. The sanctity of *Ever HaYarden*, however, came as a result of petitioning and is therefore limited.

Accordingly, it is not "first for oil." Nevertheless, it too possesses sanctity beyond that provided by mere mortals, and it is able to bring about the exalted spiritual state symbolic of complete nullification of self. Its level of nullification bears some measure of comparison to that of *Eretz Yisrael*, for which reason its oil is "second to it" — to the oil of *Eretz Yisrael*.

---

10. *Sefer HaMaamarim Kuntreisim* II, 325a.
11. *Sifri, Savo* 26:3; cf. *Yerushalmi, Bikkurim* 1:8.

This is because the sanctity of *Ever HaYarden* in fact also came about as a result of *divine illumination* and did not result from the petitions of the tribes of Gad and Reuven alone. Rather, when G-d acceded to their request, this land too was imbued by Him with an added dimension of sanctity, making its oil "second" to that of *Eretz Yisrael.*

Based on *Likkutei Sichos,* Vol. XXIV, pp. 20-24.

Chazon: A Heavenly Vision

The opening passage of *Devarim* is invariably read on the *Shabbos* that precedes the Ninth of Av, the fast that commemorates the destruction of the first and second Holy Temples. This *Shabbos* is known as *Shabbos Chazon,* because the first word of its *Haftorah* is *Chazon* ("vision").

What is the distinguishing characteristic of *Shabbos Chazon* and its relationship to this time period?

The illustrious Rabbi Levi Yitzchak of Berditchev explains that on this *Shabbos* "every Jew is shown from afar a vision of the future Holy Temple."[1]

He explains this with a parable of a father who had a precious garment sewn for his son, who promptly tore it to shreds. The father then made him a second garment, but the child tore this one up as well. Thereafter, the father had yet another garment sewn for his son. This time, however, he did not permit his son to wear it. He only allowed him to gaze upon it at appointed times, telling him that when he began to conduct himself properly he would allow him to wear it. In this way the father trained his child to act in a manner that ultimately became so ingrained that it became his second nature. At this point the father gave him the garment and allowed him to wear it.

What are some of the lessons to be gleaned from this parable?

---

1. Quoted in *Reshimos HaTzemach Tzedek LeEichah,* fn. to p. 45.

On *Shabbos Chazon* the future Temple is shown to *all* Jews. However, since the purpose of the vision is to train the child (so to speak) in proper conduct, we understand from the parable that the paramount intent is to show it to those individuals whose conduct might lead to tearing the precious garment to shreds, as it were. Moreover, the intent of displaying the garment only at certain times is, of course, to arouse a longing for it in the child's heart. This longing should be so strong that it causes the child to mend his ways, until acting in an upstanding manner becomes his second nature.

We thus understand that the revelation of *Shabbos Chazon* is of such intensity that although the Holy Temple is shown "from afar," to the degree that there are some who do not see it at all, nevertheless, it is revealed in a manner whereby it becomes *internalized* within every single Jew. It is for this reason that the sighting of the Holy Temple, which is a vision experienced by the soul, affects the person's body and animal soul as well. In fact, the impact is so great that the body and animal soul also begin following the proper path.

Additionally, since this vision is of the future Temple which is an everlasting edifice,[2] its impact too is lasting. This is so, notwithstanding the fact that this vision does not result from man's own spiritual endeavors, but is granted to him as a gift from Above.

Based on *Likkutei Sichos*, Vol. IX, pp. 24-26.

---

2. *Zohar* I, p. 28a; III, p. 221a.

Vaes'chanan   ואתחנן

Tearing Open Heaven & Earth

In describing the awesome events surrounding the giving of the Torah to the Jewish people on Sinai, Moshe says in the Torah portion of *Vaes'chanan:* "You (G-d) revealed Yourself so that it be known that the L-rd is G-d; there is none else aside from Him."[1]

The renowned commentator, *Rashi,* notes: "When G-d gave the Torah, He opened for them (the Jewish people) the 'seven heavens.' Just as He tore open the higher levels, so, too, did He tear open the nether levels. All were then able to observe that He alone existed...."[2]

Rashi first states, "He *opened* for them the 'seven heavens,'" and immediately follows this with, "Just as He *tore open* the higher levels, so, too, did He *tear open* the nether levels." *Rashi's* change of wording indicates that the "higher levels" were both "opened" and "torn open," while the nether levels were only "torn open."

The term "to open" implies revealing an additional, new level that was previously lacking or closed and concealed, an example being "to *open* new opportunities." To "tear open," however, means that something is being torn asunder and discarded. Such would be the case when something — a box or bag, for example — is *torn open* in order to give access to what lies inside it.

In terms of man's divine service, there exist two approaches, one of which involves "opening", and the other, "tearing open."

Dealing with mundane matters on a regular basis and

---

1. *Devarim* 4:35.
2. *Rashi, loc. cit.*

revealing within them their true being and ultimate intent is the spiritual service of "opening". For the material world contains sparks of holiness which are to be *revealed* by being utilized in divine service.

At times, however, man is put to a test, and is confronted by things or events that totally conceal any sparks of holiness.[3] During such times merely "opening" will not suffice; the concealment must be "torn open" and negated. Only then will holiness be revealed.

These different forms of divine service require different means. In the case of the former it suffices for the person to "open" and reveal his spiritual talents of intellect and emotion. However, when a man is tested, this will not suffice.

When confronted with a test a person must "tear himself open" and even act in a manner that is opposite to his normal spiritual nature, calling upon his power of total self-sacrifice — a power so strong that it defies limitation. By doing so "he *tears open* the higher levels," i.e., he transcends the limitations of his spirit, and is able to *"tear open* the lower levels" of his own corporeality. He will then successfully withstand the test, and reveal the latent sparks of holiness concealed within it.

In general, G-dliness is revealed within "higher levels," i.e., spiritual worlds, in quite a different fashion than it is revealed through the "nether levels" and particularly this physical world. The former does so in a manner of "opening", and the latter does so in a manner of "tearing open."

The very existence of "higher levels" reveals G-dliness and consequently is "open" to it, for "the heavens recount the glory of the Almighty; the sky proclaims His handiwork."[4] "Nether levels," and especially corporeality, not only do not reveal G-dliness; on the contrary, they exist in a fashion where their divine source is not felt within them at all.

---

3. See *Likkutei Torah, Re'eh* 19b ff.; *Derech Mitzvosecha* 186a ff.; *Sefer HaMaamarim 5680*, p. 107ff., the *maamar* beginning *Ki Menaseh*, 5708.
4. *Psalms* 19:2; see at length *Siddur im Dach*, p. 188a ff.; *Reshimos HaTzemach Tzedek (Yahel Or)* on this verse.

Revealing G-dliness in the "nether levels" must therefore come about by "tearing open" and tearing asunder their concealment. Only then will the G-dliness concealed therein be revealed.

Yet, *Rashi* says, the higher levels were not only "opened", but also "torn open." This is because the revelation at Sinai was so mighty that it was not limited to the revelation of G-dliness inherent in the "higher levels" — the level of that which is "opened". The revelation of Sinai also proclaimed that "there is *none else* besides Him." This revelation of G-d's absolute oneness required "tearing open" the "nether levels" and the "higher levels" equally. All Jews were then able to clearly see that "He alone existed."

Based on Likkutei Sichos, Vol. XXIV, pp. 36-45.

The Best of Both Temples

The *Haftorah* of the weekly reading of *Vaes'chanan* begins with the words, "Comfort, comfort My people, says your G-d."[1] The *Midrash*[2] explains that the word "comfort" appears twice because of the twofold nature of the consolation: once for the destruction of the first Holy Temple and once for the destruction of the second Holy Temple.

G-d's consolation for the destruction of the Temples lies in His promise that a third Holy Temple will be built after the coming of *Mashiach*. This Temple will contain all of the five vital elements (such as the Ark) that were found in the First Temple and lacking in the second.[3] It therefore follows that in providing consolation for the First Temple, consolation for the Second Temple is automatically included. This being so, it would seem that one consolation would suffice for the de-

---

1. *Yeshayahu* 40:1.
2. *Yalkut, Yeshayahu, Remez* 445.
3. *Yoma* 21b.

struction of both Temples. Why is there a need for a *twofold* consolation?

Although in a general sense the Second Temple was spiritually inferior to the first, nevertheless in certain respects it was superior.

The sanctity of both Temples was such that the physical materials of which they were built became refined and holy. It was for this reason that even *after* the actual sanctuaries were destroyed, the Temple area retains its sanctity.[4] Although both Temples shared this quality, there was, however, a difference in the manner in which they achieved their refinement and sanctity, just as there are two general ways through which created beings may be refined.

One manner of refinement is that which results from an illumination from Above. This is similar to a master whose method of instruction is so profound that ultimately his disciple will be able to attain wisdom alone — yet only because of what was previously taught to him by his master.

Another manner of refinement results from all creation, having G-dliness at its very core. Since this is so, creation eventually achieves such a degree of spiritual refinement that "all *flesh* will see that G-d's mouth has spoken"[5] — physicality perceives G-dliness not merely as a result of G-d's revealing Himself, but because the very world itself in its entirety is essentially united with Him.[6]

The latter means of refinement is similar to the spiritual service of a penitent. As a rule this does not result from a revelation from Above, but is rather a manifestation of his own essence. In contrast, the former means of refinement is similar to the ongoing performance of *mitzvos* by righteous individuals.

The difference between the First and Second Temples and the superior aspect of the Second Temple may be understood accordingly.

---

4. *Rambam, Hilchos Beis HaBechirah,* end of ch. 6.
5. *Yeshayahu* 40:5.
6. See *Shaar HaEmunah* of the *Mitteler Rebbe,* ch. 25.

During the time of the First Temple the service of the Jewish people was at the level of the "righteous". Consequently, the world's potential for holiness by dint of its *own* intrinsic being and divine service, was yet to be revealed.

During the time of the Second Temple, however, Jews were at the level of penitents, for it was through their repentance for the sins that destroyed the First Temple that the Second Temple came into being. Since, as we have seen, the divine service of penitents is of such intensity that under their influence physicality comes to perceive G-dliness, the Second Temple possessed a superior quality — the quality of physicality transforming itself into holiness, and becoming a Temple for G-d.

Thus, the Third Temple will contain not only those things found in the first and lacking in the second, but also those qualities found specifically in the second and lacking in the first. The verse therefore offers a twofold consolation, for the unique qualities found in each of the two Holy Temples.[7]

Based on *Likkutei Sichos*, Vol. IX, pp.61-67.

---

7. See *Zohar* III, 221a; *Likkutei Sichos*, Vol. IX, P. 27ff.

Eikev   עקב

Special Consideration

In the Torah portion of *Eikev*, Moshe described G-d's in-corruptibility in the following manner: "For G-d Your L-rd ...does not give special consideration or take bribes."[1] Comments *Rashi: "[G-d] does not give special consideration* — If you cast off His yoke; *or take bribes* — [It is impossible] to appease Him with money."[2]

Rashi's comments need clarification. It is patently obvious that only those individuals who "cast off His yoke" do not receive "special consideration." When, however, Jews per-form Torah and *mitzvos,* they are worthy of special considera-tion, and indeed receive it, as stated explicitly in the Priestly Blessing: "May G-d bestow favor upon you...."[3] What novel thought does *Rashi* impart to us by saying, "If you cast off His yoke"?

Rashi's second comment, "[It is impossible] to appease Him with money," must also be understood. "How is it possible," asks R. Eliyahu Mizrachi,[4] "to even contemplate that G-d could possibly be bribed with money?"

The matter is as follows: When *Rashi* states "If you *cast off His yoke,"* he is indicating that we are not dealing with a person who fails to perform a *mitzvah* or commits a sin. For even then he is able to beseech G-d, and receive the blessing, "May G-d bestow favor upon you."

Rather, we are dealing with a situation of *"casting off His yoke,"* i.e. with an individual who *completely* throws off the heavenly yoke and ceases to be a "servant of G-d." This

---

1. *Devarim* 10:17.
2. *Ibid.*
3. *Bamidbar* 6:26.
4. On *Devarim, loc. cit.*

person now feels free to do whatever he desires, saying, "I will follow my heart's desires."[5] Concerning such an individual the verse says: "G-d does not give special consideration" — He conducts Himself toward that individual in an exacting manner.

Accordingly, *Rashi* cannot possibly state — as do other commentators — that "or take bribes" refers to G-d's being "bribed" by the good deeds a person does, since we are dealing here with an individual who has completely thrown off the heavenly yoke. *Rashi* has already indicated that such an individual will be shown no favor, which includes not accepting his "bribe", i.e., not affording him special consideration because of his good deeds.

Rashi must therefore cite an instance where one may mistakenly be led to think that even if he has completely thrown off G-d's yoke he may still find a way of appeasing Him, and that is the case when one seeks to appease G-d with money.

The Torah stated earlier: "Do not take ransom for the life of a murderer...."[6] *Rashi* notes: "He cannot be absolved by paying money."[7]

We see here that the "bribe" of money has a twofold nature and purpose: not only is the *recipient* bribed by the benefit and pleasure he derives from the money, but money also acts as "ransom", redeeming and taking the place of the *giver;* rather than the person himself being punished he gives his money.

That money should possess the ability to substitute for a person is quite understandable: since a person can acquire lifegiving necessities by purchasing them for money, he is therefore, in a manner of speaking, giving his very life when he gives away his money.[8]

It is this latter meaning of "bribe" that the verse negates. It goes without saying that G-d cannot be bribed with money.

---

5. *Devarim* 29:18.
6. *Bamidbar* 35:31.
7. *Ibid.*
8. See *Tanya,* ch. 37 (48b).

The verse here informs us that it is fruitless for a person to give money to act as "ransom", while he blithely throws off G-d's yoke. Rather, it is *himself* whom he must offer to G-d.

There is only one way G-d can be "bribed",[9] and that is when a person truly regrets having thrown off the heavenly yoke, sincerely repents, and offers himself to G-d. Such is the power of the "bribe" of repentance that such a person receives "special consideration." His previous misdeeds are negated,[10] or — depending on his level of repentance[11] — actually transformed into merits.[12]

Based on *Likkutei Sichos*, Vol. XXIV, pp. 73-78.

---

9. *Midrash Tehillim* on *Tehillim* 17:2; *Yalkut Shimoni, loc. cit., Remez* 770.
10. See *Yoma* 86b.
11. *Ibid.*
12. See *Tanya*, conclusion of ch. 7; cf. *Likkutei Sichos*, Vol. XVII, p. 183ff.

Mezuzah: A Unique Commandment

In the Torah reading of *Eikev* we are commanded to fulfill the *mitzvah* of *mezuzah*, as the verse states: "And you shall inscribe them on the doorposts of your house and on your gates."[1] The Torah immediately goes on to state the reward for performing this command: "So that your days and the days of your children may be prolonged...."[2] The command of *mezuzah* is thus similar to a number of others, such as honoring one's parents,[3] the reward for which is stated explicitly in the Torah — but with a significant difference.

Our Sages inform us[4] that when a man affixes a *mezuzah* on the entrance of his home, G-d protects that home. This protection is not a *reward* for the performance of the command,

---

1. *Devarim* 11:20.
2. *Ibid.*, v. 21.
3. *Shmos* 20:12; *Devarim* 5:16.
4. *Avodah Zarah* 11a; *Menachos* 32b.

but "a pleasure and profit attained from the very commandment *itself*...[this being] *in addition* to the reward...."⁵
Moreover, the protection afforded by a *mezuzah* is not a secondary "pleasure and profit": it is a mainstay of the actual
commandment itself, of which *Tosafos* says, "Its *purpose* is
protection."⁶

This unique characteristic causes the performance of the
command of *mezuzah* to differ from the performance of other
commandments. Generally, the Torah cites the reward one
receives for the performance of a command in order to buttress our performance of it. After all, we are told by our
Rabbis: "One should *always* engage in Torah study and in the
performance of commandments even when they are not done
lishmah, 'for their own sake'...."⁷ Furthermore, Maimonides
explains⁸ that young children learn only when promised a
reward. It is only after a long and tedious process that one
matures and reaches the level of acting *lishmah*.

On the other hand, it is readily understandable that performance only for the sake of reward lacks completeness and
sincerity. Even when one's goal is to fulfill G-d's will, if his
motivation is clouded by hopes of personal gain, the *mitzvah*
has not been done in the best possible way.⁹

This is not the case with regard to performing the command of *mezuzah*. Since the protection it offers is not a reward
for its fulfillment but an integral component and result of the
mitzvah itself, it follows that this *mitzvah* lacks nothing when it
is done for the sake of protection. Not that one's sole motivation should be the protection it affords. For even without this
protection the individual would no doubt still have the same
desire to simply carry out G-d's will.

It follows that when one performs the *mitzvah* of *mezuzah* it
is perfectly acceptable to have in mind that the command-

---

5. *Bach, Yoreh Deah* 285.
6. *Menachos* 44a.
7. *Pesachim* 50b.
8. *Rambam, Hilchos Teshuvah* 10:5.
9. See commentary of *Iyun Yaakov* on *Ein Yaakov, Pesachim* 8a, b.

ment *itself* will ensure G-d's protection. Indeed, even if the *mitzvah* of *mezuzah* is performed *solely* for the sake of protection, Maimonides nevertheless writes[10] that those who have not yet attained a higher level are to be encouraged to perform commandments even if only for the sake of their reward.

Based on *Likkutei Sichos*, Vol. XIX, pp. 121-123.

---

10. *Pirush HaMishnayos* on Tractate *Sanhedrin*, beginning of ch. *Cheilek*.

Re'eh   ראה

Beis HaBechirah & Beis HaMikdash

The Torah portion of *Re'eh* speaks of the obligation to bring offerings "in the place that G-d will choose."[1] As explained in the *Sifri*,[2] this refers to the Sanctuary in Shiloh and to the *Beis HaMikdash*, the Holy Temple, in Jerusalem.

Although Shiloh merits the distinction of being called "a place *chosen* by G-d," nevertheless, only the *Beis HaMikdash* is known as *Beis HaBechirah*, the *"House* of [G-d's] *Choice."* Evidently the manner in which these two places were *chosen* differs.

Earlier in this portion the Torah states: "You may not worship G-d your L-rd in such a manner."[3] *Rashi* explains this to mean: "[It is prohibited] to bring offerings in whatever place [a person chooses]." The Torah goes on to say: "This you may do only on the site that G-d your L-rd will choose.... That shall be the place where you will bring your burnt offerings...."[4] A little later on the verse states: "You shall cross the Jordan.... And the site that G-d will choose as the place dedicated to His Name, there shall you bring...."[5] The *Sifri* explains that the first verse refers to Shiloh and the second verse refers to Jerusalem, where the *Beis HaMikdash* was built.[6]

It should be noted that the first verse, which relates to Shiloh, stresses those who bring the offerings — *"you* will bring your burnt offerings...." The second verse, relating to the Holy Temple in Jerusalem, emphasizes the place where

---

1. *Devarim* 14:25.
2. *Ibid.*
3. *Devarim* 12:4.
4. *Loc. cit.*, v. 5-6.
5. *Loc. cit.*, v. 10-11.
6. *Ibid.*

the offerings are to be brought — "*there* shall you bring all that I am prescribing to you...."

The reason for this is that the earlier verse is preceded by the prohibition of bringing offerings in any place a person may choose. Thus, choosing Shiloh was in effect a way of negating "all other places." However, with regard to the *Beis HaMikdash* the opposite was true: since G-d chose that place, it was therefore necessary to bring offerings there and nowhere else.

In other words, the choice of Shiloh was for the sake of the Jewish people, so that they would have a specific place to bring offerings, while the choice of Jerusalem was for G-d's sake, as it were — G-d chose His eternal dwelling place on earth.

The difference in the *manner* of choosing these places also resulted in a difference with regard to the nature of the place that was chosen. Since the intent of choosing Shiloh was to provide a specific place for bringing offerings, choosing the site itself sufficed; it was not necessary for the actual dwelling located upon the site to be singled out for special attention or to be "chosen".

The *Beis HaMikdash*, however, was "chosen" not because of external reasons but for its own sake — G-d desired an abode about which He could say, "This is My eternal resting place." It is understandable that in this instance the Sanctuary itself — even more than the location — was of primary importance. Therefore, unlike Shiloh, the *house itself* was the "House of [G-d's] Choice."

In point of fact, the Sanctuary in Jerusalem is known by both names, *Beis HaBechirah* and *Beis HaMikdash*, the "House of [G-d's] Choice" and the "House of Holiness" (i.e., the Holy Temple). Each name indicates a different and unique aspect.

Since G-d is infinite, it follows that His choice possesses infinite value as well. The name "House of [G-d's] Choice" thus indicates the Temple's limitless, intrinsic worth. However, since this is G-d's doing and not man's, it does not entirely influence and permeate the individual.

It is therefore important for man to imbue the Temple

with holiness resulting from *his own* service — service that is albeit limited, but is still of his own doing — thereby making the Temple not only the "House of [G-d's] Choice," but also a "House of Holiness."

Based on *Likkutei Sichos,* Vol. XIX, pp. 146-147; Vol. XXIV, pp. 79-83.

The Power of Repentance

The Torah portion of *Re'eh* is invariably read on the *Shabbos* on which we bless the new month of Elul, or on Rosh Chodesh Elul itself. The theme of the month of Elul is repentance,[1] and indeed, we find in the Torah portion of *Re'eh* something truly astonishing with regard to the far-reaching power of repentance.

Generally, repentance is only effective *vis-à-vis* the Heavenly Court but not in the terrestrial courts of man. As the *Gemara* says: "Those punishable by Divine excision..., if they repented they are forgiven by the Heavenly Court. As to those punishable by execution..., if they repented, they are not forgiven by the terrestrial court."[2] The reason for this is that since repentance abides mainly in the heart,[3] it is impossible for the members of a mortal court to ascertain a person's degree of repentance, if any.[4]

This is not the case with regard to the punishment of execution by sword[5] which the courts were to mete out to the inhabitants of an apostate city, wherein all (or most) of the people were found guilty of idolatry. In this instance, Maimonides rules[6] that if they repented they are forgiven. Although this ruling indicates the far-reaching effects of repentance, it is nevertheless perplexing in light of the earlier statement

---

1. See *Tur, Orach Chayim,* end of ch. 581 and commentaries *ad loc.*
2. *Makkos* 13b.
3. *Tanya,* ch. 29.
4. See *Noda BiYehudah, Orach Chayim, Mahadura Kama,* Sec. 38.
5. *Devarim* 13:16.
6. *Hilchos Avodah Zarah* 4:6.

that a mortal court cannot forgive sins for which there has been repentance.

Maimonides' statement may however be understood by prefacing another puzzling law regarding an apostate city. An individual guilty of idolatry is subject to execution by stoning. In the case of an apostate city, however, the idolators are subject to execution by the *milder* form of death by sword.

How can this be? We know that when a person is guilty of two capital offenses, the punishments for which are two manners of execution, he is to be punished with the *harsher* one.[7] Why should this rule not apply to the case of the apostate city? We must therefore say that the statement, "You must smite all the inhabitants of the city by the sword," does not apply to each of the inhabitants separately, but to all of them collectively.

This may be explained as follows: The very fact that all or most of the inhabitants became idolators causes them to become a new entity; they cease being many individuals who committed the same sin and become one entity — a *congregation* of idolators. Hence their previous *judgment* as individuals ceases as well. A new law therefore applies to them — punishment by sword.

Maimonides' statement that if the inhabitants of an apostate city repent they are forgiven, may be understood accordingly. Although it is indeed true that repentance cannot avert the punishments of terrestrial courts, yet in this instance something entirely different occurs through repentance: it causes these idolators to once again become "individuals", and the *state* of the "congregation" of an apostate city ceases to exist. Thus, Maimonides' ruling in no way contradicts the fact that repentance is not relevant to the courts of man, for in this instance repentance does not nullify the *punishment*, it only nullifies the entity of an apostate city; the nullification of the punishment simply comes about as a matter of course.

Based on *Likkutei Sichos*, Vol. IX, pp. 106-111.

---

7. *Sanhedrin*, 81b; *Rambam, Hilchos Sanhedrin* 14:4.

Shoftim   שפטים

The Purpose of a Monarch

The *mitzvah* of appointing a king is described in the portion of *Shoftim* in the following manner: "When you come to the land that G-d your L-rd is giving you...you will say, 'We would like to appoint a king....' You must appoint a king from among your brethren...."[1]

When the Jewish people asked the prophet Shmuel to appoint a king he was displeased by their request.[2] G-d, too, said: "They have rejected Me..."[3] Our Sages ask: Why were Shmuel and G-d disappointed with the request of the Jewish people which not only was legitimate, but was actually *commanded to them* in the Torah?[4] Furthermore, if their request was inappropriate, why did G-d tell Shmuel to heed it and appoint a king?

Chassidus explains[5] that there are two reasons why a king is appointed. The simple reason is that he should prescribe a proper manner of conduct for his subjects. For even when one logically knows how to conduct oneself, this alone does not yet suffice, for "the eye beholds and the heart desires";[6] one's passions may overwhelm his logic and knowledge. Fear of a king serves to guarantee that the populace will conduct itself properly. As our Sages note: "Pray for the welfare of the authorities, for were it not for the fear of them, men would swallow one another alive."[7]

---

1. *Devarim* 17:14-15.
2. *I Shmuel* 8:6.
3. *Loc. cit.*, v. 7.
4. *Abarbanel, Shoftim — HaSafek HaAsiri; Kli Yakar* on *Devarim* 17:15; *Radak* on *I Shmuel* 8:5; see *Sanhedrin* 20b; *Rambam, Hilchos Melachim* 1:2.
5. *Sefer HaMitzvos LehaTzemach Tzedek, Mitzvas Minui Melech,* chs. 1 & 3.
6. *Rashi* on *Bamidbar* 15:39.
7. *Avos* 3:2.

However, when people are on a level at which they are in full control of their emotions and are able to police themselves, a king serves no useful purpose in this regard. There are, however, certain things about which a populace may lack discernment. Only a king, being "head and shoulders above the entire populace,"[8] understands these matters. He therefore issues various decrees that his subjects faithfully obey.

On a more spiritual level: For Jews, whose true King is G-d, a corporeal king is appointed in order that he may serve as a conduit to reveal G-d's Kingship to the people.

Jews inherently believe, comprehend and feel that their life-force derives from G-d's Kingship. This should naturally result in their self-nullification to Him. When, however, this is lacking, it becomes necessary for them to have a king of flesh and blood. The fear and awe of him will eventually lead them to stand in awe and self-nullification before the King of Kings.

When Jews are as they should be and spontaneously possess this source of nullification before G-d, then appointing a physical king serves a much loftier purpose: it leads them to levels of G-dliness that they could not otherwise reach alone, inasmuch as those levels transcend their comprehension. In such an instance, a king draws down and grants the Jewish populace a measure of his own level of perception. They are then able to attain a higher and deeper level of fear of G-d, and self-nullification to Him.

The prophet Shmuel desired that the spiritual state of the Jews be such that they would attain a state of self-nullification before G-d as a result of their own efforts, without having to utilize the services of a king. The king would then help them reach a yet higher level of fear of G-d. The Jews, however, requested a "king who will rule over us *similar to all other nations*"[9] — a king who would keep them from "swallowing one another alive."

---

8. *I Shmuel* 9:2.
9. *Ibid.* 8:5, 20.

This indicated that they were not as G-d-fearing as they should have been on their own. G-d therefore said: "They have rejected Me" — they were lacking in the fear of Him.

G-d nevertheless acceded to their request and commanded that a king be appointed. For when Jews lack the fear of G-d a king must be appointed immediately to help them attain this lower level of the fear of G-d. Then, in due course, they will attain the higher level of fear provided by the king as well.

Although during the time of exile the Jewish people lack a monarch, yet our Sages say: "Who are the kings? — The Rabbis."[10] Just as Jews were commanded earlier in history to appoint a king over them, so, too, are we now commanded to accept upon ourselves the "kingship" of our rabbis and teachers; as our Sages exhort: "Provide yourself with a teacher."[11]

There are always individuals whose love and fear of G-d is greater than our own. Should we not make them our teachers?

Based on *Likkutei Sichos,* Vol. XXIV, pp. 104-106.

---

10. See *Gittin,* end of ch. 5.
11. *Avos* 1:6; 1:16.

Two Forms of Fear: Two Forms of Repentance

In the passage entitled *Shoftim* the Torah describes how the Jewish people were to prepare for war. Among the things said to the potential warriors was: "Is there any man among you who is afraid or faint-hearted? Let him go home rather than have his cowardliness demoralize his brethren."[1] *Rashi* comments on the words "afraid or faint-hearted" and explains: "R. Akiva says that this is to be understood literally, i.e., that he cannot endure the heat of battle and look upon an out-

---

1. *Devarim* 20:8.

stretched sword. R. Yosei HaGlili says, that he is fearful of his sins...."[2]

All aspects of Torah are extremely precise; the two explanations of R. Akiva and R. Yosei are directly related to the Torah portion of *Shoftim*, inasmuch as this passage is always read on the first *Shabbos* of the month of Elul, the month of repentance.[3]

The *Tur*[4] prefaces the laws of *shofar*-blowing during the month of Elul by citing the verse,[5] "G-d ascends through *teruah*, the L-rd — through the sound of the *shofar*." He immediately follows this by saying: "*Therefore* our Sages of blessed memory have instituted that the *shofar* be sounded... throughout the month of Elul so as to alert Jews to repentance...."

The words of the *Tur* must be understood, for the verse that he quotes refers to the sounding of the *shofar* on Rosh HaShanah and not during the month of Elul. We must therefore say that the repentance achieved through *shofar*-blowing during the month of Elul also encapsulates — at least in a concealed fashion — the level of repentance achieved through *shofar*-blowing on *Rosh HaShanah*.

This may be understood as follows. When Maimonides[6] explains the elusive meaning of *shofar*-blowing on *Rosh HaShanah* — that it connotes the theme of repentance — he says the following: "This means to say: 'Awaken, sleepers, from your sleep, and slumberers from your slumber, and scrutinize your deeds; return in repentance, remember your Creator... search your souls....'" Maimonides' phrasing needs clarification: "Remember your Creator" and "search your souls" are, after all, preparatory steps to repentance; when a Jew reminds himself that G-d examines the spiritual state of his soul it leads him to repentance. If so, should

---

2. Based on the *Mishnah* in *Sotah* 49a.
3. See *Tur, Orach Chayim,* end of Sec. 581 and commentaries *ad loc.*
4. *Ibid.*
5. *Tehillim* 47:6.
6. *Hilchos Teshuvah* 3:4.

Maimonides not have placed these two phrases before "return in repentance"?

The fact that he did not do so indicates that there are different manners and levels of repentance. The *primary* aspect of repentance that entails "that the sinner forsake his sin... and earnestly resolve in his heart never to repeat it"[7] is accomplished by heeding the exhortation to "awaken... and scrutinize your deeds...." The phrases "remember your Creator" and "search your souls" urge a man to *loftier* levels of repentance.

Within the primary aspect of repentance there are two general sub-levels. First comes the spiritual "awakening from sleep," for when a person is in a state of blissful slumber he cares not a wit about his spiritual status. The initial step leading to repentance is therefore to awaken and shake off his numbing slumber. Once his soul has already been roused to repentance, he must actualize this arousal by "scrutinizing his deeds" to ensure that he never transgresses again.

Rashi alludes to this in his above-mentioned commentary. First comes the comment of R. Akiva according to whom "afraid or faint-hearted" *cannot* mean "that he is fearful of his sins," for as soon as one becomes so fearful of his sins,... the essence of his soul will be roused to repentance and he will be forgiven. However, *Rashi* immediately follows this with the comment of R. Yosei, for this first level does not suffice — the arousal of the soul's essence must be fully revealed and actualized so as to ensure that the penitent will never sin again.

Based on *Likkutei Sichos*, Vol. IX, pp. 129-132.

---

7. *Ibid.* 2:2.

Seitzei   תצא

Even One Hundred Times

In the weekly reading of *Seitzei* we learn: "If you encounter a bird's nest on any tree or on the ground, and it contains baby birds or eggs, then, if the mother is sitting on the chicks or eggs, you must not take the mother so long as she is sitting on her young. You must first send away the mother, and only then may you take the young. [If you do this] you will have a good and long life."[1] *Rashi* comments: "If in the case of an easy command that involves no monetary loss, Scripture states 'you will have a good and long life,' how much greater is the reward for the more difficult commandments."[2]

The Torah then refers to another reward for performing the above command, namely, "When you build a new house...."[3] As our Sages say: "If you have fulfilled the command of 'sending away the mother bird,' you will eventually build a new house and fulfill the command of building a guard-rail [around your roof], for one good deed brings another...."[4]

According to the simple meaning of the text once the mother bird is sent away the young may be taken, and even if the mother returns she need not be sent away again. However, in the context of the law we find the rule that the mother must be sent away "even one hundred times."[5] The reason for this is that the imperative verb "send" is written in its root or infinitive form. Whenever the Torah uses such a

---

1. *Devarim* 22:6-7.
2. *Ibid.*, based on *Chullin* 142a.
3. *Ibid.*, v. 8.
4. *Midrash Tanchuma ad loc.*, quoted in *Rashi* on this verse.
5. *Chullin* 141a.

tense it implies an ongoing and constant command — "even one hundred times."

How does the above halachic principle apply in terms of man's spiritual service?

Deeds are by their very nature limited. Even when one acts out of intellectual or emotional conviction his actions will still be limited, inasmuch as his intellect and emotion themselves are finite. However, when one acts out of intense desire and surely when one acts out of the imperative of his soul's infinite essence, then his inherently limited deeds will be performed in a limitless manner. For example: a man's endeavors to extricate himself from a life-threatening situation involve not only his bodily limbs but his entire essence and being.[6] It is for this reason that when a command is stated in the root form of the imperative it means "even one hundred times."

In general, deeds are merely bound up with the power of action, since the command of the Torah is that a deed be *done*. However, a command stated in the *source* or *root* form means that the deed must be done in a manner in which the *source* is manifest: the deed must stem from an intense desire welling from the soul's essence, this being the source of all soul powers. This is why the deed is to be done "even one hundred times," for the essence of the soul transcends all limitations.

Now, although the imperative "send" is indeed written in its root form, nevertheless, according to the simple meaning of the text it only means sending away *once*. For when one is a mere novice in spiritual service — when one is only at the level of "the simple meaning of the text" — then even an arousal of the soul's source and root will only result in a limited manner of service, service which does not involve financial loss.

Nevertheless, since such an arousal did result in actual performance, albeit finite, therefore "one good deed brings another," and eventually such a person will also fulfill the

---

6. See *Sefer HaMaamarim 5706*, p. 67.

command of building a guard-rail, notwithstanding the fact
that it involves a loss of money.

All the above is also related to the month of Elul. Arousal
to repentance during this month — with regard to one's
future actions — is of a general nature, to improve one's
ways, and the like. It therefore initially succeeds only in
leading one to perform an "easy commandment." However,
since this arousal ultimately leads to fulfilling all the commandments, it is already reason enough to *immediately* earn
one a good and sweet year in all particulars.

Based on Likkutei Sichos, Vol. IX, pp. 133-142.

Building a Guard-rail

In the portion of *Seitzei* we learn: "When you build a new
house, you must place a guard-rail around your roof. Do not
allow a dangerous situation to remain in your house, since
someone can fall from [an unenclosed roof]."[1]

In spiritual terms the verse may be understood as follows.
A roof, the highest part of a house, suggests egoism and
conceit. Placing a guard-rail around one's roof means that one
must confine and limit this undesirable trait.[2] This must be
done "since someone can fall [from an unenclosed roof]" —
i.e., egoism and self-importance are at the root of every
spiritual downfall, for all evil traits stem from them.[3]

A guard-rail is placed around a roof not so much for one's
own self-protection as to protect others from falling. The
same holds true in spiritual terms. The "guard-rail" placed
around a person's egoism and conceit is important not only to
protect oneself from this ugly trait, but to ensure that one's

---

1. *Devarim* 22:8.
2. *Shaloh, Cheilek Torah Shebichsav,* end of *Seitzei;* see also *Or Torah* of the
   Maggid of Mezritch on this verse (22:8).
3. See *maamarim* beginning with the verse, *Reishis Goyim Amalek.*

ego and self-importance will not bring about the spiritual downfall of one's fellow Jew.

When a person endeavors to bring his fellow Jews closer to G-d through the observance of the commandments, and this involvement fills him with conceit, then not only is he lacking in terms of his own spiritual service, but he may cause the person whom he is trying to teach to fall as well.

That a Jew should seek the spiritual welfare of other Jews is also alluded to in this verse. "When you build a new house..." implies that a Jew ought not be satisfied merely with serving G-d himself: he should build an *edifice* for G-d, by influencing his environment, so that it too will be permeated with Judaism.[4]

When one man speaks to another with complete truth and sincerity, without thought of personal gain or self-gratification, he may be assured that his words will enter the other's heart and achieve their desired effect.

If, however, his talk is tainted by egoism and conceit, then not only will this impede his chance of bringing the other closer to Judaism, but his words may have the very opposite effect. His conceit may cause the listener to become more *distant* from Judaism, heaven forbid.

A person may well ask: Knowing as he does that he is not utterly devoid of egoism and conceit, why, then, should he embark on an enterprise whose success is in doubt? Since he does not know whether he will be able to build a proper rail around his ego to guard against his own, or his friend's, spiritual downfall, then perhaps it would be better not to "build a new house" for himself, and especially not for others.

The verse therefore begins with the blessing[5] and injunction, "You shall build a new house." A Jew can and must build a house for G-d by creating an environment of Judaism. He cannot rely on others but must build a *"new* house" — a house that is uniquely his.

---

4. Discussed at length in *Likkutei Sichos,* Vol. XIX, pp. 210, 212.
5. *Tanchuma,* quoted in *Rashi* on this verse (22:8).

Every Jew is given a portion in the world[6] that is his to purify, elevate and make "new", by transforming it into a dwelling place for G-d. He cannot rely on the spiritual service of past generations, nor on that of other Jews in his own generation. It is his task to build up *his own* portion in the world.

When one Jew meets another, this itself is an act of Divine Providence. It shows that the other's purification and spiritual elevation are in some way connected to him. He is therefore *obliged* to seek his fellow's betterment. Why should another Jew suffer because of his ego and conceit? A guard-rail must be made!

Based on *Likkutei Sichos*, Vol. XXIV, pp. 137-144.

---

6. *Tanya*, ch. 37 (p. 95).

Savo   תבוא

Gratitude to G-d & Brotherly Love

The Torah portion of *Savo* begins by saying: "When you come to the land that G-d your L-rd is giving you as a heritage, *occupying and settling it*, you shall take of the first fruits ...and go to the site that G-d will choose as the place for the indwelling of His name."[1] *Rashi* comments: "This teaches us that [the Jewish people] were not obligated to bring the first fruits until they conquered and divided the land."[2]

Offering the first fruits served the Jewish people as a gesture of thanks to G-d for leading them into *Eretz Yisrael* and allowing them to enjoy its bounty. It thus indicated that they were not ingrates.[3]

Accordingly, the following difficulty arises. Until all the land was conquered and divided there were many individuals who had already received their allotted portion; why were *they* not obligated to bring their first fruits from their land, as thanks to G-d for the good He had done for *them*, especially since their not bringing it could be construed as a sign of ingratitude?

By way of explanation: All the Jewish people are interconnected. As long as there remained a Jew who had not yet been allotted his portion in the land, the pleasure of *all* Jews was incomplete; even those who had already received their share in *Eretz Yisrael* were also lacking in joy. Since the thanks that was offered by bringing the first fruits was an expression of thanks for G-d's *all-encompassing* goodness (for which reason the first fruits were brought only of those species for which

---

1. *Devarim* 26:1-2.
2. *Ibid.*, v. 1.
3. *Rashi* on v. 3.

Eretz Yisrael was *praised*), they therefore could not be brought until the entire land was conquered and divided.

*   *   *

The above is also related to *Chai* Elul (the eighteenth day of Elul), the birthdate of two great luminaries — the Baal Shem Tov, founder of the chassidic movement, and the Alter Rebbe, founder of the *Chabad*-Lubavitch stream within that movement.

Among the fundamental principles of *Chassidus* are the obligation to love one's fellow Jew and the concept of the intrinsic unity of the Jewish people. These concepts are alluded to — as indicated above — at the beginning of the Torah portion of *Savo*, which is invariably read either on the day of *Chai* Elul itself or on the *Shabbos* that immediately precedes or follows it.

How are love and unity among Jews best achieved?

When two or more people unite, then no matter how strong their bond may be it is not absolute unity, since they are intrinsically disparate entities; their union is but an adjunct to their essential being. We thus understand that the unity of the Jewish people, which is an absolutely true and essential unity — so much so that it finds expression in "loving one's fellow as *oneself*" — stems from the fact that all Jews, by virtue of the common Source of their souls, are truly *one*.

Nevertheless, the true unity of the Jewish people finds expression specifically when Jews, *existing as distinct and separate individuals*, are even then truly united as one. Indeed, if the unity of the Jewish people were *not* to find expression among Jews who exist as distinct individuals, this would prove that their unity does not stem from the essence of their being, for an individual's essence must be found in *all* his particular and detailed aspects.[4]

This, then, was the deeper reason as to why the Jewish people were not obligated to bring their offerings of first

---

4. See *Likkutei Sichos*, Vol. VIII, p. 131.

fruits until they had conquered and divided the land — for it served as an indication of the true and absolute love and unity that existed among them, to the extent that no individual could be truly joyful so long as there existed one fellow Jew who did not yet have a portion in *Eretz Yisrael.*

And as to ourselves, by truly loving our fellow Jews, we can once again merit to "come to the land" of Israel — through our Righteous *Mashiach,* speedily and in our days.

Based on *Likkutei Sichos,* Vol. IX, pp. 152-161.

G-d's Concealed Treasure

In the portion of *Savo* Moshe says to the Jewish people: "G-d has distinguished you today, making you His special nation, as He promised you; therefore keep all his commandments."[1] *Rashi* explains[2] that "as He promised you" refers to G-d's earlier promise to the Jewish people — "You shall be My *segulah* among all nations...."[3]

Rashi explains *segulah* to mean: "A beloved treasure, as [in the verse] 'the treasure of kings'[4] — priceless vessels and gems that monarchs *conceal.* So, too, shall you be My special treasure among all nations."[5]

This analogy, which as a Torah analogy is precise, needs to be understood. What possible benefit can accrue from "priceless vessels and gems" that are *concealed?* Were these gems to be mounted in the king's crown, they would enhance his majesty and glory.[6] However, when they are concealed from the eyes of all but the king himself, they accomplish nothing at all; no one benefits from their beauty.

1. *Devarim* 26:18.
2. *Loc. cit.*
3. *Shmos* 19:5.
4. *Koheles* 2:8.
5. On *Shmos, loc. cit.*
6. See *Yeshayahu* 33:17.

The reason these priceless treasures are concealed is that *these* treasures are vital to (and on a par with) the *king himself*. Other treasures may be utilized for conducting the affairs of state,[7] or for the aggrandizement of the monarchy.[8] These *concealed* treasures, however, are bound up with the king himself. His intrinsic status as a king is inexorably connected to these treasures in which he delights.

Jews are similarly G-d's "special nation" — His "beloved treasure." The essence of the Jewish people transcends even their distinctive ability to reveal holiness and G-d's majesty in this world through performing Torah and *mitzvos;* their *very being* is an end unto itself.

Jews are one, as it were, with G-d Himself. Just as it is impossible to say that G-d exists for a particular reason, so, too, regarding His "beloved treasure," in which He delights even more than a king delights in his *concealed* treasures, it cannot be said that they exist for a special reason.

Thus, there exists an inherent difference between the Jewish people and other nations. Other nations were created for a specific purpose; Jews essentially exist for no reason other than their intrinsic being. Furthermore, even as Jews exist in this world for the purpose of transforming it into a dwelling place for G-d, here, too, the purpose is that the Divine Presence reside within *them*.[9]

This concept is alluded to by *Rashi*. On the verse, "G-d has distinguished you today," *Rashi* comments: "He has *separated you unto Him* that you be *unto Him* a distinguished nation"; Jews are utterly distinguished and separate from other nations, inasmuch as they are G-d's "beloved treasure."

This distinction results in the responsibility placed on the Jewish people to "keep *all* His commandments." That Jews are expected to observe 613 commandments while other nations are expected to keep only seven is not merely a quantitative difference, but a qualitative one as well.

---

7. See *Rambam, Hilchos Melachim* 3:4.
8. Cf. *op. cit.,* 2:5.
9. *Torah Or* 76d; cf. *Hemshech Taf-Reish-Samach-Vav,* end of p. 468ff.

Other nations, created with a specific goal in mind, were given a limited number of commandments, commensurate with their limited purpose. Jews, however, who are figuratively "one with G-d Himself," are expected to keep *all* His commandments — without any limitation.

Jews, because of their intimate connection with G-d and His Will, for "G-d and His Will are one,"[10] are completely dedicated and devoted to Him. They are ready to do whatever He commands and desires.

The above provides an invaluable lesson in the degree of care one should exercise in loving one's fellow Jew and devoting oneself to his welfare. For, whatever the Jew's revealed spiritual status, his essence is infinitely higher than that of others; the Jewish people are "the work of My hands, in which I take pride."[11] One must but seek to reveal their latent qualities.

Based on Likkutei Sichos, Vol. XXIV, pp. 157-166.

---

10. See *Toras Shalom,* end of p. 190ff.

11. *Yeshayahu* 60:21. This verse is also part of the *Haftorah* for *Parshas Savo.*

Nitzavim   נצבים

Blessing & Reigning: A Partnership

The Baal Shem Tov gave the following reason as to why we do not recite the blessing for the new month on the *Shabbos* preceding the beginning of the month of Tishrei, as we do on the *Shabbosos* that precede all other new months: "The seventh month [of the festival calendar], which is the first month of the months of the year [of the creation calendar, i.e., the month of Tishrei], is blessed by G-d Himself on *Shabbos Mevarchim*, which is the last *Shabbos* of the month of Elul. Thus empowered, the Jewish people bless the [other] months, eleven times in the year."[1]

The Baal Shem Tov then went on to explain what G-d's blessing entails: "Scripture states [in the beginning of the Torah portion of *Nitzavim*[2]], 'You are all standing today....' 'Today' refers to Rosh HaShanah, which is the day of judgment.... You (the Jewish people) stand fast and upright on this day; i.e., you are judged favorably. On the *Shabbos* preceding Rosh HaShanah, which is the last *Shabbos* of the month of Elul, we read that 'You are all standing today....' This is G-d's blessing on the *Shabbos* when we bless the 'seventh month,' [a month] that is satiated[3] and satiates all Jews with abundant goodness the year round."

We understand from the above that although the month of Tishrei is blessed by G-d Himself, nevertheless even this blessing is drawn down by the Jewish people through their

---

1. *Kovetz Michtavim, Tehillim Ohel Ysef Yitzchak*, p. 193; *YaYom Yom*, entry for 25 Elul.
2. *Devarim* 29:9.
3. In the Holy Tongue, the words for "seventh" and "satiated" share a common root; cf. *Vayikra Rabbah* 29:8.

reading of the Torah on the preceding *Shabbos*. The only difference between this and other months is that in the case of the other months the blessing itself comes from the Jewish people, while the blessing for Tishrei is recited by G-d Himself — though in order for it to be drawn down below, the Jewish people must read the portion of *Nitzavim*.

Another example — and explanation — of how something is effected by G-d but nevertheless needs the divine service of the Jewish people to bring it into actuality, is to be found with regard to Rosh HaShanah.

The *Gemara* relates[4] that G-d says to the Jewish people: "Recite unto Me on Rosh HaShanah... [verses of] kingship so that you will accept Me as your sovereign." Herein lie two opposite concepts. On the one hand, it is readily understandable that since "accepting Me as your sovereign" has yet to take place — i.e., before this acceptance G-d is *not* (as it were) a king — it would seem to be impossible for Jews to make this happen through their own spiritual service. For a "nation" can only affect that level of G-dliness concerning which the term "king" can apply; that level which *transcends* kingship and which has to be *roused* to cause the attribute of kingship to emanate, totally transcends the finite endeavors of the "nation".

It is for this reason that we say on Rosh HaShanah, "He *chooses*..." — since the spiritual flow that is drawn down on Rosh HaShanah emanates from G-d's very Essence.[5] It therefore comes about without any arousal at all on the part of created beings and purely out of His free choice.

On the other hand, since G-d Himself says, "*Recite* unto Me... [verses of] kingship *so that you will accept* Me as your sovereign" — i.e., His sovereignty is activated by the recitation of these verses by the Jewish people — it follows that G-d's essential choice of becoming King comes about because of (and through) the Jewish people. At the same time, the

---

4. *Rosh HaShanah* 16a; 34b.
5. See *maamar* beginning *Yivchar Lanu*, 5703, p. 34.

very fact that it comes about because of the Jewish people is a result of G-d's free choice.

Because the blessing of the month of Tishrei and that which is accomplished on Rosh HaShanah both result from the service of Jews, an additional measure of blessing is drawn down upon them, with all of our people being inscribed and sealed for a good and sweet year.

Based on *Likkutei Sichos*, Vol. IX, pp. 184-192.

Rosh HaShanah   ראש השנה

A Day of Shabbos: A Year of Shabbos

This year is special. Not only does the first day of Rosh HaShanah, the *head* of the year, fall on a *Shabbos*, thus providing the *body* of the entire year with *"Shabbos* delight,"[1] but the whole year is also a Sabbatical year, a year of *Shemitah*. The *Shabbos* day and the Sabbatical year, while similar in some aspects, differ in others.

Both the day of *Shabbos* and the year of *Shabbos* conclude cycles of time. *Shabbos,* the final day of the seven days of creation, is related to the creative process and consummates it.[2] Indeed, the week as a whole is sometimes called *Shabbos.*[3]

G-d created the world in such a manner that its final completion was entrusted to man[4] — the "choicest of all creatures." Man was created in G-d's image[5] and imbued with a divine soul,[6] so as to enable him[7] to bring the ultimate plan of creation to fruition.

Having been granted this capacity during the seven-day cycle of creation, man enters the framework of the cycle of the year. During this time he is expected to transform his potential capacity into actuality.

This period lasts seven years, up to and including the seventh and final year of *Shemitah*. Just as *Shabbos* vivifies all

---

1. *Yeshayahu* 58:13.
2. See *Moreh Nevuchim* II, ch. 31; *Ramban* on *Devarim* 5:12.
3. *Vayikra* 23:15.
4. See *Bereishis Rabbah* 11:6; cf. *Rashi* on *Bereishis* 2:3.
5. *Bereishis* 1:27.
6. See *Likkutei Torah* of the *AriZal* on *Bereishis* 3:23.
7. See *Bamidbar Rabbah* 12:3.

the days of the week,[8] so too does the *Shemitah* year enliven[9] all the years of the *Shemitah* cycle.[10] In a fashion parallel to the day of *Shabbos*, the whole seven-year-cycle is sometimes referred to as a "*Shabbos* of years."[11]

Man's life, too, is composed of these two cycles.[12] During his early, formative years, he undergoes the "creative process" of upbringing and character development. Thereafter come the years during which he sows the kernels of his education, so that they may blossom forth and produce the desired fruits, enabling him to live his life according to G-d's plan — to transform the world into a place in which He may reside. This is accomplished by leading one's daily life in conformance with the Torah and *mitzvos*.

These two cycles are found in a person's daily life as well. The day is begun with prayer, Torah study and charity.[13] Only after this period of preparation is a man able — accompanied by the "illumination of Torah"[14] — to venture forth "to his work, to his labor until evening."[15] He then labors in such a manner that "all [his] deeds are for the sake of heaven,"[16] and in fulfillment of the directive, "Know Him in all your ways"[17] — being cognizant of G-dliness in whatever he does.

This also explains why the *Shabbos* day differs from the *Shabbos* year with regard to the prohibition of labor. On the *Shabbos* day any and every form of creative physical labor is

---

8. See *Zohar* II, 63b, 88a; *Likkutei Amarim* of the Maggid of Mezritch (Kehot edition), Section 255; *Or HaTorah, Beshalach*, p. 636ff.

9. See *Or HaTorah, Behar*, pp. 594, 604, *et passim; Likkutei Sichos*, Vol. XIV, p. 442ff.; *ibid.*, Vol. XII, p. 247ff., and see sources noted there.

10. See *She'elos U'Teshuvos HaRashba* I, Section 9.

11. See *Vayikra* 25:8.

12. Cf. *Sefer HaMaamarim 5630*, p. 132ff.; *5678*, p. 303ff.

13. See *Shulchan Aruch, Orach Chayim* 89:3, end of Section 92, 155.

14. *Mishlei* 6:23.

15. *Tehillim* 104:23.

16. *Avos* 2:12.

17. *Mishlei* 3:6.

prohibited. During the *Shabbos* year, only intensive (agricultural) work, such as plowing and sowing, is prohibited.

Since the cycle of days that culminate in the "holy *Shabbos*" represents the period of intensive preparation for man's subsequent lifework which is carried out during the seven-year cycle, it is understandable that extreme care must be taken to ensure that each specific detail is in order. When one maps out a blueprint for life, the minutest error can translate into an ominous fault in the actual construction. And even when the blueprint is meticulously drawn, a man needs to be vigilant in the face of his own tendency to conclude that his success in life results merely from his own exertions, forgetting that it is G-d Who sustains all life.

As a member of a "wise and discerning nation,"[18] every Jew realizes that a year that begins with *Shabbos* and that is a "year of *Shabbos*," is special indeed. The resolution that is called for in such a year is clear as well: that every day of this year be sanctified, and lived in the spirit of the "holy *Shabbos*" with which it opens.

Based on *Likkutei Sichos*, Vol. XIX, pp. 605-609.

---

18. *Devarim* 4:6.

Vayeilech   וילך

Shemitah & Hakhel

In the portion of *Vayeilech* we read about the commandment of *Hakhel*.[1] This commandment involved "gathering
together" the Jewish people in the courtyard of the Holy
Temple once every seven years, *"at the end of each Shemitah,"* the
Sabbatical year. The King would read out certain passages
from the Book of *Devarim*, so that the people would "learn to
be in awe of G-d..., carefully observing all the words of this
Torah."

Since the Torah connects *Hakhel* with *Shemitah*, it is to be
understood that the inspiration provided by the *Shemitah* year
is carried over into the following six non-*Shemitah* years,
through the medium of the *Hakhel* ceremony. What is this
inspiration and how is it mirrored in the commandment of
Hakhel?

The commandment of *Shemitah* as a whole involved giving
the land a "rest period, a sabbath to G-d."[2] During this time
fields were not to be planted, and crops that sprouted spontaneously were not to be harvested.[3] *Shemitah* served to demonstrate to the Jew that "nothing was wholly his own; all was
G-d's possession."[4]

There are three general aspects to *Shemitah:* (a) *man's* rest;[5]
(b) the *earth's* rest;[6] (c) the law that the *fruits* that grow during
the *Shemitah* year are ownerless and may be eaten by all.[7] Each

---

1. *Devarim* 31:10-13.
2. *Vayikra* 25:1.
3. *Loc. cit.*, v. 4-5.
4. *Chinuch, Mitzvah* 328; cf. *ibid., Mitzvah* 84.
5. See *Rambam*, beginning of *Hilchos Shemitah VeYovel*.
6. *Vayikra* 25:2, 4-5; cf. *Likkutei Sichos*, Vol. XVII, p. 287ff., and sources
   cited there.
7. *Shmos* 23:11; cf. *Likkutei Sichos, loc. cit.*

of these three aspects emphasizes a different facet of G-d's dominion.

Man's resting during *Shemitah* from agricultural labor[8] — which was the main occupation of Jewry in ancient times — stresses G-d's dominion and supremacy over man: "I was created to serve my Master."[9] When a Jew is occupied with worldly affairs he may forget that the ultimate intent of his being created is that he be a servant of G-d.

The *Shemitah* year, during which time the Jew divorces himself completely from worldly matters and occupies himself wholly with spiritual matters, serves to reinforce his awareness of G-d's dominion. Its effect is felt not only during the *Shemitah* year itself, but also during the following six years of labor.

The *earth's resting* emphasizes G-d's dominion over the whole earth, including nature and natural laws. As the Torah says: "You may ask, 'What will we eat in the seventh year? We have not planted nor have we harvested crops.' I will direct My blessing to you in the sixth year, and [the land] will produce enough crops for three years."[10] G-d here demonstrates that when He so desires the earth produces crops through supranatural means.

This serves as a lesson to be borne in mind during the six years of labor — that ultimately, the crops produced through planting and sowing do not result from man's labor but from G-d's blessing.[11]

This third aspect of *Shemitah*, that the *fruits* of the seventh year are ownerless and may be taken freely, establishes that G-d is the proprietor of man's *possessions;* even after G-d blesses an individual with property and wealth He retains ownership.

This reminds the individual during the six years following *Shemitah*, when he may keep the fruits of his labors, that these

---

8. See *Rambam's* heading to *Hilchos Shemitah VeYovel, Mitzvah* 2.
9. End of Tractate *Kiddushin.*
10. *Vayikra* 25:20-21.
11. See *Chinuch, Mitzvah* 84.

fruits indeed belong to G-d; they were merely entrusted to him so that he may act as G-d's agent and utilize them for the fulfillment of His will.

*   *   *

Herein lies the connection of *Shemitah* and *Hakhel*. The main part of the first section read by the king during the *Hakhel* ceremony was the passage of *Shema*, which relates to the Jew's *spiritual* labors — accepting the heavenly yoke, studying Torah, and performing *mitzvos*. This is similar to *man's resting* during *Shemitah* so that he may devote himself entirely to G-d.

The second portion read during *Hakhel* deals with the material rewards for the performance of *mitzvos* — harvesting bountiful crops, and the like. This, like the second aspect of *Shemitah*, indicates that a Jew's material bounty is dependent on his relationship with G-d.

The third section read during *Hakhel* involves tithing. Like the third aspect of *Shemitah*, this indicates that G-d retains ownership of man's possessions. They are merely entrusted to him, and when G-d so desires, He directs a man to tithe, and contribute to the welfare of a fellow Jew.[12]

Based on *Likkutei Sichos*, Vol. XXIV, pp. 197-205.

---

12. See *ibid.*, *Mitzvah* 66: "We were made His messengers, so that we may benefit thereby."

Haazinu   האזינו
Shabbos Teshuvah   שבת תשובה

Close to Heaven: Close to Earth

We find in the *Sifri*[1] that Moshe was "close to heaven" and "distant from the earth." It was for this reason that he opened the Torah reading of *Haazinu* by stating, "Listen, heaven, and hear — earth." Addressing the heavens Moshe used an expression that denotes closeness *(haazinu)*, while with regard to the earth he used an expression which indicates distance, for he was "close to heaven and distant from the earth." Yeshayahu,[2] by contrast, addressed the earth with an expression of closeness, and the heavens with an expression that indicates distance. This was because he was "distant from heaven and close to earth."

This must be understood. "Listen, heaven, and hear — earth" is a verse in the *Torah*, each word of which must be a lesson (since "Torah" means "teaching") for each and every Jew as to how he is to conduct his life. Since the Torah tells *us*, "Listen, heaven, and hear — earth," we are evidently expected to attain the level of being "close to heaven and distant from earth."

This is perplexing indeed. If the towering prophet Yeshayahu was considered to be "distant from heaven and close to earth," how are we expected to be "close to heaven and distant from earth"? Alternatively, if it is indeed true that each and every Jew can attain this level, how was it that Yeshayahu found this level unattainable?

We must perforce say that Yeshayahu's words, which were said as an adjunct to Moshe's words, allude to an even loftier level than Moshe's own; only after Yeshayahu —

---

1. Beginning of *Parshas Haazinu*.
2. *Yeshayahu* 1:2.

empowered by the level of Moshe — attained the level of being "close to heaven and distant from earth," was he then able to attain the even higher level of being "distant from heaven and close to earth."

Since Yeshayahu's words are also part of the Torah, it is self-evident that his exhortation, which is even loftier than Moshe's, is also within the grasp of every Jew. After becoming "close to heaven and distant from earth," every Jew is then expected to reach the higher degree of being "distant from heaven and close to earth."

*   *   *

Since all aspects of Torah are related to the season in which they are read, we can readily understand that the above-mentioned twofold lesson of Moshe and Yeshayahu is especially pertinent during the Ten Days of Penitence, at which time we read the portion of *Haazinu*.

How are we to attain these levels?

During the whole year, a Jew's divine service mostly involves those things that have to do with "earth" — the Torah and the *mitzvos* as they are found here below. With the advent of the Ten Days of Penitence, however, every Jew feels discontented with his earthy state and desires to repent — to return and be enveloped by G-d.

Since "a person is found wholly where his desire is,"[3] it follows that the desire to be totally at one with G-d *immediately* affects such an individual, so that he attains a state of being "close to heaven" (G-dliness) and "distant from earth."

However, this is but the first step. Soon afterwards, having quenched his thirst for G-dly *revelation*, the same individual comes to the realization that G-d's *Essence* is more readily attainable by transforming the world into a dwelling place for Him. The person then feels "closer to earth and distant from heaven" — he becomes aware that nothing can be greater than earthly beings becoming vessels to contain G-d's

---

3. An aphorism of the Baal Shem Tov, quoted in *Mayim Rabim 5736*, ch. 113; *Refaeini 5698*, ch. 5.

Essence. And this is accomplished by fulfilling G-d's passion-
ate desire to have a dwelling place for His Essence in this
nethermost world.[4]

Based on Likkutei Sichos, Vol. IX, pp. 204-213.

---

4. See *Tanchuma, Naso;* see also *Bamidbar Rabbah* 13:6.

A Song of Repentance

The majority of the verses of *Parshas Haazinu* — six of the
seven sections — is taken up with Moshe's song, known as
the Song of *Haazinu.*[1] The Levites used to sing this song on
Shabbos in the Holy Temple.[2] They would divide it into six
sections, each section sung on another *Shabbos,* in the same
manner that the song is divided for the Torah reading.[3]

Maimonides explains why the Song of *Haazinu* was divided
in this fashion:[4] "...For they are [words of] admonition, so
that the people will repent." Now "admonition" and "song"
are antithetical. How are we to understand this "song" which
contains words of "admonition"?

The Song of *Haazinu* as a whole, even those parts that
contain words of admonition, has one central theme: *all* the
events that befall the Jewish people are ultimately for the
good.[5] Even those occurrences that seem to be the very
antithesis of goodness serve the purpose of leading Jews
closer to the ultimate redemption. Indeed, all occurrences in
the life of the Jewish people are steps and stages that lead in
the direction of redemption.

---

1. *Rambam, Hilchos Sefer Torah* 7:10, ch. 8 (under the heading, *Sefer Eileh HaDevarim*); *Hilchos Temidin U'Musafin* 6:9.
2. *Rosh HaShanah* 31a.
3. *Hilchos Temidin U'Musafin, loc. cit.*
4. *Hilchos Tefillah* 13:5.
5. See *Chizkuni,* end of *Parshas Vayeilech; Abarbanel* on *Parshas Haazinu.*

The portion of *Haazinu* is read most years, and this year as well, on *Shabbos Teshuvah*,[6] the *"Shabbos* of Penitence,"so called because it is the *Shabbos* that falls in the "Ten Days of Penitence."

Accordingly, it is to be understood that the passage of *Haazinu* is not only connected to these days of penitence because it contains "words of admonition, so that the people will repent," but because of the particular kind of divine service and level of repentance that characterizes *Shabbos Teshuvah.*

The mode of repentance appropriate to weekdays is *teshuvah tata'ah,* "lower-level repentance," while the mode of repentance appropriate to *Shabbos* is *teshuvah ila'ah,* "higher-level repentance."[7] In general, the former involves repenting for the commission of actual sins, while the latter is the return and cleaving of man's spirit to G-d.[8]

Since during the week man is involved with elevating mundanity to holiness,[9] his repentance revolves around the rectification of actual sins — *teshuvah tata'ah.* On *Shabbos,* however, mundane labor is forbidden, and man's spiritual service involves elevating himself from level to level within the realm of holiness.[10] This is the task of *teshuvah ila'ah*[11] — striving to come ever closer to G-d.

These levels of repentance also differ in the manner in which they are performed: *teshuvah tata'ah* proceeds from a broken and contrite heart,[12] while *teshuvah ila'ah* is done with "great joy."[13]

All this is to be found in the Song of *Haazinu.* On the one hand it includes "[words of] admonition, so that the people

---

6. See *Levush, Orach Chayim* 428:5.
7. *Iggeres HaTeshuvah,* ch. 10; cf. *Likkutei Torah, Shabbos Shuvah* 66c, *et passim.*
8. *Iggeres HaTeshuvah,* ch. 8ff.; *Likkutei Torah,* beginning of *Parshas Haazinu.*
9. *Torah Or* 13a, 65b-c, 113a; *Likkutei Torah, Balak* 72a ff., *et passim.*
10. *Ibid.*
11. *Iggeres HaTeshuvah,* ch. 10; *Likkutei Torah, Shabbos Shuvah* 66c, *et passim.*
12. *Iggeres HaTeshuvah,* ch. 7; cf. *op. cit.,* ch. 10.
13. *Op. cit.,* end of ch. 11 (beginning of p. 201).

will repent," and on the other hand it is called a "song", an expression of joy, sung by the Levites in the Holy Temple.

The connection of the Song of *Haazinu* with *teshuvah ila'ah* also accords with the plain content of the Torah portion. Moshe was commanded to write the Song of *Haazinu* "so that this song will serve Me as a witness for the Jews"[14] — it served as testimony to the Torah and the commandments, enabling the Jews to fulfill them with vitality and unswerving allegiance.

Repentance, too, especially *teshuvah ila'ah*, vitalizes the Jew and enables him to fulfill the Torah and its commandments in this manner, so that his actions thereby become "good deeds and luminous ones."[15]

Based on *Likkutei Sichos*, Vol. XIV, pp. 145-146; Vol. XXIV, pp. 229-238.

---

14. *Devarim* 31:19.
15. *Likkutei Torah, Shemini Atzeres* 85a.

# Yom Kippur						יום כפור

The Very Day Brings Atonement

There is a difference of opinion in the Gemara[1] as to how atonement is achieved on Yom Kippur. The majority of the Sages hold that "Yom Kippur atones only for those who repent"; Rebbe (Rabbi Yehudah HaNasi) holds that atonement is achieved on Yom Kippur "whether the person repents or not," the reason being that "the very day [of Yom Kippur] brings atonement." The halachic decision is rendered in favor of the Sages.[2]

The Sages do not dispute Rebbe's point that "the very day brings atonement"; they agree that the individual's penitence cannot possibly achieve the level of atonement accomplished by the day of Yom Kippur itself. Rather, the dispute centers around the manner in which one brings about the state in which "the very day brings about atonement." Rebbe maintains that as soon as Yom Kippur arrives the sanctity of the day secures atonement for an individual's sins, even if he fails to repent. The Sages, however, say that in order to achieve the atonement brought about through Yom Kippur, repentance is first necessary. Having repented, a man is then able to attain the far loftier atonement which only the day of Yom Kippur can effect.

When a Jew repents and sincerely regrets his sins he thereby expunges the pleasure he had experienced at the time, and this in turn cleanses him from the evil that attached itself to him through his sin. However, how is it possible that

---

1. Shevuos 13a.
2. Rambam, Hilchos Teshuvah 1:3, Hilchos Shegagos 3:10; cited in Shulchan Aruch Admur HaZaken 607:16.

a person's sins are erased and eradicated simply because of the day of Yom Kippur?

A Jew's attachment to G-d exists on many levels. For example, a Jew is connected to G-d by performing His commandments and by accepting upon himself the heavenly yoke; he is ready to do all that G-d commands him. There is also a deeper level of attachment, that finds expression in repentance. If a Jew transgresses G-d's commands and throws off His heavenly yoke, he weakens his relationship with G-d. Troubled by this, he repents. Because repentance emanates from a soul level that is more profound than that which prompts one to simply obey G-d's commands, it has the ability to undo all the blemishes that were caused by the sins that had weakened his revealed relationship with G-d. Hence, through repentance he achieves a higher degree of attachment.

However, the loftiest level of a Jew's relationship with G-d is that of the essential and intrinsic bond between the soul's essence and G-d's Essence, inasmuch as the soul is truly a *part* of G-d above. This bond knows no limitations and defies any form of expression, even so lofty an expression as that of repentance. For any mortal expression must by its very nature be limited, while this bond is truly without limitations.

Just as this bond is beyond expression and cannot be improved upon through man's divine service, so, too, does it remain unaffected by man's lack of service, or even by his sins. At this level of attachment, sins simply have no bearing.

On the day of Yom Kippur this essential relationship with G-d is revealed within every Jew, and then all sins are dissipated as a matter of course. The debate between the Sages and Rebbe is merely as to whether one must first repent in order for this level to be revealed; all, however, agree that once the level of Yom Kippur — "the day itself brings atonement" — is revealed, it accomplishes far more than does mere repentance.

Thus, concerning those levels within a man that are affected and blemished by sin, atonement must be *brought about* by repentance, for repentance has the capacity to strengthen his bond with G-d and nullify the sins which encumber his relationship with Him.

The atonement of Yom Kippur, however, results from the revelation in the Jew of the *supreme* level of relationship with G-d; sins lack the ability to blemish this relationship in any way.

Based on *Likkutei Sichos*, Vol. IV, pp. 1149-1152.

Sukkos   סוכות

Uniting Jews through Union with G-d

Our Sages state in the *Midrash*[1] that the *esrog, lulav, hadasim* and *aravos* used during the festival of *Sukkos* for the commandment of taking the "Four Kinds," are each symbolic of a particular category of Jew.

The *esrog*, or citron, which possesses both a tangy taste and fine fragrance, is symbolic of the Jew who possesses both Torah learning and good deeds. Since the study of Torah is an intellectual pursuit and is to be enjoyed and savored, it is likened to taste; the performance of commandments ("good deeds") through the acceptance of the Divine yoke, is likened to fragrance — something much less tangible.

The *lulav*, or palm branch, alludes to those Jews who excel in Torah study but not in their performance of *mitzvos*; like dates that grow on the palm tree they possess good taste but lack fragrance.

Hadasim, or myrtles, which have a pleasant aroma but lack any taste, are symbolic of those Jews who possess good deeds but are lacking in Torah study. Finally, *aravos,* or willow branches, lacking both taste and fragrance, are symbolic of those Jews void of both Torah and good deeds.

When the festival of Sukkos arrives G-d says, "Let all these four kinds be bound together and they will atone for one another." The festival of Sukkos thus celebrates the unity of the entire Jewish people in a very real and revealed sense.

According to the commentary of the *Midrash* it would seem that the loftiest of the "Four Kinds" is the *esrog*, inasmuch as it alludes to the highest category among the Jewish

---

1. *Vayikra Rabbah* 30:12.

people — those who excel both in Torah and good deeds. Accordingly, we must understand why the blessing for taking the "Four Kinds" is "...for taking the *lulav*," and not "...for taking the *esrog*." Our Sages answer[2] that we do so because the *lulav* is taller than the other kinds.

The shape assumed by all physical things, especially those relating to commandments, directly relates to the spiritual source from whence they derive. The *lulav's* physical height necessarily results from the fact that spiritually, as well, the *lulav* possesses a quality that makes it loftier than the other kinds.

Now how can the *lulav* possibly be loftier than the *esrog* when the *esrog* has both the pleasant taste of Torah and the fragrance of *mitzvos*, while the [fruit of the] *lulav* possesses only taste — Torah?

This may be understood by first contrasting Torah and *mitzvos*. Concerning *mitzvos* we find it written that they are the "limbs of the King."[3] Regarding the Torah our Sages state that "Torah and G-d are truly One."[4]

While the limbs of the body are nullified to the soul and its desires, they are, however, not the soul itself. The same is so with regard to *mitzvos*. Performance of *mitzvos* indicates a Jew's subservience to G-d — but he still remains a separate entity.

However, when a Jew comprehends Torah and his intellect comprehends G-d's intellect, as it were, he is then wholly united with G-d's intellect[5] which is "One with G-d Himself." Understandably, the more he devotes himself to Torah study the greater will be his attachment to G-d.

Thus the "*lulav*-Jew," the one who is wholly devoted to Torah study, achieves a greater degree of attachment to G-d than does the "*esrog*-Jew," the one who is equally devoted to the study of Torah and to the performance of its *mitzvos*.

---

2. *Sukkah* 37b; *Shulchan Aruch Admur HaZaken*, conclusion of Section 651.
3. *Tikkunei Zohar*, Tikkun 30.
4. *Likkutei Torah*, Nitzavim, quoting the *Zohar*.
5. See *Tanya*, ch. 5.

It is this greater degree of unity symbolized by the *lulav* that is at the root of the blessing which is made specifically over it. For the "Four Kinds" are taken in order to achieve unity among the Jewish people, something directly resulting from the Jews' unity with G-d[6] and best expressed by the *lulav* — total devotion to Torah.

Based on *Likkutei Sichos*, Vol. IV, pp. 1159-1161.

---

6. *Ibid.*, ch. 32.

Wine & Water: Two Forms of Joy

All Jewish festivals emphasize joy — "Festivals for rejoicing, holidays and seasons for gladness."[1] The holiday of Sukkos is particularly joyful; it is known as the "Season of Our Rejoicing."[2] Additionally, there are distinctive joyous events and *mitzvos* that take place during Sukkos.

One of these events was the drawing of water for *Nissuch HaMayim*, the water-libations, that were offered in the Holy Temple during Sukkos. These water-offerings took place in addition to the standard wine-libations that accompanied various sacrifices throughout the year.

The water would be drawn with extraordinary festivity,[3] in accordance with the verse, "You shall draw water with joy from the wellsprings of deliverance."[4] Indeed our Sages say, "He who has not witnessed the rejoicing of the water-drawing ceremonies has never in his life seen joy."[5]

Why was the water-libation unique to the festival of Sukkos; what is the connection between the two?

---

1. *Siddur*, text of the *Amidah* and *Kiddush* for the three pilgrim festivals.
2. *Ibid.*
3. *Sukkah* 48b.
4. *Yeshayahu* 12:3.
5. *Sukkah* 51a (in the *Mishnah*).

Wine, too, is indicative of joy, for which reason our Sages say, "Songs of praise [to G-d] are sung only when accompanied by wine."[6] Therefore the wine-libations, too, were joyful occasions.

However, the joy associated with wine-offerings was also bound up with man's nature. Inasmuch as wine naturally leads to joy,[7] the spiritual joy of the service of wine-offerings commingled with the inherent ability of wine to bring man temporal joy.[8] As such, it was *not* pure and unadulterated *spiritual* joy.

Water, on the other hand,[9] being flavorless and devoid of any alcoholic content does not, in and of itself, bring man to a state of joy. The joy accompanying the water-offerings was thus wholly devoid of any physical, joy-inducing quality. Rather, this joy was completely spiritual in nature, emanating solely from G-d's command that "You shall drawn water with joy...."

The joy associated with wine-offerings, coming as it did from something — wine — whose joy had a natural basis, was constricted by the confines of nature. The joy accompanying the water-offering, however, resulted solely from G-d's command. Since He is infinite, the joy was boundless as well.

*   *   *

In terms of man's spiritual service, the joy of the wine-offerings refers to joy derived from contemplation, while the joy of the water-offerings alluded to a level within an individual that transcends understanding.

When a person comprehends the great privilege G-d has granted him, in that he is able to perform *mitzvos* and become elevated thereby, becoming one, as it were, with G-d, he is

---

6. *Berachos* 35a.
7. See *Menachos* 20a and commentary of *Rashi, s.v. Adrabah.*
8. See *Siddur im Dach* 137d.
9. See *Likkutei Torah, Derushim LeSukkos* 79d; *Siddur im Dach* 268a ff.; *Hemshech VeKacha 5637,* ch. 97ff.; *U'She'avtem 5669;* see also *Likkutei Sichos,* Vol. II, p. 420ff.

filled with joy. However, since this joy results from his own inherently limited understanding, it too is necessarily limited.[10]

However, when a Jew achieves a state of total self-sacrifice to G-d, intellect becomes superfluous. In this state, as soon as he becomes aware of a Divine command, he is filled with boundless joy — joy emanating from the soul's limitless essence — that transcends the limitations of intellect.[11]

Herein lies the connection of the joy of the water-drawing with Sukkos:

The joy of Sukkos derives from the spiritual achievements of Rosh HaShanah, the Ten Days of Penitence, and most importantly, Yom Kippur.[12] On that day the Jew's essence is bound up with G-d's Essence.[13] This is revealed during Sukkos in the water-offering and in the joy accompanying the water-drawing — a joy of the Jew's essence that transcends the bounds of intellectual limitation.

Based on *Likkutei Sichos*, Vol. XXIV, pp. 246-249.

---

10. See *maamar* beginning *Samach Tesamach*, 5657, pp. 48-49.
11. *Ibid.*
12. See *Ateres Rosh, Shaar Yom HaKippurim*, 36a ff.; *Or HaTorah, Sukkos*, p. 1722ff.; *Hemshech VeKacha 5637*, ch. 84; the *maamar* beginning *VeHu KeChassan*, 5657 (Kehot, 5713), ch. 11 ff.; the *maamar* beginning *BaSukkos Teishvu*, 5738.
13. See *Likkutei Sichos*, Vol. IV, p. 1151ff.

Berachah   ברכה

Moshe & Aharon: Two Peacemakers

The Torah portion of *Berachah*, the concluding portion of
the Torah, describes the events surrounding Moshe's passing
and the fact that he was mourned by the *"Sons* of Israel"[1] for
thirty days. In describing Aharon's demise, the Torah states
earlier, "The *entire House of Israel* mourned Aharon for thirty
days."[2]

Our Sages comment: "Moshe was mourned by the men,
while Aharon was mourned both by the men and women.
This was because Aharon pursued peace and brought about
peace between man and his fellowman and between husband
and wife."[3]

The Torah portion that speaks of Moshe's passing is the
logical place to relate Moshe's qualities. Indeed, the verse does
so when it states: "His eyes were undimmed.... There has
never again arisen a prophet like Moshe...."[4] Why, then, does
it allude to a fact that accentuated the special quality of
Aharon — and by implication Moshe's failing — in connection
with Moshe's demise?

Why, indeed, did not Moshe conduct himself like Aharon
regarding the bringing of peace "between man and his fellowman and between husband and wife?" Surely this was not a
result of Moshe's lack of love for his fellow Jew, for Moshe is
extolled as "a lover of the Jewish people."[5]

In fact, Moshe not only loved the Jewish people, but also

---

1. *Devarim* 34:8.
2. *Bamidbar* 20:29.
3. *Pirkei deRabbi Eliezer*, ch. 17; *Kallah Rabasi*, ch. 3; *Rashi* in his commentary
   to the verses cited above.
4. *Devarim* 34:4, 10ff.
5. *Menachos* 65a; explained at length in *Likkutei Sichos*, Vol. XIX, p. 2ff.

provided them with their spiritual and material needs. Moshe taught them all,[6] and not only the basic laws of the Torah, but other facets of Torah as well.[7] Moreover, it was in his merit than G-d provided the people with manna during their forty-year sojourn in the desert.

The reason Moshe did not conduct himself like Aharon is that his very being, as well as his life's mission, necessitated a different form of conduct in the love of his fellow Jews and in bringing peace between them.

Our Sages relate[8] that Aharon would sometimes stretch the truth in order to bring about peace between people who were at loggerheads. The Torah condones such behavior when it is the only possible way to make peace; as our Sages say, "One may modify a statement in the interest of peace."[9]

The very essence of Moshe, however, was the personification of *truth*.[10] It was therefore impossible for him to bring about peace between people if it would necessitate his telling an untruth.[11] Although such conduct is permitted in the Torah, it went against the grain of Moshe's essence — that of complete and total honesty and truth; such conduct was more in keeping with Aharon, who personified the attribute of kindness.[12] Moshe, the "man of truth," brought about peace through truth.

Since both these manners of conduct are in accordance with the Torah, it is to be understood that each possesses a quality lacking in the other. The merit in Moshe's conduct was that he did not deviate in the slightest from the truth. The merit of Aharon's conduct was his ability to affect even so lowly an individual who could be reached only by stretching the truth.

---

6. *Eruvin* 54a.
7. *Nedarim* 38a.
8. *Avos deRabbi Nasan*, 12:3; *Kallah Rabasi, loc. cit.*; see also *Maamarei Admur HaZaken HaKetzarim*, p. 414.
9. *Yevamos* 65b.
10. *Shmos Rabbah*, ch. 5; cf. *Sanhedrin* 111a.
11. See *Binyan Yehoshua* on *Avos deRabbi Nasan, loc. cit.*
12. *Shmos Rabbah, loc. cit.*

During his lifetime, Moshe was totally occupied in his manner of service — divine service through the attribute of truth. However, on the day of his passing, having already completed his mission in this world, he was able to realize the special quality of Aharon's service — that it brought peace to *all* Jews.

Moshe, in his selfless love for the Jewish people, desired that they act toward their fellows in the best possible manner. He therefore alluded to the special quality of Aharon's service when he prophetically wrote in the Torah that he was mourned by the *"Sons* of Israel" and not by all of Israel, since his own quality of peacemaking was not as far-reaching as was Aharon's.

Based on *Likkutei Sichos,* Vol. XXIV, pp. 253-257.

Key to Proper Names

Phonetic Transliteration	Conventional Spelling
Adoniyah	Adonijah
Aharon	Aaron
Argov	Argob
Avimelech	Abimelech
Avraham	Abraham
Bas-Sheva	Bath-Sheba
Bilam	Balaam
Binyamin	Benjamin
Charan	Haran
Esav	Esau
Kehos	Kohath
Korach	Korah
Lavan	Laban
Mattisyahu	Mattathias
Moshe	Moses
Noach	Noah
Pinchas	Phinehas
Shimon	Simeon
Shlomo	Solomon
Shmuel	Samuel
Ur Casdim	Ur of the Chaldees
Yaakov	Jacob
Yehudah	Judah
Yeshayahu	Isaiah
Yirmeyahu	Jeremiah
Yishmael	Ishmael
Yisrael	Israel
Yisro	Jethro
Yitzchak	Isaac
Yosef	Joseph

Glossary

An asterisk indicates a cross-reference within this Glossary.
All non-English entries are Hebrew unless otherwise indicated.

Acharon shel Pesach (אַחֲרוֹן שֶׁל פֶּסַח): the Final Day of Passover

Akedah (עֲקֵדָה): the Binding [of Yitzchak on the altar]; see *Bereishis* 22:1-19

alef (אָלֶף): the first letter of the Heb. alphabet

Amidah (עֲמִידָה; lit., "standing"): the focal prayer, recited standing, of every service

aravos (עֲרָבוֹת): sprigs of willow bound with the **lulav*; one of the *Four Kinds

Bamidbar (בְּמִדְבַּר; lit., "in the wilderness"): *Numbers*, the fourth book of the *Chumash

bar-mitzvah (בַּר מִצְוָה): religious coming of age at 13

Bein HaMetzarim (בֵּין הַמְּצָרִים; lit., "between the straits"): the Three Weeks of semi-mourning from the *Seventeenth of Tammuz to *Tishah beAv

beis (בֵּית): the second letter of the Heb. alphabet

Beis HaBechirah (בֵּית הַבְּחִירָה; lit., "the House of [G-d's] Choice"; cf. *Devarim* 12:11): the *Beis HaMikdash

Beis HaMikdash (בֵּית הַמִּקְדָּשׁ): the (First or Second) Temple in Jerusalem

Bereishis (בְּרֵאשִׁית; lit., "in the beginning"): *Genesis*, the first book of the *Chumash

bris (בְּרִית; abbrev. for *bris milah*): the Covenant [of the Circumcision]

Chabad (חַבַּ״ד; acronym formed by the initial letters of the Heb. words *chochmah, binah* and *daas*): (a) the branch of the chassidic movement whose roots are in an intellectual approach to the service of G-d, and which was founded by R. Shneur Zalman of Liadi, the Alter Rebbe; a synonym for *Chabad* in this sense is *Lubavitch; (b) the philosophy of this school of Chassidism

Chai Elul (ח״י אֱלוּל; lit., "the eighteenth of [the month of] Elul"): the festive birthdate (in 1698) of the Baal Shem Tov, founder of the chassidic movement, and (in 1745) of R. Shneur Zalman of Liadi, founder of its *Chabad branch

challah (חַלָּה): (a) the portion of dough that is separated as a tithe; (b) a usually braided loaf baked in honor of *Shabbos

277

Chanukkah (חֲנֻכָּה; lit., "dedication"): eight-day festival beginning 25 Kislev, commemorating the Maccabees' rededication
of the Second *Beis HaMikdash* in the second century B.C.E.,
and marked by the kindling of lights

Chassidus (חֲסִידוּת): Chassidism, i.e., (a) the movement within Ortho-
dox Judaism founded in the eighteenth century by R. Yisrael,
the Baal Shem Tov, and stressing: emotional involvement in
prayer; service of G-d through the material universe; the
primacy of wholehearted earnestness in divine service; the
mystical in addition to the legalistic side of Judaism; the power
of joy, and of music; and the collective physical and moral
responsibility of the members of the informal brotherhood,
each chassid having cultivated a spiritual attachment to their
saintly and charismatic leader, the Rebbe; (b) the philosophy
and literature of the above movement

chok (חֹק; pl., *chukim*; lit., "decree"): a superrational Torah law

Chumash (חֻמָשׁ): the Five Books of Moses (the Pentateuch)

Devarim (דְּבָרִים; lit., "words"): *Deuteronomy*, the fifth book of the
Chumash

Eretz Yisrael (אֶרֶץ יִשְׂרָאֵל): the Land of Israel

esrog (אֶתְרֹג): citron, used during *Sukkos* for the *mitzvah* of the *Four
Kinds

Ever HaYarden (עֵבֶר הַיַּרְדֵּן): Trans-Jordan

Four Kinds, the (אַרְבָּעָה מִינִים): *mitzvah* performed on *Sukkos requir-
ing four species of plants — the *lulav, *esrog, *hadasim and
*aravos — which are taken in hand, and over which a blessing is
pronounced

Gemara (גְּמָרָא; Aram.): (a) that part of the *Talmud* that discusses the
Mishnah; (b) loosely, the *Talmud* as a whole

hadasim (הֲדַסִּים): sprigs of myrtle bound with the *lulav; one of the
*Four Kinds

Haftorah (הַפְטָרָה): the passage from the Prophets which is chanted
in the synagogue on *Shabbos* and festivals after the Torah
reading and related to it

Hakhel (הַקְהֵל): the seven-yearly assemblage in the *Beis HaMikdash
at which the king read out selected passages from the Torah

HaShem (הַשֵּׁם; lit., "the [divine] Name"): G-d

kabbalas ol (קַבָּלַת עוֹל; lit., "acceptance of the yoke"): self-subordination
to the Will of G-d

Kohen Gadol (כֹּהֵן גָּדוֹל): High Priest

korban (קָרְבָּן; pl., *korbanos*): sacrifice or offering

Lag baOmer (ל"ג בָּעוֹמֶר): the thirty-third day of the *Omer; a minor
festival falling between *Pesach and *Shavuos

lishmah (לִשְׁמָהּ): intended altruistically for the sake of fulfilling a
*mitzvah

Lubavitch (lit., "town of love"; Rus.): townlet in White Russia which from 1813-1915 was the center of *Chabad *Chassidism, and whose name has remained a synonym for it

lulav (לוּלָב): palm branch; one of the *Four Kinds

Mashiach (מָשִׁיחַ; lit., "the anointed one"): the Messiah

Matan Torah (מַתַּן תּוֹרָה): the Giving of the Torah

matzah (מַצָּה; pl., matzos): unleavened bread eaten on Pesach

Menorah (מְנוֹרָה): a candelabrum; specifically, the seven-branched gold candelabrum kindled daily in the *Beis HaMikdash

mesirus nefesh (מְסִירוּת נֶפֶשׁ): self-sacrifice

mezuzah (מְזוּזָה; pl., mezuzos): tiny parchment scroll affixed to doorpost, and containing the first two paragraphs of Shema (Devarim 6:4-9 and 11:13-21)

Midrash (מִדְרָשׁ): (a) any one of the classical collections of the Sages' homiletical teachings on the Torah; (b) a particular passage therefrom

Mishkan (מִשְׁכָּן): the Tabernacle, i.e., the temporary Sanctuary in the wilderness; see Shmos 25ff.

mitzvah (מִצְוָה; pl., mitzvos): a religious obligation; one of the 613 commandments

Omer (עוֹמֶר): (a) a unit of dry measure; (b) an offering of this quantity of barley flour brought to the *Beis HaMikdash each year on the second day of Pesach; (c) the period of 49 days from this date to *Shavuos

Oral Law (תּוֹרָה שֶׁבְּעַל-פֶּה): the entire body of exposition and interpretation of the Torah that Moshe Rabbeinu received together with the Written Law at Sinai, and that for centuries was handed down by oral tradition until it was ultimately committed to writing in the Talmud, Midrash, and other classical sources

parshah (פַּרְשָׁה; the common plural form is parshios): the portion of the Torah read publicly every week

Parshas... (... פַּרְשַׁת): the parshah of...

Pesach (פֶּסַח; lit., "pass over"): seven-day festival beginning on 15 Nissan, commemorating the Exodus from Egypt

Purim (פּוּרִים; lit., "lots"): one-day festival falling on 14 Adar and commemorating the miraculous salvation of the Jews of the Persian Empire in the 4th cent. B.C.E.

Rebbe (common Yid. pronunciation of רַבִּי, "my teacher [or master]"): *tzaddik who serves as spiritual guide to a following of chassidim (see *Chassidus)

Rosh Chodesh (רֹאשׁ חֹדֶשׁ; lit., "the head of the month"): either one or two semi-festive days marking the beginning of the month

Rosh HaShanah (רֹאשׁ הַשָּׁנָה; lit., "head of the year"): the New Year festival, falling on 1 and 2 Tishrei

Sanhedrin (סַנְהֶדְרִין): the supreme legislative and judicial body in Second Temple times

Seventeenth of Tammuz (שִׁבְעָה עָשָׂר בְּתַמּוּז): fast commemorating the breach of the walls of Jerusalem three weeks before the Destruction of the First *Beis HaMikdash* on *Tishah BeAv

Shabbos (שַׁבָּת): the Sabbath

Shabbos Chazon (שַׁבָּת חֲזוֹן): the *Shabbos* preceding *Tishah BeAv, whose *Haftorah* begins with the word *Chazon* ("The vision..."; *Yeshayahu* 1:1-28)

Shabbos HaGadol (שַׁבָּת הַגָּדוֹל; lit., "the Great *Shabbos*"): the *Shabbos* preceding Pesach

Shabbos Mevarchim (שַׁבָּת מְבָרְכִים; lit., "the Shabbos when one blesses"): the *Shabbos* preceding *Rosh Chodesh, marked by a prayer for the forthcoming month

Shavuos (שָׁבוּעוֹת; lit., "weeks"): festival commemorating the Giving of the Torah at Sinai; in *Eretz Yisrael* falling on 6 Sivan, and in the Diaspora on 6-7 Sivan

Shemitah (שְׁמִיטָה): the Sabbatical year (see *Vayikra* 25:1-7)

Shmos (שְׁמוֹת; lit., "names"): *Exodus*, the second book of the *Chumash*

shofar (שׁוֹפָר): ram's horn sounded on *Rosh HaShanah

Shulchan Aruch (שֻׁלְחָן עָרוּךְ; lit., "a set table"): the standard Code of Jewish Law compiled by R. Yosef Caro in the mid-sixteenth century

Sukkos (סוכות; lit., "booths"): seven-day festival beginning on 15 Tishrei, taking its name from the temporary dwelling in which one lives during this period, and marked also by the *mitzvah* of the *Four Kinds

tallis (טַלִּית): shawl worn by men during prayer and fringed with tzitzis (cf. *Bamidbar* 15:37-40)

Talmud (תַּלְמוּד): the basic compendium of Jewish law, thought, and Biblical commentary; when unspecified refers to the *Talmud Bavli*, the edition developed in Babylonia, and edited at end of the fifth century C.E.; the *Talmud Yerushalmi* is the edition compiled in *Eretz Yisrael* at end of the fourth century C.E.

Tanya (תַּנְיָא): the basic exposition of *Chabad *Chassidism by its founder, R. Shneur Zalman of Liadi

tefillin (תְּפִלִּין): small black leather cubes containing parchment scrolls inscribed with *Shema Yisrael* and other Biblical passages, bound to the arm and forehead and worn by men at weekday morning prayers; "phylacteries"

teshuvah (תְּשׁוּבָה; lit., "return"): repentance

Tishah BeAv (תִּשְׁעָה בְּאָב; lit., "the Ninth of Av"): fast commemorating the destruction of both Temples

Torah (תּוֹרָה; lit., "teaching"): (a) the *Chumash; (b) the entire body of traditional Jewish teachings, including both the Written

(Biblical) Law and the *Oral (Rabbinic) Law

Tosafos (תּוֹסָפוֹת; lit., "supplements"): classical commentaries on the
Talmud that began to appear in the mid-twelfth century

Tu biShevat (ט"ו בִּשְׁבָט; lit., "the Fifteenth of Shvat"): the New Year
of the Trees

tzaddik (צַדִּיק): a completely righteous individual

Vayikra (וַיִּקְרָא; lit., "And He called…"): *Leviticus*, the third book of the
Chumash

Yom Kippur (יוֹם כִּפּוּר): the Day of Atonement, fast day falling on
10 Tishrei and climaxing the Days of Awe

Yud-Beis Tammuz (י"ב תַּמּוּז; lit., "the twelfth of Tammuz"): chassidic
festival marking the anniversary of the release from Stalinist
incarceration (1927) of R. Yosef Yitzchak Schneersohn, the
previous Lubavitcher Rebbe, as well as his birthday

Yud-Tes Kislev (י"ט כִּסְלֵו): chassidic festival celebrating the liberation
of R. Shneur Zalman of Liadi (see *Chabad*) from capital sent-
ence and imprisonment in Petersburg (19-20 Kislev
5559l1798), after being slandered to the czarist authorities by
his opponents

Zohar (זֹהַר; lit., "radiance"): classical work containing the mystical
teachings of the *Kabbalah*

Index

A page reference often includes the following page.

Adam, 119
Aharon, see *Moshe and Aharon
Ahavas Yisrael, 42, 66, 99, 152, 272
Akiva, Rabbi, 152
Alef and *beis,* 3, 119
Alter Rebbe, 44
Angels, 33
Avimelech, 26
Avraham Avinu, 12, 18, 21, 24, 26, 28, 31, 119
Awe of G-d, 27, 236, 251
Baal Shem Tov, 150
Beis HaMikdash, see *Mishkan and Beis HaMikdash*
Body and soul, 15, 31, 174, 199, 209, 212
Calendar, 44, 73, 212, 250, 253
Candle-lighting, 142
Challah, 189
Chanukkah, 47, 49
Charity, see *Tzedakah*
Circumcision, 17, 76, 140
Commandments, see *Mitzvos*
Corporeality, 11, 14, 29, 39, 45, 54, 95, 98, 114, 150, 177, 224
Covenant, 12, 17, 204
Creation, 5, 8, 106, 128, 253
David HaMelech, 23
Education, 52, 65, 122
Eretz Yisrael, 28, 33, 187, 218, 245
Esav, 36, 38, 125
Exile, 28, 33, 38, 41, 45, 54, 56, 58, 63, 206, 211
Exodus, 26, 41
Faith, 82, 89, 187
Haftorah, 23
Hakhel, 256
Hospitality, 27
Idolatry, 77, 189

Israel, Land of, see *Eretz Yisrael
Joy, 269
Kohanim and Levi'im, 177, 194, 204
Levites, see *Kohanim and Levi'im
Love of a fellow Jew, see *Ahavas Yisrael
Love of G-d, 27
Martyrdom, see *Mesirus nefesh
Mashiach and the Messianic era, 7, 10, 35, 58, 132, 136, 193, 223
Matriarchs, 31
Mesirus nefesh, 19, 99, 153, 195, 199, 205
Messiah, see *Mashiach
Mezuzah, 228
Miracles, see *Nature and beyond nature
Mishkan and Beis HaMikdash, 94, 96, 101, 137, 145, 219, 223, 231
Mitzvos, 6, 13, 96, 104, 109, 147, 163, 197, 228, 240, 268
Monarchy, 235
Moshe and Aharon, 65, 68, 70, 99, 101, 119, 145, 183, 192, 194, 204, 259, 272
Names, 31, 111, 155
Nature and beyond nature, 15, 47, 49, 64, 66, 78, 86, 135, 190, 203
Noach, 7
Oaths, 58
Patriarchs (see also individual entries), 24, 28, 32, 45, 47, 70
Pesach, 128, 130, 155
Pinchas, 204, 206
Prayer, 185, 204
Pride and humility, 119, 160, 242, 255
Priests, see *Kohanim and Levi'im
Procreation, 10
Reason and beyond reason, 3, 7, 20, 66, 69, 71, 75, 89, 91, 109, 130, 163, 197, 271
Red Heifer, 197
Repentance, see *Teshuvah
Revelation, Divine, 7, 86, 106, 137, 173, 221, 259
Rosh HaShanah, 250
Sabbath, see *Shabbos
Sacrifices, 121, 124, 126, 137, 185, 231
Sarah, 14
Secular disciplines, 7, 91
Self-sacrifice, see *Mesirus nefesh
Shabbos, 5, 109, 128, 142, 253

Shavuos, 169, 172
Shemitah, 253, 256
Shlomo HaMelech, 23
Sukkos, 155, 157, 267, 269
Tabernacle, *see* *Mishkan and *Beis HaMikdash*
Telecommunications, 8
Temple, *see* *Mishkan and *Beis Hamikdash*
Teshuvah, 5, 21, 101, 107, 200, 226, 233, 237, 261, 264
Torah study, 3, 6, 29, 69, 229, 268
Trials, 18, 47
Tzedakah, 6
Unity of the Jewish people, 84, 112, 180, 192, 245, 267
Yaakov, 29, 31, 33, 36, 38, 47, 56, 58, 125
Yaakov, sons of, 41, 45, 47, 54
Yehudah, 52
Yeshayahu, 206, 259
Yirmeyahu, 206
Yishmael, 17, 24
Yitzchak, 17, 19, 24, 26, 28, 31
Yom Kippur, 264
Yosef, 41, 44, 54, 56, 63
Yud-Tes Kislev, 44
Yud-Beis Tammuz, 202

הוצאת ספרים

קרני הוד תורה

קה"ת

ליובאוויטש